Presencing EPIS

A Scientific Journal of Applied Phenomenology & Psychoanalysis

2016
Volume 1

EPIS Press
2026 S. 9th W. #4
Missoula, Montana 59801 USA
epispublishing1@gmail.com
www.episworldwide.com
www.episjournal.com
www.episeducation.com

Presencing EPIS is published yearly as an online journal.
ISSN 2166-5648.

Printed in the United States of America
Library of Congress
1. Phenomenology 2. Psychoanalysis 3. Lacan
4. Existential psychoanalysis 5. Philosophy 6. Shame 7. Artificial intelligence
8. Critical Theory 9. Journal I. Presencing EPIS

EPIS Journal is published as an on-line journal every Fall/Winter

ISBN 978-1-943332-09-0

Table of Contents

Letter from the Editor

Kevin Boileau, PhD

This is the 5th issue of our core journal and with it comes retrospect and review. All good things in life come from ideas, choices, and commitment. For example, in 2012, we made final preparations to develop and publish an academic and clinical journal in phenomenology, psychoanalysis, and critical theory. Five years later, we are able to look back at our hopes, acknowledge are errors, and bask in the realization that we made this journal come to presence. At the outset we contemplated a forum in which both theorists and clinicians would converge, drawing heavily from the complex trialectics involved in integrating three powerful discourses. Presently, we have come to learn how important and valuable our decision was, and still is.

This year we entertained presentations concerning the soul in mental health; a phenomenology of the unconscious; the phenomenology of symbolism and authenticity; the distinction being being and having in Marx and Aquinas; the philosophy of technology and temporality; an ontogenesis of shame; a critical look at the annihilations of terrorism; Adorno's views about psychoanalysis and the dialectical subject; the psychoanalytic view of Otto Rank; a phenomenology of the technological self; and Lacan's (psychoanalytic and phenomenological) antecedents. Coupled with year-long seminars involving the Flaubert studies, Lacan's *Ecrits*, Badiou's thoughts about being and event, and the early Husserl, it has been a challenging year of study. Being able to memorialize some of the work of some of our members is particularly rewarding, especially as we develop our post-doctoral program, the radio show, and additional seminars and programs. Thus, this year's journal is a step along our way to an unknown future.

Much of what we seek in our investigation of subjectivity is the transcendence of our heretofore fidelities and other theoretical commitments. In this endeavor, we hope for creative solutions to the aporias and lucanae of our own thinking history, and chances for work that provides us with a more palatable meaning to our existence. This community of thinkers has had the rare chance of meeting regularly, in some cases for several times per year for well over a decade. We know not where this shall lead, but we are already planning the next, and are grateful for this year's work. As such, it feels appropriate to thank everyone who has contributed to this journal over the past five years. It has been a singular pleasure, a labor of love, and a well-spent investment in the future of this psychoanalytic organization and community.

From the desk of Kevin Boileau
Writing in Missoula
August, 2016

Author Bios

Loray Daws, PhD

Loray is a Registered Clinical Psychologist with the Health Professions Counsel of South Africa and a Registered Psychologist with the College of Psychologists of British Columbia, Canada. He graduated from the University of Pretoria and served as a full time lecturer from 1998 to 2006. Academically, as well as clinically, Loray's areas of interest include Mastersonian psychoanalysis and its various research and clinical applications to developmental trauma, philosophy and ethics of mental health and the question of human freedom and agency, and integrating various existential theorists with psychoanalytic traumatology. Never far from the academic field Loray serves as assistant editor for the Global Journal of Health Sciences, evaluator and international advisory board member of the International Journal of Psychotherapy (IJP), assistant editor and psychoanalytic candidate at EPIS (Existential Psychoanalytic Institute and Society) and has published various articles and chapters on dreaming, psychosomatic disorders and the disorders of the self. Loray supervises and teaches in South Africa, Canada, the United States, Australia and Turkey as faculty member of the International Masterson Institute.

Vic Schermer, PhD

Victor L. Schermer is a psychologist in private practice in Philadelphia, PA. He is a Life Fellow of the American Group Psychotherapy Association. Schermer has edited and authored numerous journal articles and eight books, most recently author of *Meaning Mind and Self Transformation: Psychoanalytic Interpretation and the Interpretation of Psychoanalysis.* He is a frequent presenter of lectures, workshops, and panels internationally.

Daniel Bradley, PhD

Daniel O'Dea Bradley graduated from Gonzaga with degrees in Biology and Philosophy in late 1990s. At the National University of Ireland in Galway, he earned a Masters in Ethics and Cultural Studies and in 2008 was awarded a PhD in philosophy for his dissertation, "The Ambiguity of Desire: Truth and Illusion in the Discernment of the Divine." Dan is now an Associate Professor at Gonzaga University where he has been teaching in the philosophy department for the last eight years. He regularly teaches Human Nature, Ethics, Phenomenology, and Hermeneutics, along with an array of less regular courses in more specialized areas. His research focuses on the intersection of phenomenology and religion, particularly around questions of presence, desire, illusion, and the sacred. He has recently written on Plato, Richard Kearney, Ricoeur, Augustine, Kierkegaard, Teresa of Avila, Julia Kristeva, Hossein Nasr, and the philosophy of film. In Galway he met his wife Róisín who is now an adjunct lecturer, also in the philosophy department at Gonzaga. The two of them live with their three children in Spokane.

Róisín Lally, PhD

Rósín Lally is teaching in Gonzaga University. She was awarded her PhD from the National University Ireland, Galway, June 2016. Her research interests includes the ontology of technology, contemporary philosophy, specifically Heidegger and Husserl, philosophy of technology, and speculative idealism.

Andrew Nutt, MA

Andrew has a degree in theology and biblical studies from Moody Theological Seminary and currently is finishing a degree in counseling psychology. He is an itinerant speaker and adjunct professor addressing suffering from a phenomenological and theological perspective. His research interest is in intersubjective ontology and the philosophic foundations of counseling theories, specifically relational models of healing. Andrew is a member of EPIS and lives in Alaska when he is not traveling or studying.

Michel Valentin, PhD

Michel Valentin is teaching French literature and textual/critical/postmodern theory at the University of Montana (Missoula). Valentin teaches and applies Lacanian theory to the unravelling of any textual surface (graphic, written, filmic...). He also uses theory to enhance the socio-cultural critique of our contemporaneity and publishes in his area of expertise. He is a long-time EPIS member.

Julian von Will, PhD

I was born in Seattle Washington. I focus on Kant, German idealism, phenomenology, Frankfurt School sociocultural criticism, psychoanalysis, philosophy of war and military history. I try to relate them through a dialectic of reason and contradiction in self-consciousness. I concentrate on Kant, Hegel, Husserl, Heidegger, Adorno, Freud and Clausewitz. I'm trained in psychoanalysis, clinical sexology and family therapy. I just finished a book on Theodor W. Adorno's metacritique of modern German idealism entitled: *Inverted World.*

Julio R. Costa, MS

Sociologist with experience in teaching and field research. In his professional career, researched underserved communities in Brazil, developing actions with diversified social actors, such as producer's associations, municipalities, worker's unions, government agencies, NGOs and social movements, aiming the building of social capital and the promotion of local development. Has published articles on Sociology of Development, Environmental Responsibility, Participatory Research, Cultural Studies, and the book "To Be More Person: a reading of Otto Rank", and related topics.

Gary Kolb, PhD

I am a therapist and have worked full-time at Harbor Crest Behavioral Health hospital inpatient treatment center for chemical dependency for 15 years. I have both a PhD and a Psy.D. and have a private psychotherapy practice. I am also a psychoanalytic candidate at the Existential Psychoanalytic Institute and Society. I have been married for 43 years to the same woman, raised 8 adopted children, and re-assemble old car parts in my spare time.

Ellie Ragland, PhD

Ellie Ragland is Professor or English and Honorary French Professor as well as Frederick A. Middlebush Chair at The University of Missouri where she teaches psychoanalytic theory and world literature. She is author of eight authored and edited books on Lacanian psychoanalysis. She is a practicing psychoanalyst and a member of the New Lacanian School and the World Association of Psychoanalysis.

Fundamentals of Taxonomy: The Rise of the DSM as a Medical **Hortus Siccus** *and the Need for a Soul in Mental Health*

Loray Daws, PhD

Abstract

This essay aims to explore the historical importance of empirical import in the domain of clinical psychiatry. It will be argued that the empirical import, although an achievement in logical construction, has not taken into full account its implications, or even its political agenda. As such, without this awareness it can be argued that psychiatry (or psychology for that matter) merely becomes a complex language and praxis 'signal' for the application of pre-existing institutional arrangements, facilitating an *estrangement* between the scientific/ symbolic/materialist realms and Being *per se*. What is needed is not so much knowledge of knowledge and taxonomy, but rather how it is constructed, held (in institutions, in mind), communicated, and carried 'across' toward *Being/the Other, facilitating an* indwelling and meditative thinking so as to retain mystery and openness to experience. Diagnostic thinking, taxonomy and classification as *hortus siccus*, focusing on *Being as cut and dry* so to speak, has had immense 'narrowing' implications on the Other. These implications will be explored through Heidegger's philosophical thought on calculative and meditative thinking, Eric Craig's Dasein-analytic description of Soul, and brought 'to life' through various case studies.

Key words: Taxonomy, classification, diagnostic and statistical manual for mental disorders, soul, deficit-correction model, Soul.

Introduction

"To care for people is more important than to care for ideas"

Harry Guntrip

The doctor is the patient's fate

Karl Jaspers

It is difficult to ignore the reality that the use of diagnosis greatly aids the clinician in organizing an array of symptoms into coherent and communicable structures. Since the work of Hempel (Fulford, Thorton & Graham, 2006) much emphasis has been given to the inherent taxonomy of psychiatric diagnostic systems. Embedded in logical empiricism and the need for "audit trails" (p. 328) (ensuring reliability and validity), psychiatric classification has seen much change over the decades and although seemingly the domain of logical empiricism, empirical import *per se* may be more elusive and complex than originally thought. Various theorists such as Thomas Szasz have been vocal about the reification of taxonomy, and its contemporary hegemony could lead to various ethical difficulties evident in post-modern theories such as feminism and deconstructionism. It will be the aim in this section to discuss the philosophical-clinical importance of the latter through,

- A brief history of the use of classification and taxonomy—its strengths and weaknesses.
- Its 'use' and application and relationship to the Other, and as
- Political tool

The debate will also conclude with case studies and the notion of 'Soul', as defined by the Daseinanalyst Eric Craig (2008) as it is deemed important to bridge the contemporary tendency to separate calculative thinking from meditative thinking. Through 'Soul-care-as-dialogism' it may be possible to develop anthropological approaches of what I refer to as *triangular dialogism.*

The use of diagnosis: a brief history on the use of classification and taxonomy

Based on early Greek and Latin, the word "diagnosis" has been synonymous with discernment, to distinguish (therefore 'dia' referring to apart or 'a' -part), the ability to 'know' or to 'come to know'. A true testament of both Cartesian and Galilean worldviews where "I think therefore I am", scaffolded later theorists such as Locke and others to follow in constructing a dominant approach to sense impressions. Many post-modern thinkers and schools have taken issue with this view in mental health. They include thinkers from existentialist phenomenology, constructionism and Lacanian psychoanalysis, wherein naïve materialism is said the basis of various (catastrophic) errors[1] in logic when applied to man.

To return to diagnosis and its natural 'offspring' so to speak, i.e., taxonomy and classification, Kendell (2002) stated that any good classification system has as its aim the grouping together of similar observable phenomena—giving it a common name, a denomination (de-'nominal'-tion), qualifying the group and making it clinical relevant (qualification). In doing so ensures a measure of prediction in terms of 'its' course and treatment. This seemed very evident when reading early psychiatric pioneers such as Kraepelin's inspiring observations of manic depressive psychosis (1921, in Wolperd, 1977, pp. 33-35). A taxonomy should be (a) comprehensive, (b) easy to use, (c) clinical significant[2], (d) be reliable, and (e) be valid, and in doing so remain 'true' or 'evident' over many context and culture thereby (e) *serving* the needs of its 'users'[3]. The latter seems of

1 A beautiful example of such exploration can be found in Lacan's Ècrits (2006) and Badiou's 'Theory of the subject' (2009).
2 For mental health and especially clinical psychology and psychiatry this would mean it's a 'harmful' 'dysfunction' either to the individual or to society.
3 A fascinating need as it implies a shared value system. Clearly, out of the example to follow this was not the case at all. Taxonomy and diagnoses can be

importance—the *needs of its users*!

Before a deeper exploration concerning the epistemology of mental health classification and the needs of the user, I would for a moment return to Fulford's (in Bloch and Green, 2009, p. 70) good strawberries' (like 'bodily disorder') and 'good pictures' (like 'mental disorder') description as a simplified way to organize the debate to follow. According to Fulford (in Bloch et al., 2009) there is a clear difference between what constitutes a good strawberry versus what constitutes a good picture, that is, there is a difference between said factual and evaluative meanings of that which we observe. When considering a strawberry it is not difficult to contemplate or describe in detail what constitutes a good strawberry, even a bad strawberry for that matter. Although it may have different shapes, be cultivated in different parts of the world, its color and texture (irrespective of size) usually constitutes it as a 'good' strawberry. There is a comfort in the clarity of its 'goodness' and 'badness'. However if one considers a picture, of for example a house, what is perceived as good or bad could be more challenging to 'frame'. That is, what constitutes a good or bad picture may have physical elements that could be measured- such as its size, the amount of paint used, its dominant or predominant style or school of technique ('a' Monet, renaissance art and the like) such as clarity (I am sure a vague picture may lead to uncertainty) for most it remains secondary to what the picture 'means' to or for the observer. A good strawberry remains (retains?) a good strawberry even if the observer decides it not so[4]. A picture could be perceived as art/good as it represents for this person a good example of a Monet, for another is good

used to keep 'a part' clients experiencing much mental anguish and society as well as the clinicians treating them.

4 I have to mention in academic honesty that the more I work with the example the more I am aware that the example does have a naughty logic imbedded, i.e., although the senses I rely on to distinguish factual and evaluative meanings, ocular ad oral meanings may lead to different systems of thought, each with its factual and evaluative meanings per se. I can certainly eat my picture by gobbling it up greedily visually, creating a hunger – a visual pica. Visual pornography has such a state of mind, both factually and evaluative. Also in itself, only since I eat strawberries has it become subject to my factual and evaluative system. It existed in nature before man's use of it, and although bad for me to eat a bad strawberry- in terms of nature decay is seen as healthy and nurturing (i.e., compost). The latter was debated thoroughly as part of the philosophy of statesman Jan Smuts (Savage, 1998).

as its reminds them of their childhood home, for another the childhood they never had and the like. Certainly the strawberry could evoke similar associations (the strawberry as a memory of having Sunday lunches with grandma) but for the aim of the current debate suffice it to say that the strawberry lends itself to empirical import easier than a representation (the picture).

Factual and Evaluative Meaning	
Strawberries	**Pictures**

☺☺	☹☺
Agreement	***No agreement***
Over what makes a good strawberry (=sweet, clean skinned, etc.)	Over what makes a good picture
Hence	***Hence***
The term "good strawberry" has acquired the factual meaning "sweet, clean skinned, etc"	The meaning of "good picture" has acquired no consistent factual meaning
Parallels	***Parallels***
Concepts of disorder in physical medicine	Concepts of disorder in psychiatry

Figure 4.'Good strawberries' (like 'bodily disorder') and 'good pictures' (like 'mental disorder') (in Fulford in Bloch and Green, 2009, p. 70)

Given the figures as structure it could also be stated that when considering factual realities such as bipolarity, Alzheimer disease and schizophrenia, it would prove difficult in contemporary mental health contexts to ignore both its factual and evaluative meanings. Certainly as tensile structure and the inherent 'keeping apart' (diagnosis) one may come to predominate over the other (factual > evaluative meanings). To 'know' or come to know the factual of such diseases (Heidegger's calculative thinking) in psychiatry as a profession has been instrumental in containing such devastating realities. As practitioner this has been evident in my practice. So, on the one hand one could share Kendell's biological optimism- but if one considers personality disorders, sexual disorders and others, Szasz's concerns seems very evidentiary. That is, mental health may be ecologized or neurologized leading to a colonization of the Real through the symbolic order (in the guise of topology, classification and thus calculative thinking) leading to the 'Tortion' (Badiou, 2009) of man as Being, swallowing autochthony, the subjective and meditative thinking. These concerns are also evident in modern day psychiatry. The work of Dr Allen Frances, past principle investigator of the DSM *IV* Task force added 'concerning' modern trends such as diagnostic inflation (under the auspices of prevention), homogenizing tendencies in modern culture medicalizing difference, elastic diagnostic labels swallowing up newly recruited patients, cultural perfectionism (that feeds the problematizing approach to general problems in living) that not only sells happiness[5] but controls and even demands it, and last, but not least, 'the power to label is the power to destroy', i.e., mental illness creates willingly or not stigma;

> "Being normal and fitting in with the pack are a key to survival. Evolution has wired into human nature an uncharitable wariness and lack of compassion for those who are different and don't satisfy tribal expectations. Having a mental disorder 'marks' someone in ways that can cause much secondary harm. Stigma can take many forms, comes from all directions, is sometimes blatantly overt, but can also be remarkably subtle. It is the cruel

5 Please see a very important article entitled "A proposal to classify happiness as a psychiatric disorder" by Richard P. Bentall (1992). Thank you to Mr. Andrew Nutt for providing me with the article.

comment, the unkind smirk, the exclusion from the group, the lost job opportunity, the rejected marriage proposal, the ineligibility for life insurance, the inability to adopt children or pilot a plane. ...And the secondary psychological and practical harms of having a mental disorder come only partly from how others see you. A great deal of trouble comes from a change in how you see yourself-the sense of being damaged goods, feeling not normal or worthy, not a full fledged member of a group." (in Allen,2013. P. 109).

A more detailed example, given by the now psychologist Eleanor Longden, may serve as educator. The following excerpt can be found in Ted Talk[6] (2013) and introduces a contemporary voice of concern. This is a transcript of her talk:

The day I left home for the first time to go to university was a bright day brimming with hope and optimism. I'd done well at school. Expectations for me were high, and I gleefully entered the student life of lectures, parties and traffic cone theft.

Now appearances, of course, can be deceptive, and to an extent, this feisty, energetic persona of lecture-going and traffic cone stealing was a veneer, albeit a very well-crafted and convincing one. Underneath, I was actually deeply unhappy, insecure and fundamentally frightened -- frightened of other people, of the future, of failure and of the emptiness that I felt was within me. But I was skilled at hiding it, and from the outside appeared to be someone with everything to hope for and aspire to. This fantasy of invulnerability was so complete that I even deceived myself, and as the first semester ended and the second began, there was no way that anyone could have predicted what was just about to happen.

I was leaving a seminar when it started, humming to myself, fumbling with my bag just as I'd done a hundred times

6 http://www.ted.com/talks/eleanor_longden_the_voices_in_my_head/transcript?language=en
Eleanor Longden
The voices in my head
Posted Aug 2013
Permission obtained for both presentation and publication by The Media Requests Team, 15 July 2016

before, when suddenly I heard a voice calmly observe, "She is leaving the room."

I looked around, and there was no one there, but the clarity and decisiveness of the comment was unmistakable. Shaken, I left my books on the stairs and hurried home, and there it was again. "She is opening the door."

This was the beginning. The voice had arrived. And the voice persisted, days and then weeks of it, on and on, narrating everything I did in the third person.

"She is going to the library."

"She is going to a lecture." It was neutral, impassive and even, after a while, strangely companionate and reassuring, although I did notice that its calm exterior sometimes slipped and that it occasionally mirrored my own unexpressed emotion. So, for example, if I was angry and had to hide it, which I often did, being very adept at concealing how I really felt, then the voice would sound frustrated. Otherwise, it was neither sinister nor disturbing, although even at that point it was clear that it had something to communicate to me about my emotions, particularly emotions which were remote and inaccessible.

Now it was then that I made a fatal mistake, in that I told a friend about the voice, and she was horrified. A subtle conditioning process had begun, the implication that normal people don't hear voices and the fact that I did meant that something was very seriously wrong. Such fear and mistrust was infectious. Suddenly the voice didn't seem quite so benign anymore, and when she insisted that I seek medical attention, I duly complied, and which proved to be mistake number two.

I spent some time telling the college G.P. about what I perceived to be the real problem: anxiety, low self-worth, fears about the future, and was met with bored indifference until I mentioned the voice, upon which he dropped his pen, swung round and began to question me with a show of real interest. And to be fair, I was desperate for interest and help, and I began to tell him about my strange commentator. And I always wish, at this point, the voice had said, "She is digging her own grave."

I was referred to a psychiatrist, who likewise took a grim view of the voice's presence, subsequently interpreting everything I said through a lens of latent insanity. For example, I was part of a student TV station that broadcast news bulletins around the campus, and during an appointment which was running very late, I said, "I'm sorry, doctor, I've got to go. I'm reading the news at six." Now it's down on my medical records that Eleanor has delusions that she's a television news broadcaster.

It was at this point that events began to rapidly overtake me. A hospital admission followed, the first of many, a diagnosis of schizophrenia came next, and then, worst of all, a toxic, tormenting sense of hopelessness, humiliation and despair about myself and my prospects.

But having been encouraged to see the voice not as an experience but as a symptom, my fear and resistance towards it intensified. Now essentially, this represented taking an aggressive stance towards my own mind, a kind of psychic civil war, and in turn this caused the number of voices to increase and grow progressively hostile and menacing. Helplessly and hopelessly, I began to retreat into this nightmarish inner world in which the voices were destined to become both my persecutors and my only perceived companions. They told me, for example, that if I proved myself worthy of their help, then they could change my life back to how it had been, and a series of increasingly bizarre tasks was set, a kind of labor of Hercules. It started off quite small, for example, pull out three strands of hair, but gradually it grew more extreme, culminating in commands to harm myself, and a particularly dramatic instruction:

"You see that tutor over there? You see that glass of water? Well, you have to go over and pour it over him in front of the other students."

Which I actually did, and which needless to say did not endear me to the faculty.

In effect, a vicious cycle of fear, avoidance, mistrust and misunderstanding had been established, and this was a battle in which I felt powerless and incapable of establishing any kind of peace or reconciliation.

Two years later, and the deterioration was dramatic. By now, I had the whole frenzied repertoire: terrifying voices, grotesque visions, bizarre, intractable delusions. My mental health status had been a catalyst for discrimination, verbal abuse, and physical and sexual assault, and I'd been told by my psychiatrist, "Eleanor, you'd be better off with cancer, because cancer is easier to cure than schizophrenia." I'd been diagnosed, drugged and discarded, and was by now so tormented by the voices that I attempted to drill a hole in my head in order to get them out.

Now looking back on the wreckage and despair of those years, it seems to me now as if someone died in that place, and yet, someone else was saved. A broken and haunted person began that journey, but the person who emerged was a survivor and would ultimately grow into the person I was destined to be.

Many people have harmed me in my life, and I remember them all, but the memories grow pale and faint in comparison with the people who've helped me. The fellow survivors, the fellow voice-hearers, the comrades and collaborators; the mother who never gave up on me, who knew that one day I would come back to her and was willing to wait for me for as long as it took; the doctor who only worked with me for a brief time but who reinforced his belief that recovery was not only possible but inevitable, and during a devastating period of relapse told my terrified family, "Don't give up hope. I believe that Eleanor can get through this. Sometimes, you know, it snows as late as May, but summer always comes eventually."

Fourteen minutes is not enough time to fully credit those good and generous people who fought with me and for me and who waited to welcome me back from that agonized, lonely place. But together, they forged a blend of courage, creativity, integrity, and an unshakeable belief that my shattered self could become healed and whole. I used to say that these people saved me, but what I now know is they did something even more important in that they empowered me to save myself, and crucially, they helped me to understand something which I'd always suspected: that my voices were a meaningful response to traumatic life events, particularly childhood events, and as such were not my enemies but a source of insight into solvable emotional problems.

Now, at first, this was very difficult to believe, not least because the voices appeared so hostile and menacing, so in this respect, a vital first step was learning to separate out a metaphorical meaning from what I'd previously interpreted to be a literal truth. So for example, voices which threatened to attack my home I learned to interpret as my own sense of fear and insecurity in the world, rather than an actual, objective danger.

Now at first, I would have believed them. I remember, for example, sitting up one night on guard outside my parents' room to protect them from what I thought was a genuine threat from the voices. Because I'd had such a bad problem with self-injury that most of the cutlery in the house had been hidden, so I ended up arming myself with a plastic fork, kind of like picnic ware, and sort of sat outside the room clutching it and waiting to spring into action should anything happen. It was like, "Don't mess with me. I've got a plastic fork, don't you know?" Strategic.

But a later response, and much more useful, would be to try and deconstruct the message[7] behind the words, so when the voices warned me not to leave the house, then I would thank them for drawing my attention to how unsafe I felt -- because if I was aware of it, then I could do something positive about it --but go on to reassure both them and myself that we were safe and didn't need to feel frightened anymore. I would set boundaries for the voices, and try to interact with them in a way that was assertive yet respectful, establishing a slow process of

7 "There may be modes of thinking to which no known realization has so far been found to approximate. Hallucinosis, hypochondriasis and other mental 'diseases' may have a logic, a grammar, and a corresponding realization, none of which has so far been discovered. They may be difficult to discover because they are obscured by a 'memory', or a 'desire', or an 'understanding', to which they are supposed -wrongly- to approximate. Unless the obscurity can be circumvented or penetrated it will remain unobserved, as the galactic centre or the origin of the universe remains unobserved." (W. R. Bion, A Memoir of the Future, 1990, p. ix).

communication and collaboration in which we could learn to work together and support one another.

Throughout all of this, what I would ultimately realize was that each voice was closely related to aspects of myself, and that each of them carried overwhelming emotions that I'd never had an opportunity to process or resolve, memories of sexual trauma and abuse, of anger, shame, guilt, low self-worth. The voices took the place of this pain and gave words to it, and possibly one of the greatest revelations was when I realized that the most hostile and aggressive voices actually represented the parts of me that had been hurt most profoundly, and as such, it was these voices that needed to be shown the greatest compassion and care.

It was armed with this knowledge that ultimately I would gather together my shattered self, each fragment represented by a different voice, gradually withdraw from all my medication, and return to psychiatry, only this time from the other side. Ten years after the voice first came, I finally graduated, this time with the highest degree in psychology the university had ever given, and one year later, the highest masters, which shall we say isn't bad for a madwoman. In fact, one of the voices actually dictated the answers during the exam, which technically possibly counts as cheating.

And to be honest, sometimes I quite enjoyed their attention as well. As Oscar Wilde has said, the only thing worse than being talked about is not being talked about. It also makes you very good at eavesdropping, because you can listen to two conversations simultaneously. So it's not all bad.

I worked in mental health services, I spoke at conferences, I published book chapters and academic articles, and I argued, and continue to do so, the relevance of the following concept: that an important question in psychiatry shouldn't be what's wrong with you but rather what's happened to you. And all the while, I listened to my voices, with whom I'd finally learned to live with peace and respect and which in turn reflected a growing sense of compassion, acceptance and respect towards myself. And I remember the most moving and extraordinary moment when supporting another young woman who was terrorized by her voices, and becoming fully aware, for the very first time, that I no longer felt that way myself but was finally able to help someone else who was.

I'm now very proud to be a part of Intervoice, the organizational body of the International Hearing Voices Movement, an initiative inspired by the work of Professor Marius Romme and Dr. Sandra Escher, which locates voice hearing as a survival strategy, a sane reaction to insane circumstances, not as an aberrant symptom of schizophrenia to be endured, but a complex, significant and meaningful experience to be explored. Together, we envisage and enact a society that understands and respects voice hearing, supports the needs of individuals who hear voices, and which values them as full citizens. This type of society is not only possible, it's already on its way. To paraphrase Chavez, once social change begins, it cannot be reversed. You cannot humiliate the person who feels pride. You cannot oppress the people who are not afraid anymore.

For me, the achievements of the Hearing Voices Movement are a reminder that empathy, fellowship, justice and respect are more than words; they are convictions and beliefs, and that beliefs can change the world. In the last 20 years, the Hearing Voices Movement has established hearing voices networks in 26 countries across five continents, working together to promote dignity, solidarity and empowerment for individuals in mental distress, to create a new language and practice of hope, which, at its very center, lies an unshakable belief in the power of the individual.

As Peter Levine has said, the human animal is a unique being endowed with an instinctual capacity to heal and the intellectual spirit to harness this innate capacity. In this respect, for members of society, there is no greater honor or privilege than facilitating that process of healing for someone, to bear witness, to reach out a hand, to share the burden of someone's suffering, and to hold the hope for their recovery. And likewise, for survivors of distress and adversity, that we remember we don't have to live our lives forever defined by the damaging things that have happened to us. We are unique. We are irreplaceable. What lies within us can never be truly colonized, contorted, or taken away. The light never goes out.

As a very wonderful doctor once said to me, "Don't tell me what other people have told you about yourself. Tell me about you."

In short, and similar to various existentialist scholars' phrase *'existence precedes essences'* the section is a beautiful reminder of the two realities the therapeutic or mental health couple constantly face. Firstly, the experiences described would easily fall into Kendell's biological optimism and structures articulated throughout the many ages, i.e., that the symptoms described by the writer would 'fall' under the classification of a psychotic disorder, more specifically schizophrenia. It is of importance to note that the 'schizophrenia- out -there' (i.e., essentialist approach) forgets[8] that the 'out there' is someone's 'in here'! The latter is currently actively explored by various feminist theories of caring (Thomas & Longden, 2013), and argues that the technological approaches to mental health fails to adequately address the meaning and contextual factors of mental illness, even psychosis. Even if the latter is paired with psychological interventions such as CBT they share in principle the basic attitude that mental health difficulty can be ascribed to disordered mechanisms in either physiology or psychology (deficit correction models of mind), that these mechanisms can be accounted for "independently of the particular contexts in which they occur" (Thomas & Longden, 2013), and that *technological interventions can be designed and used independently of human relationships, values or "narratives"* (p. 20). From the transcript it is of interest to note that what brought about changes *per se* were not so much technological interventions, but an existential basis for caring where "happening"[9] could be understood. Through 'caring', narrative (of trauma and Being someone that experiences

8 Although not the most prudent of word choices in illustrating a complex intellectual and ethical process (diagnosis), I have yet to find descriptors able to both respect essentialist traditions and carry such practices and states of mind across into the domain of mental health without running the risk of violence to a sense of self already burdened by illness.

9 I take it this is what Badiou (2009) would refer to philosophically as "an event".

events), and moral imagination, science may become a *guardian, if not servant,* to caring and *through caring*. Similar to Emannuel Levinas's notion that philosophy is not love of wisdom but wisdom of love- *a thinking heart.* If, as articulated by Jeff Coultier and David Ingelby "psychiatric diagnosis is merely a 'signal' for the application of pre-existing institutional arrangements" (Montcrieff, 2010, p. 371) *estrangement* will follow with a greater disparity between scientific/ symbolic / materialist realms and Being *per se*. That is, 'matter' (materiality and 'objectivity) transformed into 'it/what matters' is a matter of urgency and in need of ethical resolve (if not Badiou's revolt!).What is needed is not so much knowledge of knowledge and taxonomy, rather *how it is held, communicated, constructed and carried across in relation to the Other*. The latter could also be combined with indwelling and meditative thinking so as to retain mystery and openness to experience—only then is *Eigenlichkeit* possible (Heidegger, **1959/1966**) to the imaginary, the symbolic, and the Real (Lacan, 2006).

The sceptic reader may mention that taking individual cases may be an oversimplification, and that medicine and medical diagnosis has helped many adapt to complex illnesses. Clients also actively seek diagnostic procedures for their difficulties and feel most in control of their illness if they have a diagnosis. This is certainly the case and meaningful in itself. An example may suffice: a client treated by me had the utmost respect for diagnostic nomenclature after he could successfully find a diagnosis to explain what he felt was 'wrong' with him. Paradoxically it took this particular client two decades to *convince* physicians and psychiatrist that something was amiss! At first glance I accepted the notion until spontaneously we started making sense that his search for a diagnosis had *multiple meanings*. Being the son of a mother that suffered period psychotic symptoms and a very strict demanding father it came as no surprise, to use the concept of the superego a bit freely, that he was exposed since an early age to immense pressures of perfectionism ('my world is damaged—I have to be perfect, together, never needy') and other chaotic superego demands (i.e., 'be independent- but do as I say'). He was also frequently blamed for his own difficulty and given no sensitive regard or benign parental direction- a true Orphan of the Real

(Grotstein in Allen & Collins, 1996). By 'finding' a diagnosis (finding ensured also agency!), that seemed to truly 'fit' (an explanation that could 'tie up', so to speak, his biological self as well as various contextual factors that included making sense of the other's gaze as congruent and non-judgmental [treatment team], i.e. "it now makes sense why they [parents] said I was loud and aggressive-it is part of my biology, I am not a failure and just difficult!", separating and protecting a budding psychological self), he could protect his own intuition/ perception that he was 'different' (vs. 'bad') , gain an objective if not self-observing understanding in a system (in medicine and psychotherapy) that proved to supply symbolic protection[10] against a brutalizing internal mother and father, and lend an supportive environment full of benign professionals (helpful humans compared to brutalizing parenting) that helped re-interpret his understanding of himself over time. *Diagnosis here served as guardian, protector, elucidator, enhancer, clarifier and scaffolder of a reconstituted self* ("I am rebuilding myself after I not only collapsed but was *gutted* by what happened in my life").He even received grants and other support, that although at times brought its own complexity, did serve him well. The use of medication, as *initiated by his own free will can still be viewed as part of eigenlichkeit*—it facilitated a releasement toward the world. Philosophers such as Martin Heidegger (**1959/1966)** view releasement towards things, as well as an openness to the mystery of things central to finding a true relationship between nature and man,

> Releasement[11] towards things and openness to the mystery belong together. They grant us the possibility of dwelling in the world in a totally different way. They promise us a new ground and foundation upon which we can stand and endure in the world of technology without being imperiled by it. Releasement towards things and openness to the mystery give us a vision of a new autochthony which someday even might be fit to recapture the old and now rapidly disappearing autochthony in a changed form... (Heidegger, **1959/1966,** p. 55)

10 He once mentioned that he would have liked to tell his parents that if all of us as learned people say there is something biological wrong they would know he is not to blame and thus stupid and a disappointment.

11 As opposed to, or in relationship with, comportment and classification.

For Heidegger there are two distinct ways of dwelling in the world- through calculative thinking[12] and meditative thinking. Calculative thinking is central to the natural sciences, to topology and diagnosis. Heidegger does not scorn such a way of thinking but does mention that,

> [This] assertion is valid in the sense that the approaching tide of technological revolution in the atomic age could so captivate, bewitch, dazzle, and beguile man that calculative thinking may someday come to be accepted and practiced as *the only way* of thinking (p. 56).

As mentioned earlier the very difficulties facing the mental health practitioner is not calculative thinking *per se* , but that it is seen and used as the *only way to approach a mental health difficulty*, i.e., an indifference and rejection of meditative thinking, a total 'thought'lessness or 'thinking- less- ness' to other ways of being in the world, of man's Soul,

Then man would have denied and thrown away his own special nature—that he is a meditative being. Therefore, the issue is saving of man's essential nature. Therefore, the issue is keeping meditative thinking alive (Heidegger, **1959/1966, p. 56**)

Another way to illustrate this reality is through literary examples,

12 "There are, then, two kinds of thinking, each justified and needed in its own way: calculative thinking and meditative thinking. This meditative thinking is what we have in mind when we say that contemporary man is in flight-from-thinking. Yet you may protest: mere meditative thinking finds itself floating unaware above reality. It loses touch. It is worthless for dealing with current business. It profits nothing in carrying out practical affairs" (p.46). Calculative thinking computes, it "races from one prospect to the next. Calculative thinking is not meditative thinking, not thinking which contemplates the meaning which reigns in everything that is" (p.46)... "...meditative thinking does not just happen by itself any more than does calculative thinking. At times it requires a greater effort. It demands more practice. It is in need of even more delicate care than any other genuine craft. But it must also be able to bide its time, to await as does the farmer, whether the seed will come up and ripen" (p. 47).

Calculative thinking's impact on the native self - The Little Prince:	*Meditative thinking: Albert Camus (1955/1983)—The Absurd Walls—*
If I've told you these details about Asteroid B-612 and if I've given you its number, *it is on account of the grown-ups. Grown-ups like numbers. When you tell them about a new friend, they never ask questions about what really matters. They never ask: "What does his voice sound like?" "What games does he like best?" "Does he collect butterflies?" They ask: "How old is he?" "How many brothers does he have?" "How much does he weigh?" "How much money does his father make?" Only then do they think they know him. If you tell grown-ups, "I saw a beautiful red brick house, with geraniums at the windows and doves on the roof they won't be able to imagine such a house. You have to tell them, "I saw a house worth a hundred thousand francs." Then they exclaim, "What a pretty house!"*(de Saint-Exupèry, 1943/2000, p.10)	Like great works, deep feelings always mean more than they are conscious of saying. The regularity of an impulse or a repulsion in a soul is encountered again in habits of doing and thinking, is reproduced in consequences of which the soul itself knows nothing. *Great feelings have with them their own universe, splendid or abject ...It is probably true that a man remains forever unknown to us and that there is in him something irreducible that escapes us. But practically I know men and recognize them by their behaviour, by the totality of their deeds, by the consequences caused in life by their presence.* Likewise, all those irrational feelings which offer no purchase to analysis. *I can define then practically, appreciate them practically, by gathering together the sum of their consequences in the domain of intelligence, by seizing and noting all their aspects, by outlining their universe. It is certain that apparently, though I have seen the same actor a 100 times, I shall not for that reason know him any better personally.* Yet if I add up the heroes he has personified and if I say that I know him a little better at the hundredth character counted off, this will be felt to contain an element of truth... *But it is also evident that that method is one of analysis and not of knowledge.* For methods imply metaphysics, unconsciously they disclose conclusions that they often claim not to know yet. Similarly, the last pages of a book are already contained in the first pages. Such a link is inevitable. *The method defined here acknowledges the feeling that all true knowledge is impossible...* (pp. 10-12) (italics added).

To return to Longden, one reads the difference of approach in the essay by Longden's two experiences with different physicians:

Psychiatrist one [calculative thinking]:**"Eleanor, you'd be better off with cancer, because cancer is easier to cure than schizophrenia."** [Language about being diseased- no *eigenlichkeit* and no releasement, only an *I-It* relationship and thus enslaved autochthony].

Psychiatrist/Doctor two [meditative thinking]: "**As a very wonderful doctor once said to me, "Don't tell me what other people have told you about yourself (alterity). Tell me about you (autochthony)."** [Recognition of autochthony (eigenlichkeit) facilitating a releasement towards the world (alterity)]

Heidegger (1959/1966) augments his opinion in that "[Yet] releasement towards things and openness to the mystery never happen of themselves. They do not befall us accidentally. Both flourish only through persistent, courageous thinking... if releasement[13] towards things and openness to the mystery awaken within us, then we should arrive at a path that will lead to a new ground for foundation. In that ground the creativity which produces lasting works could strike new roots" (Heidegger, 1959/1966, p. 56-57). Again Longden gives us many examples of being open to her own voices, the cumulative effort of understanding her own history and current being within her world. Diagnosis as *hortus siccus* can only be of use if it meets the very thing it describes-a human being. But only a human being is alive and has freedom to choose- diagnosis is the fruit of such a reality. In itself it can only accumulate further distinction, more symptoms and serve calculative thinking, at worst, oppressive superego technologies. It is even more of a concern if the use of such a reality (the mental health provider) only serves as vessel to its calculative reality.

13 This is an important word as many technologies on identity actually keeps the Other not only hidden but language and cultural practices confines the ill! Newer superego technologies may give rise to greater internal and mental forms of institutionalization under the banner of the good.

The Soul in need of articulation within Calculative logic

I also include here thinking on "Soul" as the definition provided by the existential psychoanalyst Eric Craig may not only scaffold psychiatric thinking, but may support all clinicians to follow an anthropological view to man's psychological lived world suffering possibly integrating both modes of being- calculative as well as meditative. According Craig (2008) the word Soul is most often used to "disclose the crux of the individuals own human existence, the quintessence of one's one and only life as lived" (Graig, 2008, p.256). More specifically , and again according to Craig " The best I can put this tacitly held understanding, phenomenologically, is that the soul or 'life of the soul', is an individual's very own situated gathering of lived experience" (p. 257). It is the unique and singular way an individual has collected, organized, processed, symbolized [put to "meaningful account"] his or her "ongoing stream of lived experience while wending [our way] through life" (257). As seen in our contemporary analytic work this being in the *lifeworld* may contain known and unknown elements. Never the less, being in the world implies an ongoing relationship, *an ongoing gathering together,* in Winnicottian terms. It should be mentioned that an individual's "gathering" is by no means calculable, an end product in itself; " it is the human being as a whole, no ego, no self, no body, no world alone, but an *entire existence that gathers all that it lives through and endures as a whole.*" (Graig, 2008, p. 257, Italics mine).

Combined with *Soul as one's gathering of lived experience,* Craig also emphasizes *Soul as one's going on being as 'stretching along'* and borrows from Donald Winnicott's notion that gathering implies a continuity of being. The gathering of life experience has ontic and ontological significance, and only through disclosure of such world design may the Soul be evident, if at all, as *situated.* "In saying that the gathering of lived-lived experience is situated, I mean only that as *Da-sein,* our gathering of experience is unavoidably contextualized, that is, shaped and structured by the manifold social, historical, existential, genetic, biological, and evolutionary contexts from which each of our existences arise." (p.259). Furthermore:

> "The circumstances (a) that we are the kind of being we call human being, a being that has evolved in its own kind of way and not some other way (e.g., not like the way of an insect, bird, cat, dog, dolphin, or gorilla); (b) that we are embodied as we are, not only as a particular species, but as both distinct and gendered individuals; (c) that we are cast into a very particular geological region and climate and not any other; (d) that we each appear at a particular time in history with its own cultural, socio-economic, political, and power dynamics; (e) that we also appear within a certain locally ethnic, economic and linguistic community; and (f) that we are thrown, rather haphazardly I'm afraid, into particular existential situations, that not only manifest the specific worlds of a geography, a particular community, and, especially, a particular family but also manifest all of these contexts in a peculiar, only-once-in cosmic-history manner; all these circumstances, shape our experiences and how we gather them in such pervasive and largely invisible ways we can in no way separate from them what we call ourselves, what we call our very soul" (p 259).

Despite the Soul *being situated*, i.e., that we are thrown into various situations, situations that may, given it being either good or bad, evoke the most fleeting of thoughts and feelings, existence in the final analysis belongs to the person who lives it, and only that person. The *Soul is thus one's very own; existence remains one's own responsibility.* Without delving into Dasein analytic technique, or any psychotherapeutic approach, Craig's *language of Soul* does allow some remediation in my view supportive of more 'whole'-some' attitudes to mental suffering. It can be said that when faced with mental pain there may be desperate attempts to remake the world, active or inactive approaches to alter lived experience of time, space, body sense, social relationships, a reworking, a re-languaging and envisioning of one's unique world view (world design, the physical world [Umwelt], the social and interpersonal [Mitwelt], and/or personal subjective world [Eigenwelt]). The change may be conscious or unknown, uncanny as it seems foreign or not me experiences. Given the abovementioned concerns, our access to both calculative and meditative thinking one could envision a languaging of another, a dialogue of togetherness wherein both modes of thinking can be used in such a way that diagnostic thinking does not become a deadening objectifying discourse, enacting an experience distant contact in a period of another's life where mutuality, solidarity and non-problematizing is central for the Soul's gathering and stretching forward in hope [stones]. Put another way, could we find a way of dialoguing that ensures a third (triangular dialogism), a looking together at, an I –thou 'at', vs. the I –It inherent in empiricism. *Mental health triangular dialogism* can thus become, (similarly) in the work of Brazilian educator and philosopher Paulo Freire a pedagogy of communication, mutuality, solidarity, hope and a thinking heart. Again, as beautifully articulated by Langdon:

> As Peter Levine has said, the human animal is a unique being endowed with an instinctual capacity to heal and the intellectual spirit to harness this innate capacity. In this respect, for members of society, there is no greater honor or privilege than facilitating that process of healing for someone, to bear witness, to reach out a hand, to share the burden of someone's suffering, and to hold the hope for their recovery. *And likewise, for survivors of distress and adversity, that we remember we don't have to live our lives forever defined by the damaging things that have happened to us. We are unique. We are irreplaceable. What lies within us can never be truly colonized, contorted, or taken away. The light never goes out.*

Conclusion

Man's empirical and transcendental self, man's Soul language, invites both calculative and meditative modes of being. Although both are of importance, it seems evident that contemporary culture tends to act, for complex reasons in itself, as if only calculative thinking, and thus the empirical, is of importance in the study and relating to man. It especially becomes an area of concern when the empirical gives rise to technological interventions designed and used independently of human relationships, their values and their own 'Soul voice (s)'. Soul thinking, or *triangular dialogism*, may serve as guardian and ensure the development and refinement of our moral imagination, and as such, our deepest level of care towards our fellow human beings. As stated by Martin Buber:

> "In certain cases, a therapist is terrified by what he is doing because he begins to suspect that, at least in such cases, but finally, perhaps, in all, something entirely other is demanded of him (or her). Something...dangerously threatening...is demanded of him: that he step forth out of the role of professional superiority, achieved and guaranteed by long training and practice, into the elementary situation between one who calls and one who is called. The abyss does not call to his confidently functioning security of action, but to the abyss, that is to the self of the doctor, that selfhood that is hidden under the structures erected through training and practice, that is itself encompassed by chaos, itself familiar with demons, but is graced with the humble power of wrestling and overcoming, and is ready to wrestle and overcome thus ever anew." (in Agassi, 1999, pp.18-19)

Acknowledgements

Special thanks to Prof Kevin Boileau for his thorough and critical reading of the article, as well as the anonymous reader. Your perceptive reading enhanced the paper's core concerns—I am deeply grateful.

Bibliography

Agassi, J.B. (1999). *Martin Buber on psychology and psychotherapy. Essays, letters, and dialogue.* USA: Syracuse University Press.

Allen, J.G. & Collins, D.T. (1996).*Contemporary treatment of psychosis. Healing the relationship in the era of the brain.* Northvale, New Jersey: Jason Aronson, Inc.

Angel, K. (2012). Contested psychiatric ontology and feminist critique: Female sexual dysfunction and the DSM. *History of Human Sciences, 25 (4)*, 3-24.

Badiou, A. (2009). T*heory of the Subject.* London and New York: Continuum International Publishing Group.

Bion, W.R. (1990). *A Memoir of the Future. Book 1-3.* London: Karnac Books.

Bloch, S. & Green, S.A. (Eds.). (2009). *Psychiatric ethics (4th edition).* London: Oxford University Press.

Bromme, M.R. (2006). Taxonomy and ontology in Psychiatry: a survey of recent literature. *Philosophy, Psychiatry and Psychology, 13 (4)*, 303-319.

Camus, A. (1955/1983). *The myth of Sisyphus and other essays.* New York: Vintage Int.

Craig, E. (2008). The human and the hidden: existential wonderings about depth, Soul and the unconscious. *The Humanistic Psychologist, 36*, 227-282.

de Saint- Exupèry, A. (1943/2000).*The Little Prince.* New York: Houghton Mifflin Harcourt.

Frances, A. (2013). *Saving normal.* NY, NY: HarperCollins Publishers.

Grotstein, J. S. (1997). Integrating one person and two person psychologies: Autochthony and Alterity in counterpoint. *Psychoanal Q.*, 66, 403-430.

Fulford, K.W.M., Thorton, T. & Graham, G. (2006). *Oxford textbook of philosophy and psychiatry.* UK: Oxford University Press.

Heidegger, M. (1959/1966). *Discourse on thinking.* New York: Harper Perennial.

Henry, M. (1987/2004). *Barbarism.* London and New York: Continuum International Publishing group.

Lacan, J. (2006). *Ecrits.* New York: W.W. Norton and Company. Translation from French by Bruce Fink.

Moncrieff, J. (2010). Psychiatric diagnosis as political device. *Social Theory and Health, 8(4)*, 370-382.

Savage, H. (1998). *An Introduction to Holism.* Pretoria: Wessa.

Thomas, P. & Longden, E. (2013). Madness, childhood adversity and narrative psychiatry: caring and the moral imagination. *Med Humanit*, 39, 119-125.

Von Broembsen, F. (1999).*The sovereign self: toward a phenomenology of self-experience.* Northvale, New Jersey: Jason Aronson, Inc.

From Image to Imago: Reflections on Phenomenology, Psychological Depth, and the Unconscious

Vic Schermer, PhD

Abstract

Phenomenology and psychoanalysis appear to be at opposite poles of understanding, with phenomenology positing consciousness as subsuming the totality of all experience, while psychoanalysis holds that many experiences are repressed or otherwise concealed from consciousness. In this article, it is proposed that these two seemingly mutually exclusive points of view are reconcilable through an examination of the phenomenological reduction and psychoanalytic method.

The relationship between an image and an *imago*, an image that contains deep and hidden symbolism and meaning, provides a basis for linking phenomenology and psychoanalysis, using Husserl's concept of horizon. At the horizons of the "things themselves" are potential ambiguities, contradictions, and gaps that provide a ground for metaphor and in-depth understanding and constitute evidence for psychoanalytic investigation of the unconscious. There are locations within the phenomenological field of perception, imagination, and judgment that allow for concealment. The unconscious can be understood phenomenologically as that which is hidden and ambiguous at the horizon, facilitated by imagination and dream, what Merleau-Ponty called the *oneiric*, and what psychoanalysis calls fantasy.

Key Words: Edmund Husserl; Sigmund Freud; Maurice Merleau-Ponty; phenomenological reduction; unconscious fantasy; horizon; oneiric; empiricism.

Axioms are not axioms until they are proved upon our pulses.
—*John Keats*

Edmund Husserl conceptualized phenomenology as the investigation of the things themselves as they appear in consciousness: the noesis-neoma relationship disclosed by the epoche (Husserl, 1980). By contrast, psychoanalysis is the pursuit of that which eludes and escapes consciousness, the repressed or otherwise sequestered unconscious conflicts of which the subject is unaware but which continue to influence his or her thought and behavior.

As such, phenomenology and psychoanalysis are at opposite poles of understanding, the former subsuming the totality of experience within consciousness, and the latter positing consciousness as but a small segment of the total psychosomatic mind-body complex that is largely unconscious. However, in what follows, I will argue that these seemingly diametrically opposed ways of understanding the mind can be reconciled and understood in terms of one another.

To do so, I will consider the problem of how an image, a dream, a work of art, or a symptom, understood through descriptive phenomenology, can become a deep image, an *imago* that has hidden complex meanings, thus susceptible to deep analysis. I will do this from the standpoint of the phenomenological reduction but with some reference to post-Husserlian thought, especially the work of Merleau-Ponty on perception and imagination. I will try to show that the phenomenological "I" and world, as they constitute themselves in perception, imagination, and judgment include ambiguities, gaps, fragmentations, and "hiding places" which remained in the background for Husserl and which Freud discovered in his analytic work. It is precisely in this overlapping region of phenomenological complexity and psychoanalytic understanding of the depths that much of post-Heideggerian Continental philosophy came about. However, this essay goes back to the beginnings because in the philosophical storm that ensued, some matters vital to Husserl and Freud were neglected.

Although Freud and Husserl lived and worked during the same time period and intellectual climate (the transition from the enlightenment and romantic eras to modernism), and even though they acquired similar ideas about psychology and intentionality from their studies with Franz Brentano, and despite their similar purpose to create an over-riding meta-theory for understanding that transcended and disclosed truths beyond the empiricist thinking of their time, Husserl and Freud went in divergent directions and left a yawning gap between their two points of view. Husserl sought the transcendent truth of consciousness from which psychology and the natural order arose, while Freud sought psychological truth consistent with nature but outside of consciousness. It would appear that never the twain could meet, but I will contend that they do indeed converge in the place of pre-reflective thought, the world where images rule.

The gap between a philosophy of all-encompassing consciousness versus a psychology of consciousness as a mere gateway to things concealed has persisted despite the efforts of psychiatrists, social thinkers, and Continental philosophers who have tried to close it, as well as the more recent efforts of some psychoanalysts (e.g. Atwoood and Stolorow, 2014) to incorporate phenomenology in psychoanalysis. Unmoved by these attempts at synthesis, contemporary phenomenologists still struggle to free themselves from the naturalism and empirical science that Freud and most of his followers employed. Thus, in the *Cambridge Companion to Husserl* (Smith and Smith, 1995), an end-of-the-century retrospective on Husserl's work, there is not a single reference to Freud or psychoanalysis. Conversely, Husserl's major preoccupation, the rigors of the phenomenological reduction, are rarely if ever discussed by psychoanalysts. For the most part, psychoanalysis continues to accept the natural world as a given, make empirical claims to validity, and assume biosocial, linguistic, and narrative views of the self and the organism rather than emphasizing the ground of phenomenology as such.

Thus, while there have been a number of efforts to discuss the interplay of Husserl's and Freud's ideas, the problematic that remains unresolved is whether and if so, how a philosophy that emphasizes the primacy of consciousness can be reconciled with a psychology that regards consciousness as the mere tip of an iceberg in which the mental life is mostly hidden and below the surface. That is the problem I hope to address, recognizing that there may be other paths to the same goal, as well as significant objections to such point of view in any form. My purpose in recalling how my ideas took shape is not so much to draw hard and fast conclusions as to stimulate thinking about how a depth psychology of what might be called the implicate order (a quantum understanding of nature as having an underlying flow posited by the physicist David Bohm, 1980) may emerge from the Husserlian reduction, which seeks and demonstrates transparency in all phenomena. How does an image, which, after all, is only an appearance, take on a deeper, concealed meaning? In attempting to answer this question, I take a different tack from Heidegger's linguistic/hermeneutical turn from epistemology to ontology, and from Lacan's emphasis on language and the symbolic order, rather focusing on pre-reflective thought, which Heidegger (1962) called the "present-at-hand" and which Lacan relegated to the "imaginary" and "real" components of the signifier-signified relationship. In my view, phenomenology and psychoanalysis share the common realization that we live in a sea of images, and that language, the life world, and psychology are ways in which we give these images further sense and meaning in communication and collectivity.

Dreams, Images, and Art as Phenomena with Depth

My attention was drawn to the apparent discrepancy between phenomenology and psychoanalytic interpretation by two experiences. The first was my realization of the difficulties of remembering and reporting dreams. The second was a conversation with a poet about a poem that initially seemed like an iteration of discrepant images, with a puzzle as to how to arrive at its underlying meaning. I will tell you a bit about both experiences and how they brought me to this point.

A patient reported a dream in which he, an architect, was standing in the construction area near a half-completed building. He was with his pet dog from adolescence, a dog who was his companion during a time of family upheaval that led to his being forced to leave them against his will to attend a boarding school far away from home. I had worked with him for several years, and the interpretation came to me quite naturally. I said that the dream spoke to his feelings of incompleteness and failure for which he sought comfort from me. Aware of counter-transference, I added that I may have sometimes neglected his need for understanding in this regard. The patient validated my interpretation with memories of his dog being "therapeutic" and elaborating on his insecurities about his work, further acknowledging that, yes, he felt more support from his dog than from me.

Sometime later, when I was reflecting on this dream while working on a book (Schermer, 2014) that included a section on phenomenology, I realized that many details of the dream escaped me: the location of the building, the clothes the patient was wearing, his posture and facial expression, the appearance and position of the dog, the light and shadows, and the position, emotions and attitude of the dreamer who dreamed the dream (Grotstein, 2000). In other words, I lacked an eidetic description of the dream. I didn't know the dream at all. I only knew it vaguely within the narrative of a waking individual that was furthermore intersubjectively internalized into my own experience. I only knew the dream as a projection of myself in dialogue with the dreamer. That was not unimportant for therapy, but the dream as the thing itself, as phenomenon, remained hidden, a secret.

The truth is that no one has ever interpreted a dream-as-dream. As a private experience occurring during sleep, details are quickly lost when the dreamer awakens, and once he reports selected elements, they are assimilated into an intersubjective conversation and narrative, and ultimately into a historical and cultural context. The pure phenomenology of the dream-as-dream is lost. It can be partly recovered by detailed introspection, immersing oneself in the dream world in a way that the Romantic philosopher Herder described as "feeling ones way into" a person or literary work, pursing the phenomena until they become vivid inside us (Forster, 2007).

Even so, the dream as dreamed is quickly lost in the transition from sleep to wakefulness.

That realization led to the further thought that, while difficult to bring to light, some of the dream's meanings must somehow reside in the dream as dreamed, not in projections and introspection based on waking conversation and analysis. While psychologists have debated whether dreams have meaning, people through the ages have been drawn to them on the basis of such a belief. I surmised that the dream images must acquire meaning from within their own organization. In that way, they become *imagos*, deep meaningful experiences having significance, depth, and history embedded within them.

The second occurrence that brought me to a similar place was a discussion I had with a friend[14] about a poem by the late James Wright, one of the poets of the "deep image" (Haskell, 1979), a phrase used to depict the use of shifting images as opposed to narrative verse to convey emotions and implications about the human condition. My poet friend and I were discussing one of Wright's poems called "The Jewel" (Wright, 1990, p. 122):

> There is this cave
> In the air behind my body
> That nobody is going to touch:
> A cloister, a silence
> Closing around a blossom of fire.
> When I stand upright in the wind,
> My bones turn to dark emeralds.

Wright (1975) ironically said his poems were "carefully dreamed", and this poem is more like a dream, free association, or stream of consciousness than a real life narrative. As in a dream, the images at first seem randomly chosen: cave, air, body, cloister, bloss

om, fire, emeralds. Yet there is an undeniable power in these images as combined and spoken by the poet: a private space in need of protection, defiance, a choice having consequences. Their power gives them intuitive meaningful presence

14 Michael Graves, poet and literary critic, New York City

contained in the images and words as such.

My poet friend, who knew Wright personally and had studied his work with him, gave me insights into the poem through allusions to other sources and contexts: Plato's cave, references to blossoms and fire in other of his poems, connections to Yeats' preoccupation with the occult, the mythic significance of emeralds, Wright's alcoholic psychoses. I thought these were all pertinent and interesting, but I felt that the images themselves and their juxtaposition possessed depth in and of themselves. I suggested that we just immerse ourselves in the images as what Husserl called "the things themselves." We agreed that the images were paradoxical: a cave in the air; a blossom of fire, bones turning into dark emeralds. Their power seemed to emerge from their ambiguous, contradictory, and disparate nature, exactly what struck Freud about dreams and symptoms.

These two experiences—with a patient and with a poem—led me to believe that an image, as simply an occurrence, can by a special intentional act acquire an intuitive depth of meaning prior to any reflection about it. Moreover, the meanings may not always be transparent through the epoche, but, under certain circumstances, present themselves therein as ambiguous and with gaps and contradictions, which, in turn are what give the images depth. Let me try to say what I mean, with special reference to dreams, but with all types of images in mind.

Images, Horizons, and Depth

The word "image" has several meanings. For our purposes here, an image is any mental appearance, usually sensory, that may or may not have a meaning, object or thought process assigned to it. [15] Thus, an image is a percept prior to its being attached to a specific idea about it, for example, a Rorsach inkblot, a blotch of paint on a canvas, or a sound before we identify its source or form. Through intentionality, images acquire meanings through the noesis-noema relationhip. (It could be argued, in agreement with Husserl, that there are no percepts prior to intentions, even if the object is not identified as such, that even "meaninglessness" is intended. For the current purposes, I am saying that many images

15 This definition is to be distinguished from the definition of an image as a representation.

are available to consciousness and that only some are selected by intentional acts.)

Thus, by my definition, images have no object unless they are assigned one. As in Lacan's mirror stage, the child's image in the mirror has no meaning until he recognizes that it is of himself. (Until then, he lives in a world of images, of imagination, in which meanings are highly variable and paradoxical, what Freud called the primary process.) Most often the epoche discloses that an image is assigned an object in an intentional act. (I look at the moon, and it is the moon, not the image on my retina, that I "see.") In most cases, when we apply the phenomenological reduction, we find their noema to be organized objects, whether the color red or an automobile or a unicorn or the number one. They may or may not represent something in the natural world, but they always have a "thing-ness" about them and a singular consistent meaning. The ideality of such things (or beings, what Heidegger called the "ontic") allows us to reflect on them, think about them. This is what Husserl's transcendent ego discloses to us. This is his legacy from Plato, Descartes, and Kant.

The concept from Husserl that via Heidegger caused a tectonic shift in twentieth-century philosophy is his notion of horizon. Noema have features that are implicit, not evident, like the back of a person who is facing me. Consciousness intends the whole object and its context without necessarily having *prima facie* evidence for it. We see a chair, which includes its unseen back, its familiarity, and its use. The noema includes ever-widening circles or layers, all of which are aspects of the same bracketed experience. Some of these horizons may be infinite or unknown. Thus, if I see a chair, it is in a room, which is in a house, which is in a neighborhood. Moreover, it has its use, which is also intended. These are the horizons of the experience of that particular chair that I see before me. The horizon contains the unseen and unknown.

Heidegger went further than Husserl and held that at the horizon of all beings is Being, *Dasein*, thrownness into time, mortality, Being that cares for its existence. This was the hermeneutical turn: for Heidegger, rigorous phenomenology disclosed at the horizon the interpretive necessity that permeated all of existence, the historicity and facticity of human life. This was the ontological bombshell that startled so many of his students and other thinkers of his time. It is a mind-blowing idea that we still struggle to come to grips with in its fullness and implications.

Without in any way diminishing Heidegger's epoch-making insights, I wish to take a step back and look at the notion of horizon in a somewhat different way. I do this because I feel that something important was lost in the existential storm, something that takes us closer to Freud and his intentions. It is this: as we pursue the horizon of the noema, the ambiguity and uncertainty of its meaning increases. For example, when I look at this person who faces me, behind him may be a gift or a dagger. And as I am aware of his temporality and historicity, there is increasing ambiguity about their details. So if we start with an image like a dream or perhaps Rembrandt's "Self-Portrait as the Apostle Paul" (Rembrandt von Rijn, 1662; see reproduction), and move to their horizons, we encounter complex meanings in the person, place, and action encountered in the beings that are there.

As I gaze at Rembrandt's man with the turban and a manuscript shrouded in darkness except for the illumined face and the corner of the manuscript, I experience an ambiguity that calls for interpretation and understanding. The image takes me to a place of wanting to know something more about the man and his relationship to the manuscript. The darkness of most of the painting stimulates this pursuit of the unseen and unknown. The "fusion of horizons" of self and other (person, artwork, historical period, etc.) is, according to Gadamer (1997, p. 302), what prompts us to enter into a dialogue with the image and a conversation about it. This is the basis of metaphor and metonymy in language and of dream interpretation. I want to assert that the initial approach to ambiguous meaning is pre-reflective, already present in the horizon. This will bring phenomenology into conjunction with psychoanalysis.

From Phenomenology to Hermeneutics: How Images Constitute Meanings

An essential insight from phenomenology is that most of our lived experience is intuited, known to us well before we begin to think and reflect upon it in speech and language. It is "already there" and we live within it. Perception, memory, judgment, and imagination are intentions that constitute a lived experience. Language, science, logic, and the *cogito* serve to communicate, explain, clarify, and refine our lived experience.

Merleau-Ponty (1976) conceptualized the phenomenology of perception and lived experience in a way that potentially provides a way to understand what Freud called "unconscious" as constituted phenomenologically and prior to language and the symbolic order. For Merleau-Ponty, our pre-reflective perception of the world and the people who inhabit it emerges from and is an extension of our own body.[16] This principle of the embodiment of all experience connects to Freud's notion of erogenous zones and, more generally, to Melanie Klein's statement that "The child is an intensely embodied person" (Ashbach and

16 "... now it is precisely my body which perceives the body of another person, and discovers in that other body a miraculous prolongation of my own intention, a familiar way of dealing with the world." - M. Merleau-Ponty, M. (1976, p. 354)

Schermer, 1987, p. 37). The phenomenological body is the center of the lifeworld, and the two are intertwined. Merleau-Ponty (1968, pp. 130-155) thus argues for the interpenetration of the embodied self and the world. For example, when we touch an object, we sense both our fingers and the surface it touches: the two are inseparable. Developmentally, the infant experiences its mind, body, and world as what Balint (1968) called an "interpenetrating harmonious mixup." In certain respects, psychoanalysis may be seen to be a phenomenology of the embodied self and its interpenetration with the world. A patient of mine became pregnant during the course of her treatment. In the later stages of her pregnancy, the weight and activity of the little being inside her affected her sense of self as well as my own perceptions of the room, my own body, and my moods. The presence of the third living being in the consulting room was known to me phenomenologically as my own bodily experience. If I had bracketed off my knowledge of the natural world in the manner of Husserl's epoche, I would have described a change in myself and the space, rather than a physical being inside the mother. The former is a phenomenon of pre-reflective thought, while the latter is an inference about nature.

Another area of great interest to Merleau-Ponty was the imagination ((Merleau-Ponty 1993, p. 126). He contended that the imagination informs all experience, including our perceptions of self and world. For Merleau-Ponty, dreams, myths, imaginary people and places, are all as much a part of our life world as are our perceptions of the natural world. They are as "real" to us as nature herself, even to be found within nature. Merleau-Ponty called the realm of the imagination the *oneiric*, linking it directly to dreams as the prototype. Phenomenologically, imagination and the oneiric precede and interpenetrate the natural world. The child lives in a world of imagination which gradually, and based on feedback from its actions (reality testing) and socialization, develops a semblance of a so-called "realistic" perception of a world which it can hopefully navigate successfully.[17] Like the child, we all start out with images, and we weave stories and metaphors about them.

17 The same is surprisingly true of the hard sciences. Newton's dreams and alchemical interests preceded his discovery of the laws of motion. Kekule disovered the shape of the benzene ring through a dream. Einstein used a series of "thought experiments" to formulate the special theory of relativity. Imagination is the midwife of theory.

Stories and metaphors are important means of establishing mutual understanding (Lakoff and Johnson, 1980). They are essential components of hermeneutics and interpretation.

Images, Psychic Depth, and the Unconscious

Images acquire meaning within and through the noesis-noema relationship. They take on "sense" through the intentional act. So I see a chair or the moon, not merely the sensory features that compose them. So my patient dreamt about a familiar dog and a building. The dream images acquire sense. So James Wright wrote about things like caves and blossoms and wind rather than just making utterances absent the things themselves. The relevant questions for psychoanalysis are 1) how do these meanings within the noesis-noema relationship acquire depth? 2) How do they come to be related to the "I," the self, the patient or poet, and his history? 3) How do they come to be ambiguous, contradictory. and concealed?

With regard to the first question, I have already hinted at an answer. Psychological depth opens up as the horizon expands, in what Heidegger (2008) called *alatheia*, Being disclosing itself. At that shifting horizon of disclosure is ambiguity. Ambiguity calls for something to generate sense and reference, completeness and transparency of the noema. But since direct apprehension is no longer possible, the noesis-noema relationship is completed through possibility, and this is done is through metaphor, a likeness to what it might be. The horizon and its metaphorical incompleteness create the experience of psychological depth. Thus, in the Wright poem, the image of a cave in the air creates an ambiguous horizon. Somewhere in the horizon of the image of a cave there is a relationship to a metaphorical enclosure in the air rather than the earth.. Consciousness begins to stretch the image. The cave shelters, conceals. The air is everywhere. The cave in the air affords shelter and secrecy from omnipresent transparency. As we begin to reflect on the meaning, we might compare the cave that no one is going to touch with Levinas' (1999) "alterity," the unknowability of the other; and Winnicott's (1965, p. 187) "incommunicado core," the secret aspects of the self. These are meanings generated by reason and understanding, but they require the ambiguous aspect of the image at the horizon to even be considered at all.

With regard to the second question, the psychoanalyst is primarily concerned with the image as it emerges from the patient, from a singular being who is present with him. How does an image become related to the "I," a subject, the self, if indeed the two can ever be considered separately from one another? For Husserl and Merleau-Ponty, the "I," is the embodied hub or center of the experience of the lifeworld. By contrast, many images and objects in daily life are typically perceived in a detached manner, not identified with the self.[18] There are objects, and then there are objects that engage the self. People rarely regard dreams, poems, and works of art—at least the ones they appreciate—with detachment. They position themselves in such a way as to find the imagery personally meaningful objects of identification. The curious thing about some symptoms, is that they are experienced in a detached manner as patterns that come from an unknown source. The symptom is understood when the patient discovers its source in his own mental life. Freud's famous statement, "Where id was, there ego shall be" ("Wo Es war, soll Ich werden") literally translates as "Where it was, there I shall be" (Freud, 1991, p. 112). The presence of self in its identification with the object transforms the mundane and detached to an experience of depth and implication.

The third question is of singular importance with respect to the unconscious: how do images and their intended objects come to be concealed, hidden, inaccessible to consciousness and discourse? The answer that I propose resides in the nature of pre-reflective perception and imagination. The pre-symbolic infant and child inhabit a sea of images that are a concatenation of perceptions and imagination. The perceptual component acquires three dimensions through the binocular and binaural senses as well as movement within the sea of evolving experience. Such sensory-motor configurations configure the phenomenological world that we are born into. Experiences soon take on the quality of noema, of things themselves. So, for example, the child comes to think of "mother" as an object

18 Indeed, the scientific view, at least until recently, is based on the de-subjecitivizing of the natural world.

(and later, a subject) outside of itself. But at the horizons of these noema, there are places in the child's imagination-infused three-dimensional world that are concealed, hidden from view. Moreover, they are not yet identified by the child as "mind" or "matter," as *cogito* versus substance. (Research on "mentalization" (Fonagy, et al., 2002) suggests that the child only gradually develops a concept of mind and of subjects other than itself.) It is through the possibility of concealment within the sea of images that what Freud called the "unconscious" paradoxically becomes part of the phenomenological world.

Within its evolving world of experience, the child discovers that there are horizons of things that are hiding places, "file cabinets" where it can put things away that it doesn't like or are disapproved by others. It can put those contents inside something, or behind something, or at a great distance. It can retrieve some of those, but it can also banish them as the evil one in the kingdom is banished forever in fairy tales. As it begins to make hiding places, the child is creating within its phenomenological world regions of the hidden and even the imprisoned or unknown. Its horizons include enclaves of parts of self, relationships, phantasms, dreams, real and fictional characters, all of which become temporarily or permanently inaccessible. There are smaller worlds within worlds that are sequestered, like the private diary of secret thoughts kept by an adolescent. Those that are not encountered for a long period of time are forgotten. But, paradoxically, they are in the phenomenological world, yet a concealed part of it. Slap and Slap-Shelton (1991) captured some of this idea in their concept of "sequestered schema," whereby the cognitive schemas the child uses to understand its experience can become "sequestered," inaccessible to the child's subsequent experience. Slap and Slap are referring to the child's cognitions as understood by Piaget and Inhelder (1958), while I am talking about phenomenology, implying that sequestering develops before the child can think conceptually and is processing images in a pre-reflective way, which Piaget and Inhelder incorporate in the sensori-motor and pre-operational stages of intellectual development.

While psychoanalysis is still largely framed within a

neo-Kantian (cf. Bion, 1962) and/or empirical epistemology, or in existential and Lacanian thought in terms of discourse, one can find echoes of phenomenology there as well. One example that has escaped the net of theorizing, although clinical examples abound, is Melanie Klein's (1977) depiction of the defense mechanism of projective identification, as a *fantasy*. She says that the infant has a *fantasy* of putting the bad parts (pain, frustration, etc) of its experience into the mother's breast until, as a result of mother's care, it feels safe to retrieve them. This is an interesting idea with which even Klein herself could not fully come to grips: that defense "mechanisms" are not the result of "drives," but the use of imagination for purposes of safety and security: the phenomenology of defense.

Bettleheim's (1976) *The Use of Enchantment* provides many illustrations of the ways in which the child makes use of fairy tales and imagination to organize his or her inner world. While Bettleheim uses Freudian theory to interpret and explain these stories, it is sufficient for the present purpose to see how the child's imagination works to make a world that allows it to cope with threat. Bettleheim's (1983) *Freud and Man's Soul* makes the further point that, based upon a medical model rather than Freud's own subjective understanding, many English translations of Freud converted his concepts of self and mind into the mechanistic language of reductionist science. In other words, the subjective and phenomenological aspects of Freud's theories were lost in translation.

An illustration of how images may be concealed within other images was provided to me by a colleague (Cohen and Schermer, 2004). A woman patient recalled that as a child, she would sometimes read books that incurred her mother's disapproval. When her mother came into the room, she would put her secret "little book" underneath a "big book" so that her mother would not see what she was reading. The patient said that this was what she sometimes did in therapy, i.e, hide her real feelings under an intellectualizing façade, an insight that furthered her therapeutic progress. My colleague and I considered that at least some coping mechanisms and defenses are aspects of concealment within conscious phenomenological experience. The natural world, discourse, and the imagination afford many opportunities to put things "out of sight, out of mind."

What I have said so far suggests that if they had engaged in a serious dialogue, Husserl and Freud could have found much common ground for reconciling their points of view, which of course never happened. And there isn't much documentation to suggest that they had any knowledge of or interest in one another's ideas. I believe their all too neglected commonalities can be seen in their common interests in images, interpretation and meaning, and how consciousness and ideas constitute themselves. However, each had strong philosophical and theoretical biases which were antithetical to one another. This is an unfortunate reality the consequences of which are still manifest several generations later. My purpose has been to demonstrate a strong commonality between them that is hidden by their opposing assumptions. I conclude my musings about Freud and Husserl with a slightly humorous aside by saying how their respective world views would have made each other's ideas literal "nightmares" for each other. A rapprochement between their ideas, which is retrospectively quite possible, would have been difficult for them at the time.

Freud's Nightmare: Interpretation is Not an Empirical Science

Here is a fictitious "dream" of the great neuroscientist and psychiatrist Sigmund Freud:

> Freud wakes up terrified from a dream in which he is in the medical laboratory of his mentor, Ernst Brucke, who chastises him for his recent paper concluding that hysterical symptoms are psychological rather than chemical in origin. Just then, a flask explodes and the shattering glass blinds him in one eye.

Freud was steeped in the empirical reductionist neuroscience of his day. He made a major departure from the *zeitgeists* of the emerging fields of neuroscience and psychiatry when he wrote *The Interpretation of Dreams*, where he used an interpretive method rather than one that emphasized empirical causes. In Dilthey's terms, he shifted from causal explanation of natural events to subjective, intersubjective, and existential understanding of human experience (Lessing, Makkreel, and Pozzo, 2011). Freud attempted to unify the empirical and the hermeneutical by using Aristotle's notion of representation, holding that conscious ideas represented unconscious processes that had an instinctual, somatic origin. He thus made himself vulnerable to a kind of "mentalism" in which biological necessity included "thoughts" that were not conscious. This led him erroneously to believe that an interpretive method could provide causal explanations of natural phenomena. Philosophers like Popper (1959) and Grunbaum (1984) have pointed to the fallacies and dangers attendant on confounding these two distinctly different paradigms of causality versus meaning. (This does not mean that Freud was wrong in his discoveries, only that his methods of verification were flawed.)

Freud, regardless of his own interests in art, philosophy, and the humanities, and his own statements that his basic ideas had long been expressed in literature and theater, was heavily invested in presenting psychoanalysis to the world as an empirical science, guarding against accusations of Jewish mysticism, quackery, and defection from the psychiatric profession (Gay, 1988). Imagine if Freud had come out and said, "Like my philosophical counterpart, Husserl, I am a phenomenologist. My real accomplishment has been to perceive and describe the full range of the lifeworld from birth to death and how our everyday understanding and discourse is but a small and self-protective part of a much richer and more complex life world." His own claim to a scientific revolution would have been shattered, and his detached objectivizing world view that was so much influenced by Enlightenment science would have run aground. Freud, whose ideas were so profoundly immersed in the human experience, was nevertheless compelled to maintain a position based on empirical science rather than the interpretive method central to the psychoanalytic situation.

Husserl's Nightmare: The Phenomenological Self and World as Ambiguous, Disruptive, and Hidden

Husserl falls asleep while monitoring a lecture by his student, Heidegger. While dozing off, he has a dream in which he is attempting a phenomenological reduction of his pet cat. As he is writing it down, the cat hisses at him and disappears beneath the sofa. When he wakes up, the whole class is surrounding him, comforting him, asking him if he is all right.

Husserl recognized and probably was put off by the difference between the unpredictable "cat-like" stream of consciousness and the phenomenology of the noesis-noema relationship. I don't think he was quite able to articulate how the two are related to one another. His purpose, expressed in the notion of the transcendental ego, was to show how all ideas presuppose and are conditional upon experience that constitutes itself from the intentional relationship between the thinker and the thought. In other words, he sought to demonstrate through bracketing and the reduction that the building blocks of explanation and understanding were not sensations but irreducible phenomena that manifest in consciousness. Husserl, true to the idealist legacy, believed that the phenomenological reduction would reveal an orderly relationship of direct experience to thetic explanation and understanding. In a way, he anticipated Russell's later idea of a universal science (Korhoven, 2013), although from a point of view different from the analytic philosophers.

In this respect, Husserl was blind to the "falling into death" that Heidegger saw behind all phenomena, and more importantly for the present purpose, the contradictory and troubled nature of human experience as it presents itself in the stream of consciousness. He incorporated some of the complexity and turbulence of the stream in his notion of the life-world, but he always distinguished between the life world and a coherent philosophical and psychological understanding of consciousness. My purpose here has been to suggest that there is no escape, not even through the epoche and phenomenological reduction, from the gaps, deceptions, and complex dynamic and developmental in-folding that informs experience as it constitutes itself in consciousness. In this, I stand with Heidegger, Sartre, and especially Merleau-Ponty. My intention has been to show that Freud as phenomenologist played a major role in deconstructing the idea of a coherent, orderly consciousness, while at the same time uniquely relating his understanding to clinical phenomena and the consulting room. For Husserl, this might have constituted an excursion into some personal Hell. But I think that if Freud and Husserl had both emphasized their discovery of the importance of images in the thought process, they might have found much in common.

References

Ashbach, C. and Schermer, V.L. (1987). *Object relations, the self, and the group: A conceptual paradigm*. London: Routledge

Atwood, G. E. & Stolorow, R. D. (2014). *Structures of sujectivity: Explorations in pychoanalytic penomenology and contextualism*. London: Routledge.

Balint, M. (1968). *The basic fault: Therapeutic aspects of regression*. London: Tavistock.

Bettleheim, B. (1976). *The uses of enchantment: The meaning and importance of fairy tales*. New York: Vintage.

Bettleheim, B. (1983). *Freud and man's soul*. New York: Vintage.

Bion, W. R. (1962). A theory of thinking. *International journal of psychoanalysis, 43*: 306-310.

Bohm, D. (1980). *Wholeness and the implicate order*. London: Routledge.

Cohen, B.D. and Schermer, V.L. (2004). Self transformation and the unconscious in contemporary psychoanalytic therapy: The problem of "depth" within a relational and intersubjective perspective. *Psychoanalytic psychology*, 21, 4: 580-600.

Fonagy, P., Gergely, G., Jurist, E. L., & Target, M. (2002). *Affect regulation, mentalization, and the development of the self*. New York: Other Press.

Forster, M. (2007). Johann Gottfried von Herder. *Stanford encyclopedia of philosophy*. Web page: http://plato.stanford.edu/entries/herder/ (last accessed August 15, 2016).

Freud, S. (1991). The dissection of the psychical personality. In *New introductory lectures on psychoanalysis*, (Trans. James Strachey). London: Penguin Books. (Originally published 1932.)

Gadamer, H-G. (1997). *Truth and method.* New York: Continuum, 1997

Gay, P. (1988). *Freud: A life for our times.* New York: Norton.

Grotstein, J. S. (2000). *Who is the dreamer who dreams the dream.* Hillsdale, NJ: The Analytic Press.

Grunbaum, A. (1984). *The foundations of psychoanalysis: A philosophical critique.* (Pittsburgh Series in Philosophy and History of Science). Berkeley, CA: University of California Press.

Haskell, D. (1979). The modern american poetry of deep image. *Southern Review* [Australia], 12: 137-166.

Heidegger, M. (1962). *Being and time.* (J. Macquarrie & E. Robinson, Trans.). San Franscisco: HarperCollins. (Originally published in German, 1927.)

Heidegger. M. (2008). On the origin of the work of art. In *Basic writings* (Ed. D.F. Krell.) New York: HarperCollins, 143-212.

Husserl, E. (1980). The thesis of the natural standpoint and its suspension. In R.C.Solomon (Ed.), *Phenomenology and Existentialism.* Lanham, MD :Rowman & Littleford, 112-117.

Klein, M. (1977). Notes on some schizoid mechanisms. In: *Envy and gratitude and other works: 1946-1963* (pp. 1-24). New York: Delta. (Originally published: 1946.)

Korhoven, A. (2013). *Logic as universal science: Russell's early logicism and its philosophical context.* London: Palgrave Macmillan.

Lakoff, G., & Johnson, M. (1980). *Metaphors we live by.* Chicago: University of Chicago Press.

Levinas, I. (1999). *Alterity and transcendence* (M. B. Smith, Trans.). New York: Columbia University Press. (Originally published 1970).

Lessing, H.U., Makkreel, R.A., and Pozzo, R., Eds. (2011). *Recent contributions to Dilthey's philosophy of the human sciences.* Stuttgart, Germany: Frommann-Holzboog.

Merleau-Ponty, M. (1968). *The visible and invisible.* Evanston, IL: Northwestern University Press.

Merleau-Ponty, M. (1976). *Phenomenology of perception.* (C. Smith, Trans.). London: Routledge & Kegan Paul.

Merleau-Ponty, M. (1993). Eye and mind. In Johnson, G. (Ed.). *The Merleau-Ponty aesthetics reader: Philosophy and painting*. Evanston, IL: Northwestern University Press, 121-149. (Original work published 1961).

Piaget, J. and Inhelder, B. (1958), *The growth of logical thinking from childhood to adolescence.* New York: Basic Books.

Popper, K. (1959). *The Logic of scientific discovery*. London: Hutchinson.

Rembrandt von Rijn. (1662). Self portrait as the apostle Paul. Web location:

https://www.flickr.com/photos/gandalfsgallery/5228901563 (last accessed August 15, 2016).

Schermer, V.L. (2014) *Meaning, mind, and self-transformation: Psychoanalytic interpretation and the interpretation of psychoanalysis.* London: Karnac Books.

Slap, J.W. and Slap-Shelton, L. (1991). *The schema in clinical psychoanalysis*. London: The Analytic Press.

Smith, B. and Smith, D.W., eds. (1995). *The Cambridge companion to Husserl.* Cambridge, UK: Cambridge University Press.

Winnicott, D. W. (1965). Communicating and not communicating leading to a study of certain opposites. In: *The Maturational processes and the facilitating environment*. London: Hogarth, 179-192.

Wright, J. (1975). James Wright, The art of poetry XIX. (Interview with Peter Stitt). *Paris Review*, 16, 62: 34-61.

Wright, J. (1990). *Above the river: The complete poems*. New York: Farrar Strauss and Giroux.

Having and Being: A Thomistic Critique of Private Property as an Absolute Right

Daniel Bradley, PhD

Abstract

A great deal of our contemporary thinking and the structures of power that dominate our lives are rooted in the Lockean notion of private property as an absolute and inalienable right. This toxic and alienating ideology sickens our most important relations, including our relation to the beauty of nature, to our neighbors as companions to which we are bound by moral obligation and civic friendship, to the animals and plants with which we share our world, to our labor as a rich and creative expression of our human nature, to the things we use as lasting sources of satisfaction and cultural heritage, and to our urban spaces as centers of civic and cultural life. In this article, I turn to the work of Thomas Aquinas to challenge the pernicious ideology of private property as absolute. For Aquinas rights to property are not a product of natural law, but are a human construction rooted in the pursuit of human flourishing. Thus, property claims are not inalienable, but always amenable to human wisdom and judgments in the context of human needs. This has important implications for challenging the dominant Lockean ideology.

Keywords: Thomas Aquinas, Private Property, Locke, Ideology, Critique, Political Economy

It is a widely held assumption in contemporary philosophy that religion plays an important ideological role in legitimating the current structures of power, and in many cases this assumption can be an important hermeneutic key for understanding certain aspects of religion. In this paper, however, I will argue that Catholic philosophy offers a powerful critique of the contemporary notion of the absolute right to private property and thus provides an important challenge to the ideological foundation of the current Capitalist structures of power that dominate our world. In our current political and economic situation, then, Catholic thought is counter-ideological—at least on the question of property.

In particular, I will turn to the thought of the great medieval Dominican, Thomas Aquinas. This may seem a strange choice in looking for Catholic allies in challenging contemporary notions of private property. We could look at the ideas of John Ball, Lollard Priest and spiritual leader of the 1381 Peasants revolt in England, the French worker-priest movement of the 1940s, the Liberation theology of the Latin American Jesuits in the later parts of the 20th century, among others. Those are all worthwhile projects, but for this paper I will focus on Aquinas. Partly this is because, while there is a mountain of literature on the critiques of property in these other Catholic traditions, there is a great lack of work on Aquinas' critique of property as an absolute right that I would like to begin to ameliorate. Partly this is because Aquinas' thinking is generally extremely balanced and his arguments insightful, thus making his work a perennially valuable resource. Perhaps most importantly to many of the readers of this journal, though, the turn to Aquinas is important because it offers an underdeveloped resource for those who wish to challenge many of the worst aspects of our contemporary political economy while retaining a place for some version of private property that is more amenable to the practice of wisdom in response to particular contexts and human needs. Finally, for my own purposes, this article is also a step towards a larger project that argues against the claim that the more radical Catholic movements are aberrations or at best minorities that represent only the left fringes of Catholic thinking and defends the idea that, by its very nature, Catholic philosophy is unified in its rejection of universal and inalienable property rights.

Aquinas' careful study of Aristotle taught him a wonderfully nuanced and balanced approach to the intellectual life, for unlike Plato's disdain for common opinion, Aristotle was committed to always trying to find a way to harmonize the conflicts between "the wise and the many" or between different authorities by showing how both sides in the apparent dispute contained aspects of truth, but were approaching the same subject in different contexts or at different levels of reality or of human development. In the case of private property we see Aquinas at his most intellectually charitable, in this regard. He notes that important authorities, including the Apostles in the New Testament and many of the church fathers argued for communal property, and yet others such as St Augustine argued for private property. Both must be right, says Aquinas, on the basis of the distinction between the "use" of things, which we must consider common to all, and the "procuring and dispensing" or possession of things, which can be properly relegated to the individual. So, Aquinas does defend the legitimacy of private property; however, it is crucial to see that he explicitly rejects the claim that private property is a natural or inalienable right. According to Aquinas' argument, by natural all things are given in common to all; thus, "the division of possessions is not according to the natural law, but rather arose from human agreement which belongs to positive law."[1]

This social construction is justified based on what it accomplishes. In particular, the institution of private property, with regard to the possession of things, effects three important goals, for Aquinas.

> Firstly, because everyone is more solicitous about procuring what belongs to himself alone than that which is common to all or many, since each shunning labour leaves to another what is the common burden of all, as happens with a multitude of servants. Secondly, because

> human affairs are conducted in a more orderly fashion if each has his own duty of procuring a certain thing, while there would be confusion if each should procure things haphazard. Thirdly, because in this way the peace of men is better preserved, for each is content with his own. Whence we see that strife more frequently arises among those who hold a thing in common than individually.[2]

Thus, for Aquinas private property is valuable *because* it raises us above the level of servants by making us more solicitous, that is more attentive, careful, and invested in our work. It allows us to be less haphazard, working in fits in starts here and there, and helps to keep our relation to our work orderly and sustained. Finally, there will be more peaceful and harmonious relations among people if they are not constantly trying to negotiate who gets to use which of the common goods. In sum we can see that Aquinas thinks private property is legitimate because it leads to a healthier relation to one's work and to better relations among people, thus enabling the creative activity by which we are the stewards of nature in the fulfillment of our human nature.

This puts Aquinas much closer to Marx than to modern Liberals in their agreement on the criteria by which to judge the legitimacy of private property. The difference between the two is that Marx believes the conditions that once justified private property no longer hold. As Marx writes in his 1844 manuscripts, "precisely in the fact that *division of labor* and *exchange* are embodiments of private property lies the two-fold proof, on the one hand that *human* life required *private property* for its realization, and on the other hand that it now requires the supersession of private property"[3]

So, the stronger challenge to the status quo, stemming from Thomist constructivism, would be the claim that the conditions under which private property is a wise policy have passed, that what was appropriate for the pre-modern world no longer holds. But that terrain has been well-traversed by the Liberation theologians and Catholic Socialists. The weaker version, which I will pursue here, accepts that Aquinas' view of property still holds, but looks to the ways that his rejection of the Lockean claim of private property as a natural right challenges our contemporary political economy by changing our understanding of the grounds on which property is philosophically justified.

Private Property as Wise Social Construction

In order to see the alternative offered by Aquinas, we must briefly characterize the contemporary position to which it offers a challenge, and, of course, it is John Locke who provides the definitive argument for the dominant contemporary understanding of property:

> Though the Earth...be common to all Men, yet every Man has a Property in his own Person. This no Body has any Right to but himself. The Labor of his Body, and the Work of his Hands, we may say, are properly his. Whatsoever then he removes out of the State that Nature hath provided, and left it in, he hath mixed his Labor with, and joyned to it something that is his own, and thereby makes it his Property. It being by him removed from the common state Nature placed it in, it hath by this labor something annexed to it, that excludes the common right of other Men.[4]

At the heart of the argument lie two intuitions: (1) when I work, the fruit of that labor becomes mine, by right, to do with as I alone please and without interference, as long as (2) that fruit was obtained without violating anyone else's right to private property, in other words as long as I produce something using only property to which no one else has a legitimate claim. The first claim is not true, as we will see below, and the accompanying condition never applies completely to any actual situation, for even a brief look at history suggests that most property was not originally taken justly from the public domain by settlers coming to virgin land or by explorers venturing in unspoiled wilderness. Almost every property was at one point or another unjustly pillaged by colonizers from the people who originally lived in a place and used those resources. But this means that any advantages a person has are not *just* the result of property that was gifted to him or her by someone who earned it or to whom it was given in turn by someone who did earn it. Rather it means that inherited property is, at least in part, the result of original injustices.[5]

This problem could theoretically be solved in a society where children are taken at birth from their families and raised by the state under conditions of equal opportunity, rather like the scenario that, for different reasons, Plato suggested. The implausibility of this proposal does not mean we should neglect to work for restorative justice in the case of historical wrong-doing, but it does highlight the problem with an absolute understanding of rights. In reality rights are always partially conflicting. This is why contemporary combatants over abortion and universal health care cannot even enter into conversation, for when a woman has an absolute right to her body and a fetus has an absolute right to life or when one person has an absolute right to life-saving health care and another person has an absolute right to do whatever he wants with his money (i.e. not to be taxed for someone else's health care bills) then rational discussion becomes fruitless and decisions are made, not by discussion and persuasion, but by those with the brute political power to silence their opposition.

Absolute Natural Right/Result of Human Needs

For modern liberals who see property as an absolute and foundational right these disputes between rival rights-claims remain insoluble. For Aquinas, on the other hand, property rights are not absolute but are a social response to deeper philosophical truths about the human condition and our place in the cosmos, thus opening a space for dialogue about conflicting rights claims through appeal to something more fundamental on which both claims depend. In fact, according to Aquinas, before we can ask whether private property is legitimate, we have to ask whether there can legitimately be any kind of human property, personal or communal, for as he notes Psalm 23 says, "The earth is the Lord's, and everything in it," a line quoted again by St. Paul in the Christian Scriptures. To solve this problem Aquinas distinguishes between ownership as power of the will over a thing's nature verses ownership as use. The former is only appropriate to God, for only God, and not human beings, have the right to change a thing's nature, according to Aquinas. But humans do, he argues, have a legitimate right to use the things of nature. Aquinas writes, "God has sovereign dominion over all things: and He, according to His providence, directed certain things to the sustenance of man's body. For this reason man has a natural dominion over things, as regards the power to make use of them."[6] We must not forget this in the turn to positive law. After the discussion of private property as a social construction, Aquinas reminds us, "Wherefore the division and appropriation of things which are based on human law, do not preclude the fact that man's needs have to be remedied by means of these very things."[7]

So the legitimacy of any claim to possess the things of nature at all is rooted in our need for them in order to live and to thrive. Further, Aquinas links this need to our ability to reason as constitutive of our human nature. This rational capacity explains why, for Aquinas, it is morally reasonable for a human to kill a deer to feed a hungry neighbor, but not morally permissible to kill a human to feed your dog, but it also points to the fact that for humans reason is not a luxury added to our animal nature, but a necessity for a being for whom instincts alone are not enough to ensure survival. Rather, as the Thomist, Jarrett Bede, writes:

> the human animal is bound by the law of his own being to provide against the necessities of the future. He has, therefore, the right to acquire not merely what will suffice for the instant, but to look forward and arrange against the time when his power of work shall have lessened, or the objects which suffice for his personal needs become scarcer or more difficult of attainment. Property, therefore, of some kind or other, says Aquinas, is required by the very nature of man. Individual possessions are not a mere adventitious luxury which time has accustomed him to imagine as something he can hardly do without, nor are they the result of civilised culture, which by the law of its own development creates fresh needs for each fresh demand supplied; but in some form or other they are an absolute and dire necessity, without which life could not be lived at all. Not simply for his "well-being," but for his very existence, man finds them [possessions] to be a sacred need. Thus as they follow directly from the nature of creation, we can term them "natural."[8]

For even the earliest human beings, tools replaced fur and claws, and without these possessions we cannot live. But this means that property is not a foundational truth but a response to needs that are themselves only to be understood as obstacles to human flourishing. Thus it is human flourishing that is foundational, and property, in whatever form, is legitimated only to the extent that it serves human flourishing.

Inalienable Right/Conditioned Right

From this understanding of property in general as a response to human need, it follows that private property is not rooted solely in the individual possessor. Rather, its use must be responsive to the social conditions that surround it. For example, in response to the argument made by Ambrose who says: "Let no man call his own that which is common," Aquinas argues that Ambrose is "speaking of ownership as regards use, wherefore he adds: 'He who spends too much is a robber.'" Use is socially constructed and legitimated by the needs of human beings, and so when a person spends wastefully while others are in need, this is an illegitimate use of private property, as morally reprehensible as theft. Further, not only is the right to property not unconditional, it is not inalienable. As Aquinas writes,

> Now according to the natural order established by Divine Providence, inferior things are ordained for the purpose of succoring man's needs by their means. Wherefore the division and appropriation of things which are based on human law, do not preclude the fact that man's needs have to be remedied by means of these very things. Hence whatever certain people have in superabundance is due, by natural law, to the purpose of succoring the poor. For this reason Ambrose says, "It is the hungry man's bread that you withhold, the naked man's cloak that you store away, the money that you bury in the earth is the price of the poor man's ransom and freedom." Since, however, there are many who are in need, while it is impossible for all to be succored by means of the same thing, each one is entrusted with the stewardship of his own things, so that out of them he may come to the aid of those who are in need. Nevertheless, if the need be so manifest and urgent, that it is evident that the present need must be remedied by whatever means be at hand (for instance when a person is in some imminent danger, and there is no other possible

> remedy), then it is lawful for a man to succor his own need by means of another's property, by taking it either openly or secretly: nor is this properly speaking theft or robbery.[9]

For the Modern follower of Locke, the rights to justly obtained property are inalienable, for the Thomist the legitimacy of possession is only upheld by continued moral use of a resource. In particular we have a moral obligation to use our possessions in ways that help those in need. Even more radically, those in dire need have a right to those things necessary for human life that supersedes the right to property, for as we have seen rights-language derives its legitimacy only from the more fundamental natural need for the use of possessions that make possible human life.

Wealth as Deserved/ Wealth as Gift

If the notion of property as absolute and self-grounding is undermined from below, so to speak, by the recognition of a more fundamental reality on which claims to property must be based, namely characteristically human needs, property as absolute and self-grounding is also undermined "from above" by the turn to metaphysics, which yields an understanding of property as gift rather than desert. Thus, we must return to Locke's conditions for the acquisition of private property. As we have already sketched, first occupancy conditions never hold absolutely and thus cannot be the grounds of absolute rights to private property. Now we must argue that the claim that I deserve the fruits of my labors is not absolutely true. This is hard to see in a culture where we get paid by the hour or based on our productivity under conditions of carefully controlled industrial production. If I work longer hours or pick more pounds of strawberries or perform more surgeries, I expect to get paid more. And this is proper, but it is the result of social institutions into which I was born, not a result of some universal moral law. The hunter who often returns empty-handed to camp, and the farmer who faces ruin from a stretch of bad weather know that there is no universal and necessary link between labor and reward. Thus, for these workers it is much easier to see the fruit of their labors with gratitude as a gift. First this is a gift from all those others who make society possible, from those who gave me the gift of life and the nurturing of my talents, and from the goodness of nature, but for Aquinas wealth is ultimately a gift from a divine source. He tells us that the "the rich man is reproved [by Jesus] for deeming external things to belong to him principally, as though he had not received them from another, namely from God."[10] Further, this understanding of property as a providential gift extends not just to the fact that I have anything at all, but even to discrepancies in wealth. Aquinas quotes Basil approvingly, "Why are you rich while another is poor, unless it be that you may have the merit of a good stewardship, and he the reward of patience?"[11] Wealth is not understood as the deserved and expected result of one's labor but as a gift of providence, and greater wealth is not understood as the result of harder work, but as the missioning of a task through which I cultivate my own character while helping others, while less wealth is not understood as the result of less merit but as the gift of the opportunity to grow through reliance on others.

Private property as rise from barbarism/ as fall from grace.

Finally we see a major difference between the contemporary liberal[12] claim for the absolute right to private property and the traditional writings of the Thomist tradition in the place in history to which private property is assigned. According to most modern liberals the original human condition is one of savagery out of which we have slowly climbed in a progressive march towards freer and freer markets and ever greater peaks of civilization.[13] We hear from von Mises,

> The history of private ownership of the means of production coincides with the history of the development of mankind from an animal-like condition to the highest reaches of modern civilization... Nowhere and at no time has there ever been a people which has raised itself without private property above a condition of the most oppressive penury and savagery scarcely distinguishable from animal existence.[14]

According to the traditional Catholic model, on the other hand, private property is a result of the corruption of humanity in its falling away from an originally superior position. As Bede Jarrett writes,

> Created in original justice, as the phrase ran, the powers of man's soul were in perfect harmony. His sensitive nature, *i.e.* his passions, were in subjection to his will, his will to his reason, his reason to God. Had man continued in this state of innocence, government, slavery, and private property would never have been required. But Adam fell, and in his fall, said these Christian doctors, the whole conditions of his being were disturbed.[15]

Rather than a glorious peak of human achievement, private property is understood, on the analogy of slavery, as a necessary evil. This falling away from a higher state in an immemorial or mythical past is mirrored in historical time after the original apostolic fervor of the early Church in the first century of the Common Era is found to be unsustainable and the socialist economics of the first Christian communities are abandoned. However, even in society contemporary to the Medieval theorists, the fall into the inferior social arrangement of private property was not considered absolute, for among monks and nuns a life lived in community was possible and indeed considered by many a more elevated life than that of the secular clergy or laity.

Conclusion

A Thomist view of private property, as a social construction legitimated by its success at promoting the flourishing of the rational and social human animal, will provide a myriad of challenges to our society, in which the dominant power structures are rooted in a Lockean conception of absolute rights to private property. Certain tentative starts on developing the implications of this project in terms of particular economic, political, and cultural questions have been made, but the territory is largely uncharted. So let me end by tentatively pointing to a few starting points for developing a Thomist critique of private property in the American context. Where many liberals see wealth as the deserved reward for hard work and thus property as an absolute right which is the beginning and end of political economy, Aquinas sees wealth as a gift to human beings that makes possible their flourishing and the development of their character, thus showing political economy, not as an autonomous discipline but as pointing towards a metaphysical background out of which it springs and forward to its completion in ethics and cultural studies. Thus, whereas many Americans understand their culture as defined by their allegiance to particular economy, for a Thomist the economy is supposed to serve the culture, and the study of economics ought to be subservient to both metaphysics and the liberal arts.

Where many Americans see charity to the poor as supererogatory or an optional personal virtue best left to individual choice, Aquinas sees it as a requirement of justice and in fact posits the right of the poor to life as more fundamental than the right of the rich to their property, thus placing the question of charity in the civic square and opening it to rational debate in our communal discussions of ethics and politics. Where many liberals see private property as an inalienable right subject only to my will, Aquinas sees private property as legitimate only for possessions which are held by an individual in good stewardship, while allowing for common use. This has important practical political implications for welfare, public health care, city planning and zoning, but the dearest to my heart is the challenge it provides to claims to private ownership of our most beautiful places, including the natural beauty of our rivers, the seaside, and mountaintop land, that bars access of others to these goods.

Where many liberals sees private property as the glorious culmination of human history, Aquinas sees private property as a necessary evil resulting from our falling away from the great socialist high points of the past, namely the Garden of Eden and the Apostolic community, and as unnecessary for the more spiritually cultivated such as members of a religious order. This emphasis on private property as an amelioration of our human condition that has not always been necessary and is still not necessary among certain communities, which society at large can aim to imitate, is a deep challenge to a triumphalist neo-liberalism that would impose its economic system, as the only possible rational choice, on the world.

For the Thomist, who would critique Capitalist ideology on the grounds that human flourishing is more fundamental than property rights, there remains much work to be done.

Endnotes

1 *Summa Theologiae*, II,II, Q 66, Art. 2.

2 *Summa Theologiae*, II,II, Q 66, Art. 1

3 Marx, *The Economic and Philosophic Manuscripts of 1844*, p. 134.

4 *Two Treatises on Government*. 1988 [1689], II, para. 27)

5 For a particularly powerful account of this truth see Ta-Nehisi Coates, "The Case for Reparations," *The Atlantic*, June 2014.

6 *ST*, II,II. 66. 1

7 *ST*, II,II. 66. 7

8 Bede Jarrett, *Medieval Socialism*, Ch. 4 "The Schoolmen." Originally Published, London: T.C. and E.C. Jack, 1913. Accessed through Internet Archive: https://archive.org/details/mediaevalsociali00jarr

9 *ST*, II,II. 66. 7

10 *ST*, II,II. 66. 1

11 *ST*, II,II. 66. 2

12 Words matter, and I see it as unfortunate that defenders of absolute rights to private property are now often called "conservative," when they are properly described as "liberals." See von Mises: "The program of liberalism, therefore, if condensed into a single word, would have to read: *property*, that is, private ownership of the means of production."

13 Which is why free market apologists, like von Mises, are most properly described as progressive liberals.

14 Von Mises, *Liberalism*, San Francisco: Cobden Press, 2002. p. 60.

15 Bede Jarrett, *Medieval Socialism*, Ch. 1 "Introduction."

Revolutionary Technologies: *Praxical* Time as a Way of Overcoming Reification

Róisín Lally, PhD

Abstract

This article argues that by recognizing the fundamental relationship between praxical time and dwelling as a matrix of interweaving modes of being, society can subvert the potential reification of humanity by technology. This can only be achieved through a democratic process that involves participatory agents not only at the design level but also in the event of naming future innovations. By looking at the work of Alain Badiou, it is shown how a fusion of Heideggerian-inspired phenomenology and speculative ontology is critical for the advancement of social theory, as revolutionary technologies become increasingly immersive.

Key Words: Heidegger, Feenberg, Badiou, speculative ontology, reification, dwelling, revolutionary technology, *praxical* time, naming.

Introduction

Much of the recent pre-occupation with the "IT revolution" is rooted in the drive towards efficiency and control, which, according to Martin Heidegger, is a 20th century phenomenon where time itself is reduced to a calculable value, something not to be wasted. As a consequence humans regard everything, including humanity, as a product of technical reason and action. Symptomatic of this is our total absorption in communication technologies, which has led to an exponential increase in online interactions, commonly referred to as virtual relations. However, the language of modern internet technology points to an ambiguity. This ambiguity can be summarized using Herbert Marcuse's (1964) understanding of technological consciousness as a twofold structure of practical and representational thinking,[1] which he develops from Martin Heidegger's twofold understanding of technology as crafting and calculating. The former is characteristic of experiential knowledge, the latter epistemological knowledge, which Heidegger later formulates as a distinction between poetic and enframing consciousness. Enframing is intimately related to what Lukács (1971) calls the "reification of consciousness"[2] where human beings become subsumed by the predominance of the rational structures that govern modern communication technologies, leading to a distortion of human relations. Given the language of the internet,[3] which is dominated by Cartesian ideology with its emphasis on the interior self, the possibility of a thoughtful or contemplative life within a shared community remains closed off. Heidegger argues that thinking in terms of assertion as proof of existence has been inherited historically from the Greeks. However, he also reminds us that latent in the Greek's notion of truth (alētheia) lies the tension between poiēsis and enframing. Truth, therefore, is not static; it is a building up

1 Herbert Marcuse, One-Dimensional Man, (Boston: Beacon, 1964), p. 1.
2 Georg Lukács, History of Class Consciousness, trans., Rodney Livingstone (Cambridge, Massachusetts: The MIT Press, 1971), 93.
3 Language such as "selfies", "i-phones", and "i-tunes".

and working out of a culture. For Heidegger, building means to dwell-in-the-world. In *Contributions to Philosophy (From Enowing)*, (1999), Heidegger refers to dwelling as an *event*, or the truth of being.[4] Events, as opposed to universal truths, are ongoing transformations that *endure* until their cultural time passes. Because revolutionary technologies are, by their very nature, new, the event of modern internet technologies is ongoing. In other words we are still building up and working out the political and social landscape of these technologies. But do these technologies by their very nature reify humanity?

Thus Section I will begin by outlining Heidegger's departure from traditional ontology. By extending Heidegger's *dwelling-in-the-world* thesis in Section II, Andrew Feenberg develops his *secondary instrumentalization* theory to overcome the objectification of humanity by technology. Like Heidegger, Feenberg sees our technologies not as a construction or forming of the self but rather as an ongoing process of receiving and transforming. This ongoing process is a time of praxis, or *praxical* time. The twofold problematic of praxical time concerns (i) the culture are we building and (ii) the naming of these transformative technologies. Therefore, in Section III, we will see that although naming does not signify truth, it nevertheless leads to the reification of things as objects. Therefore, the process of naming is at least as important as the objects we invent. As we invent new technologies that transform notions of the self and our relations to others in virtual space, we must name these technologies with care, so that the social and political are embedded into the technologies prior to production. In this way reification can become a communal and participatory event in which human creativity is engaged in an ongoing relationality rather than a dehumanizing process in which we stand forever as isolated subjects before a frozen and alienated collection of objects.

Dwelling-in-the-World

While the Heidegger of *Being and Time* (2010) situated the ontological priority of being as temporality, his later philosophy

4 Martin Heidegger, Contributions to Philosophy (From Enowing), trans., Parvis Emad and Kenneth Maly (Bloomington and Indianapolis: Indianan University Press, 1999), p. 42.

focuses on the sociopolitical context of being's dwelling. The former was structured as a transcendental hermeneutical-phenomenological analysis of being-in-the-world, the latter as the ontological priority of dwelling-in-the-world. This move towards dwelling is an attempt by Heidegger to address the final questions he poses in *Being and Time* concerning the "reification of consciousness", a response to Georg Lukács' *History and Class Consciousness* (1971). Heidegger writes in the final lines of his Magnus Opus:

> We have long known that ancient ontology deals with "reified concepts" and that the danger exists of "reifying consciousness". But what does reifying mean? Where does it arise from? Why is being "initially" "conceived" in terms of what is objectively present, *and not* in terms of things at hand that do, after all, lie *still nearer* to us? *Why* does this reification come to dominate again and again? How is the being of "consciousness" *positively* structured so that reification remains inappropriate to it? Is the "distinction" between "consciousness" and "thing" sufficient at all for a primordial unfolding of the ontological problematic?[5]

Heidegger's entire project in *Being and Time* is the groundwork to restructure the sedimentation of the Cartesian object and subject division. This destabilization of objects as an ongoing process of disclosure as opposed to the objectification of things and people, is what preoccupied Heidegger for the remainder of his career, as he continually sought new ways to talk about human subjects and their relations.

In his essay 'The Thing' (1971) Heidegger establishes how each thing "worlds", or opens up a web of relations.[6] Uncovering the

5 Martin Heidegger, Being and Time: A Translation of Sein und Zeit, trans., Joan Stambaugh, revised by Dennis J. Schmidt (Albany, New York: State University of New York Press, 2010), 437. All notes from Being and Time are taken from Joan Stambaugh.

6 GA 79: Bremer and Freiburger Vorträge. Edited by Petra Jaeger, 1994. Parts of this volume were first published in Vorträge und Aufsätze, 1954 (See GA 7.) Bremen and Freiburg Lectures: Insight into That Which Is and Basic Principles of Thinking, transl., Andrew J. Mitchell (Bloomington: Indiana University Press, 2012). [Earlier, from the lecture series "Einblick in das was ist" (1949):] GA 79: 5–21 (= GA 7: 165–87), "Das Ding" = "The Thing." In Poetry, Language, Thought, trans., Albert Hofstadter, 165–186, (New York: Harper & Row, 1971). Hereafter PLT.

etymology of the term "thing" he finds it to mean *das Ding, res, causa, Rosa, chose*, words that describe a gathering movement towards "that which bears on or concerns man," that which is present, "as standing forth-here".[7] In other words, a thing is not a representation or a sign that signifies something, nor is it, first of all, an object. Rather, a thing is a relational gathering that perdures. A thing perdures in the fourfold: earth, air, mortals, and divinities. When a thing is not simply an essence with its own limits, but is in relation with other entities, then it is worldly. For example, a jug gathers a world to itself, a gathering to which the potter merely contributes by shaping the clay. For Heidegger, in opposition to Husserl, the jug is not an object revealing itself with each new aspect, and in opposition to Aristotle the form of the jug is not contained in the mind of the potter, nor much less in the Platonic sense of an outward appearance as idea. Rather the jug emerges from its own void and is only "a thing in so far as it things".[8]

Using the old Germanic meaning of the word thing, (gathering) he uncovers the essential nature of the jug as a "poured gift".[9] The outpouring distinguishes it from other objects, say for example a hammer, and makes the jug a jug. The jug is an aggregate vessel which "holds" wine or water, a thing "made" from the earth; it "sits on" the earth, with sides and a bottom, and "holds" substances such as air and atoms which can be replaced by liquids. The world depends on the unity of the four. The worlding is the joining together of each of these separate natures into a "onefold". The thing (jug) stays, no longer in the process of being made, but in the gathering and uniting the fourfold.

> The thing things. In thinging, it stays earth and sky, divinities and mortals. Staying, the thing brings the four, in their remoteness, near to one another. This bringing-near is nearing. Nearing is the presencing of nearness.[10]

Things exist within a fourfold structure of being. In my interpretation the fourfold indicates both nature and culture.

---

7 *PLT*, 173, 174.
8 *Ibid*, 175.
9 *Ibid*, 170.
10 *Ibid*, 175. See also, 177, 178, and 180

Earth and sky signify the potentiality for a thing coming into being and the giftedness of actuality. While mortals and divinities are representative of the human ability to understand, and create a cultural context in which to move around and relate. The entire structure of being comes together into a unity (oneness) within the horizon of intelligibility. As such, the thing is not a delimiting object but an unfolding of the fourfold.

Things in this context have inherent meaning and cannot be viewed in isolation. The jug is only a jug insofar as it used for pouring. The form (jug) follows from its function (out pouring). The function of the jug is what makes a jug, a jug. This is not the scientific way of thinking of function as an aggregate of individual causes arising out of the past, nor of the Modern idea of function as the purpose in the mind of the user. Rather the jug is an event of being. As an event (of the fourfold) it brings something to light; it quenches thirst, or is used as libation, but in either case the event occurs within a context of possibilities becoming actualized or presented and others withdrawing from presence. The thing (jug), things (pours). In pouring it gives, but also holds something back. We do not see the well from which the water was drawn, or the ocean as its storehouse from which the rains continually arise. These things are concealed; they remain invisible. The jug can only be truly known when it forms a unity within the manifoldness of being. In other words, the truth of the jug is not alone the material out of which it is made, its shape, or the purpose to which it is put, all which stand out there in appearance. Phenomenologically Heidegger discloses the nature of a thing as an event of being.

To understand truth, then, we appear to be looking within a framework of a complex mode of being, rather than any mere assertion of truth or falsity. Heidegger calls it *alētheia*, by means of which something is shown and something is, it is necessarily, forgotten. The thing hovers within a rift of oppositions; truth and untruth, being and non-being, revealing and concealing. The jug sets itself into work.[11] The work presences as this work, at this time, in this particular way. The essence of the jug as the outpouring, cannot be reduced to form. It is the function of the

11 Ibid, 185, 186, 187. This is analogous to the act of founding a state as sacrifice of both a giving and receiving.

jug that is essential to the jug's nature. But we must remember that function is itself irreducible to the subject's purposes, for our purposes are always responses to the functions made possible by the web of inter-relations of which we are a part.

In his essay 'The Question Concerning Technology' (1993) Heidegger interchanges between *wesen* (essence) and *Anwesen* (presencing) to denote the event-like meaning of essence. *An-wesen* is coming to presence whereas *wesen* in the traditional sense is the stable condition of an entity. In normal usage there is no hyphen in this word; by using the hyphen Heidegger intends to emphasize the prefix *an* (to, at, toward) to indicate essence as a "coming to presence"[12] as a way of challenging the philosophical tradition that he sees as reifying the notion of essence and thus losing its event-like, historical, and relational nature.

Drawing on the original meaning of the verb form, Heidegger accords to the word *wesen* a crucial role in his speaking of the happening of being. Moreover, he asserts that *wesen* is "not whatness, *quidditias*, but enduring as presence, presencing, and absenting".[13] In 2000 and again in 1982 he associates *Wesen* [essence] with Aristotle's expression to *ti ēn einai* ("what [it] was to be"), which, like *Wesen*, has to do with the past: meaning what a thing was, or has been, before it is actualized, and what we understand "earlier", already or *a priori* about something.[14] Essence is also identified as *währen*, to endure, as Heidegger states: "The noun is derived from the verb *wesen* and is the same as to last or endure (*währen*)".[15] It is in the enduring that the being of *what-is*, as presencing [*An-wesen*], governs everything that, maintaining itself on-goingly in its own particularity, presents itself by way of time as a temporal duration for the essence is opened out by way of man and lived out by him.[16]

12 Martin Heidegger, 'The Question Concerning Technology' in *Basic Writings*, ed., David Farrell Krell (London; New York: Routledge, 1993), p.314.
13 Note: this is Heidegger's translation from *Pathmarks* on page 208. Also, IM, p. 59.
14 *The Basic Problems of Phenomenology*, trans., A Hofstadter (Bloomington: Indiana University Press, 1982), p.120. GA 24: *Die Grundprobleme der Phänomenologie*, ed., Friedrich-Wilhelm von Herrmann, 1975.
15 QCT, 161.
16 Martin Heidegger, 'Time and Being', in *On Time and Being*, trans., Joan Stambaugh (Chicago: University of Chicago Press, 2002); originally New York: Harper & Row, 1972. p. 12.

Heidegger's creative use of etymologies also links *wesen* to *sein*, to be in.[17] This then creates resonances with his etymologies in 'Building, Dwelling, Thinking' (1993) where he links the *bin* of the interiority of the Cartesian *Ich bin* (I am) to the exteriority of ancient *bauen* (building), and recasts it as *buan* (dwelling). Thus, as with Plato we must think of essence in terms of the fullness of being, but Heidegger wants us to see being, not as a static, absolute truth separate from the realm of becoming, human involvement, and human experience, but more akin to the sheltering and stable (but not eternal) space for meaning created in a home that fits harmoniously into the rhythms of human life in a particular setting. In a similar vein Heidegger reminds us in that a gathering of the assembly of free people in ancient Germanic societies was called a thing (*ding*).[18] Thus, Heidegger's answer to the problem of reification is to recast it as the question: Why is being "initially" "conceived" in terms of what is objectively present, *and not* in terms of things at hand that do, after all, lie *still nearer* to us? His solution is to remind us that to be a thing (*ding*) is to have an essential nature but that his nature is tied to living, temporal communities and shared ways of life.

This rejection of things as mere abstractions, separate from content and meaning, is not just a matter of changing one's thinking; it requires a confrontation with the iron cage of rationality which conceals the immediate character of things as things. In advanced industrial and technological societies, things becomes reified in the form of a rational order, including human consciousness where, as Lukács observes, the fate of the worker is that "this self-objectification, this transformation of human function into a commodity reveals in all its starkness the dehumanized and dehumanizing function of the commodity relation". [19] The capitalist system subordinates the worker to use-values where nature, culture, and human relations become objects or commodities. Latent in the commodity exchange are relations between people, the objects used, and the labor they produce. Heidegger's analysis of the metaphysical underpinnings of this process of "enframing," by which these relations are obscured, is of central importance and has had a

17 *Ibid.* Also, Lovitt et al., p.253, IM, p. 59.
18 BW, 355.
19 Lukács, 1971, 92.

profound impact on philosophy around the world since *Being and Time* was published almost a hundred years ago, producing a vast secondary literature. But in order to overcome reification, we must *also* engage in a more directly political account of contemporary technologies. So with Heideggerian tools we have gathered, we turn to the more overtly political analysis of technology in the work of Andrew Feenberg, a thinker deeply influenced by both Heidegger and Marx, via his teacher Marcuse.

Secondary Instrumentalization as Dwelling

Feenberg's *Critical Theory of Technology* (1991) projects a general analysis of technology and its relation to culture, with the aim of opening opportunities for democratic development. In his view technology does not have an essential nature but is a socially constructed historical phenomenon. He develops this idea further in *Questioning Technology* (1999), where he argues that technology does not have an essential nature but exists within a matrix of social and political agents: firstly the technological master actors (technicians and programmers), and secondly the subordinate actors (users of technology) who influence the ongoing evolution of the technological design.[20]These two types of activity are what make up the technological phenomenon. The first is based on a positivist world view, in which production is central and technology is devoid of meaning. Thinking of technology exclusively in these terms, what Heidegger calls present-at-hand (object-being), eliminates the history of technology and its socio-historical context of use. The second is based on life-experiences, i.e., the ready-to-hand (work-being).

Our understanding of technology needs to encompass this complexity, and Feenberg offers us an enrichment of Heidegger's concept of dwelling that is more applicable to our increasingly high-tech lives. The modern house is full of meaning and is not merely a device. While a house is the centre of an electrical, communications, heating, plumbing, and mechanised system designed and created by the master actors, a house is more than that. Dwellers live in the house and often romanticize about the house by hiding and concealing devices,

20 Andrew Feenberg, *Questioning Technology* (London, New York: Routledge, 1999), p. xii.

in traditional facades, such as gas burners in a faux wood fireplace. Dwelling *in* the house obscures its technical character. In a paradoxical way, the house has become the "*machine* for *living*". While it belongs to our lifeworld, it is also an efficient device. Its goal is to shelter us from the weather, but the house also belongs to the realm of meaning. The essentialist response to this argument is that the duality of the house of devices is different to the house as a human environment: One belongs to the realm of technology and the analytic domain, the other to the life-world. The distinction is between the electric circuit as technology, and the experience of warmth and light in the space we occupy. However, Feenberg argues persuasively that these two "practices" (dwelling and devises) cannot be separated. The experience of these two dimensions – device and meaning, technical and life-world practise – are intrinsic to each other, as the user is aware of the technical source of warmth in the home and this awareness helps to shape its meaning.[21] While I agree with Feenberg's argument, it is not clear that this is entirely at odds with Heidegger's encounter with modern technology. In fact it was his work that made us acutely aware of the relation between devices and dwelling. In 'Building Dwelling Thinking' Heidegger's highway bridge is a paradigmatic example. The spatial hyperbola of a bridge defines the river. It "gathers" the earth and sky. It preserves itself as a crossing over a river and at the same time "grants mortals the way".[22] Like the Cathedral square, villages etc., bridges gather the fourfold into what Albert Borgmann calls "focal practices" which function to gather peoples. "The bridge *gathers* as a passage that crosses."[23] This "Gathering is called 'thing'".[24] Thus, the bridge is not merely an unknown entity that determines people's views in an essentialist manner. Because of the bridge's existence it draws into itself a *site*, a place that is freed for settlement and lodging with a boundary; a horizon of being. Bridges are constructions that create a hyperbolic space providing a *locale* in which dwelling can occur, to the extent that people respond to this invitation. As such the technology of bridge building is always rooted in the larger project of being's dwelling. And while the

21 Andrew Feenberg, *Critical Theory of Technology* (New York; Oxford: Oxford University Press, 1991), xii.
22 BW, 354.
23 *Ibid*, 355.
24 *Ibid.*

technological understanding of being can be disassociated from technological devices, it is not necessarily so. Like Feenberg's example of the house, the highway bridge is not separated from the experience of drawing two communities together by crossing over the bridge, nor from their awareness of the social and political implications of this river crossing.

Highway bridges are not just an aid for human activity, they "reshape" those activities and meanings. Technology has in effect created multifarious worlds. While the foundation for understanding this diversity is laid by Heidegger, he does not develop the political implications of dwelling far enough to make sense of our contemporary situation, nor does he give a detailed account of many of the technologies we use. So to augment Heidegger's reflection on the bridge, we will turn to Langdon Winner's analysis of the automobile.[25] Drivers and pedestrians use bridges to arrive at their destination. However, both those activities reveal different worlds. Prior to the highway bridge, neighbors would bike or walk. With the development of the highway bridge, the car driver and pedestrian live in their own world, and any attempt to extend a greeting is complicated by the presence of the enclosed technological device that is the car. Communication between neighbours is "shaped by the incompatibility" of two forms of locomotion – one known as walking, the newer one, driving an automobile. Thus, the instrumental/functional knowledge of automobiles is not adequate to develop our understanding of how automobiles affect the "texture" of modern life."[26] Winner writes "[i]ndividual habits, perceptions, concepts of self, ideas of space and time, social relationships, and moral and political boundaries have all been powerfully restructured in the course of technological development".[27] The side effects or "secondary consequences" of these transformations of technology are to repeatedly enter into a series of social contracts, the terms of which are revealed only *after* the signing of the contract. Winner calls this a state of "technological somnambulism". He describes this as wilfully sleepwalking through the process by which technological entities reshape and condition our social

25 Langdon Winner, *The Whale and the Reactor: A Search for Limits in an Age of High Technology* (Chicago: University of Chicago Press, 1986).
26 *Ibid*, 106.
27 *Ibid*, 107.

and moral life.

Winner suggests that in the continuing activity of material and social production the instruments and processes together with the production of the life world must be accounted for. This leads Winner to investigate the ways modern technology creates new forms of political life. In *The Whale and Reactor* Winner examines two ways artefacts can embody political implications. The first occurs when human beings specifically make or produce technologies that solve political problems such as Robert Moses' Long Island parkway overpasses.[28] These overpasses were designed to restrict the use of buses and, by implication, access by the urban poor. The second case includes technologies that, independent of any human intention, embody certain inherent political implications.

Feenberg, extending Winner's secondary consequences, develops the political aspect of technology further by examining in detail how politics is embedded in tools or instruments. In a short essay "Subversive Rationalization", he offers the example given by Pinch and Bijker of the ways that the technological design of the bicycle has been influenced socially and politically.

> The object we take to be a self-evident "black box" actually started out as two very different devices, a sportsman's racer and a utilitarian transportation vehicle. The high front wheel of the sportsman's bike was necessary at the time to attain high speeds, but it also caused instability. Equal sized wheels made for a safer but less exciting ride. These two designs meet different needs and were in fact different technologies with many shared elements.[29]

But once closure is in place, social origins are forgotten. Accordingly closure produces a "black box" effect.[30] The artefact that is no longer called into question is taken for

28 Carl Mitcham, *Thinking Through Technology The Path between Engineering and Philosophy* (London, Chicago: Chicago University Press, 1994), 187- 188, and Winner (1986), 22-25.
29 Andrew Feenberg, Subversive Rationalization: Technology, Power and Democracy, *Inquiry*, 35: 3 - 4, 1992. This paper expands on Chapter 1 of *Critical Theory of Technology* delivered at the American Philosophical Association, Dec., 28, 1991.
30 Feenberg, 1999, 11.

granted. The artefact appears purely technical, even inevitable. However, a de-sedimentation of this process by way of a genetic phenomenology, can remind us that the final object may have been arrived at through a democratic and socially participatory process. The rejection of Heidegger's exclusive emphasis on *enframing* is apparent here. Instead of thinking of modern technology as a particular state of consciousness determined by a particular metaphysical epoch, technology is often designed and modified as a result of practice and use, socially and politically. This Feenbergian account brings to light even more of the engaged social relations that make a particular technology possible, for unlike Winner who sees the political emerging after the technological invention, Feenberg sees it as embedded in the technology already at the stage of design.

This affirms the phenomenological account that the essence of the bike is its function and not form. Heidegger's ontology of technology is directed at the function of the bike. The function is prior to the black-boxed or reified effect. The inner structure or being of the bike is the metaphysical blueprint for a way of engaging the world that allows for the invention of the bike in the first place. How that bike is used, or what gave rise to modifications in the design, are merely superficial attributes. This does not deny variations in the bike, nor does it deny that the bike can be used for good or evil. Rather the bike, as opposed to a horse drawn carriage, has the political and social already embedded into it, for it opens certain ways of engaging the world and closes others, and these ways of engaging the world are productive of our meanings and identity. Another good example of this interweaving of culture, identity, and politics in design is the domestic use of solar energy and the whole complex of meanings that arises from this use. As Feenberg writes: "A solar house that gets its heat from the sun rather than from burning fossil fuels internalizes environmental constraints in its design, making them in some sense part of the "machinery".

For both Feenberg and Heidegger the world gives itself to be transformed. Humanity does not "form" or construct the world, it receives it as it is given. If that disclosure is rational, then human beings interpret it as such, creating instruments that are rationally constructed (including the bicycle). This is different to an essentialism that suggests that we have always been destined to the current technological era. Instead, humanity's receptivity is always already a response to the world, together with the metaphysical possibilities it presents. Thus we have seen so far that Feenberg's work is not a radical break, but an important correction to Heidegger's understanding of technology as dwelling to more completely reveal the social relations that are often embedded in modern technologies, but easy to forget as those technologies become taken for granted. This gives us some clues to the ways that we can overcome reification by making more apparent, and also inclusive and participatory, these social relations embedded in the design and use of technology particularly for more modern technologies such as the solar panel, that Heidegger never lived to see.

Nonetheless, even Feenberg and Winner's analysis, attentive to the political as it is, remains underdeveloped for a contemporary understanding of technology. The automobile certainly has political and ontological implications as it changes the way we move, as the solar panel does for the way we heat our houses, but they do not provide the more radical rupture with the past that virtual technologies are bringing about. Virtual reality has the power to bring distant worlds into the same proximity and imaginative worlds into proximity with the real, in radical more powerful ways than can our previous communications technologies such as story-telling, novels, television, letters, and telephones could do. These immersive technologies are no longer merely science fiction; they are with us to stay.

Virtual reality[31] is different to the virtual reality world or VR world in so far as in the former where the material gets inverted in the virtual world where relations foreclose on a full-body sensory experience. Thus, we might say as with Deleuze that virtual relations submit to bodies without organs, where language is reduced to machine code and communication is achieved through the development of complex avatars. On the other hand, the VR world is an immersive technology that

31 See for example, Feenberg, 1999, Baudrillard, 1994, Borgmann, 1999, Ihde, 2002, Zimmerman, 1990 for a discussion on virtual reality.

involves a full-embodied experience. For example, Oculus Rift is an immersive interactive environment within the VR world that became available to the public in March of 2016. It is a wearable headset that goes over the eyes like a clunky pair of scuba goggles. The user is then transported into a 360-degree virtual world. Combined with "Leap Motion," which is a camera affixed to the Rift, elements of the outside world - including the body - are added to the VR world, eliminating the need for a keyboard or mouse. In this way, users can interact with the environment: They can grab a chair, their partner's hand, or engage in full-bodied sexual acts. The Oculus Rift is based on an optical illusion, in much the same way as photography, mirrors, and film. But whereas we always turned away from the picture or the film back to "real-life," the enhancements of virtual-life, in this way, is becoming part of the real-life experience for many people, blurring the distinction between real-life and virtual-life.[32]

This new technology has the same dual nature of previous technologies. It is a device and a space for dwelling.

As a space for dwelling, humanity will continue to seek to transcend the rational objectification of the rational character of the machine and thus to overcome our tendency to reify the world and ourselves. As shown above, to dwell is to exist within a shared community, a place to build up and work out a culture. However, there is something different about the Oculus Rift and the automobile. The car is an extension of a process that has been with us for generations, namely the Industrial Revolution, a change in technological production to which we have had a long time to adapt, for example by the creation of the welfare state and the rise of labor unions in order to attempt to overcome reification and make our society more participatory. Virtual Reality is part of a new event, the IT revolution. For this revolution, the work still lies ahead of us. Because these spaces are revolutionary, we need to encompass the entire matrix of actors and inventors as Feenberg suggests, where design must incorporate the political and social, the artistic, and the philosophical. As an aid in this daunting process, it will be

32 Aurora Snow, 'Welcome to Oculus XXX: In-Your-Face 3D is the Future of Porn', *The Daily Beast*. http://www.thedailybeast.com/articles/2016/05/31/smart-car-meet-the-smart-city.html. Accessed 7/13/2016

helpful to be clearer about the nature of a revolution. So in our final section, we turn to the nature of time and its relation to the act of naming as central to understanding our responsibly in creating transformative technologies that give rise to virtual relations in revolutionary new spaces.

Dwelling in Praxical (Revolutionary) Time

The move to democratize technology has become all the more urgent the more modern information technology pervades the lifeworld. However an aporia arises in the democratic process with regards revolutionary technologies: Revolutionary technologies by their very nature are new, yet the process of naming is retroactive, which necessarily reifies them. Once reified, the technology can no longer be thought of new. Further complications arise from the paradoxical structure of these technologies which is based on purely rational formalism while simultaneously remaining the site of human interactions and relations. To unravel these paradoxes we will need to understand the relation between modern information technology and truth – truth as reason and truth as alētheia. It is the contention of this paper that these dichotomous forces confront each other in immersive technologies where calculative and crafting come together in a new way. Because we are still hypothesizing about the possible effects of such technologies they can be considered revolutionary technologies. But because naming has the potential to reify objects, the question is how do we maintain a space of dwelling without reifying human relations?

Ordinarily we think of the computer technology as a tool for calculation which submits to immanent repetitions. This is because the computer is designed in the language of Boolean logic and set-theory; a language of logical instructions. The infinite set of looping algorithms repeat continuously, devoid of meaning. This language gets translated into the language of higher level programming languages used by Information technology, such as Hypertext Markup Language (HTML), from which all other interface languages have evolved. Truth in this formal system becomes stripped of its "meaning," i.e. of its content and intuition. The only meaning that exists is the one given by the formal rules of the system, with no reference to either intuitive truth or relation to reality. Truth, here remains wholly mechanistic and algorithmic, for mathematical operations become nothing but a sequence of operations deduced from given axioms, which appeal to nothing beyond themselves.

This notion of truth, so dominant in postmodernism, has been challenged by Badiou. In *Being and Event* (2005) he masterfully works out the conditions under which the new occurs. He posits that novelty is contingent on truth, by drawing a distinction between truth and knowledge. Truth is first and foremost something new. Knowledge on the other hand is what is transmitted or repeated; he calls this "encyclopedic" knowledge. Truth, on the other hand, is about action, or "intervention".[33] One does not simply know or contemplate a truth, one acts on it as a "subject". *Praxis* subsists in the truth procedures of political action amongst others. According to Badiou, truths are made, not as the effect of an order, but by rupturing with the order which supports truth. This is what he calls 'event'. Thus, truth is newness, and the emergence of truth is strictly incalculable. It is subject to contingency, only named truth after the fact. In fact, the truth may never come to pass, and when it does emerge, it emerges as infinite—but it is made possible by finite subjects. Truth in general (as opposed to 'veridicity') is known only through retroaction, a 'will have been' that is the structure of an event. So as we can see with both Heidegger and Badiou, events are revolutionary by their very nature, once we hear the ambiguous sense of revolution as both destroying and instituting, *and* returning and repeating.

Within events, time emerges in and through the orders of doing *(praxis)* and making (*poiēsis* or *chronos*). Doing (praxis) is a process whereby something happens or an event takes place. Praxis is oriented toward a goal, but it is not contained in the future; rather it is the moment between past and future that is the temporal dimension of decision. The ontological structure of sequential time is making. Chronos and its measures are ontologically prior; it constitutes the "between" moments that allow for the praxical situation of revolutionary action. Human

33 Alain Badiou, *Being and Even,* trans., Oliver Feltham (London, New York: Continuum, 2005), Part 7, Meditation 31.

beings are agents in and through time who disclose the practical constitution of temporality. To elucidate this, Badiou appeals to the Christ Event as a time of revolution[34], an example already used by Kant in *Religion within the Limits of Reason Alone*. There Kant argues that Christianity was not a mere continuation of the old. Instead it was the introduction of a new moral religion in place of the old worship, to which the people were all too well habituated. Christianity arose suddenly, though not unprepared for, from Judaism. Kant adds, this new teaching "effected a thoroughgoing revolution in doctrines of faith".[35]However, while the Romans were provoked and awestruck at the revolution that was taking place, as is made clear by the persecution of the Christians, they failed to mention Christianity in their official public discourse. It was only after a lapse of a century that the Romans instituted inquiries into the nature of the change of faith, and "Christianity" as such is born. As Badiou teaches, the new situation is only named retroactively.

The event constitutes and creates a subjectivity in which, and through which, the event is manifested as a universal singularity. St. Paul is an example of the "faithful subject" to the event, but it should be remembered that Badiou's subject is not the individual. The subject, for Badiou, it is not egological, psychical, substantial, nor conscious, and to participate in its constitution is an anonymous dispersal into the variations of a procedural beginning.[36] The task of St. Paul, as a creative inventor, was to choose fidelity to the situation and accept the consequence of a "judgment" or decision against the continuity of his old life. Christians and followers of Christ were faithful to the Christ Event. The contingency of the Event, means it may not come to pass at all, as in the case of the still-born Spartacus Event, or it may perdure for centuries through the faithfulness of its subjects. The Christ event has lasted for 2,000 years. But this does not have to be the case, and more recently Christianity has been replaced by Secularism. No event lasts forever, and, no matter how long or short, each event participates in an

34 Badiou, 2005, Part 5, Meditation 21.
35 Immanuel Kant, *Religion Within the Limits of Reason*. (Illinois: The Open Court House Publishing Company, 1934), 118.
36 Alain Badiou, *The Concept of Model: An Introduction to the Materialist Epistemology* of Mathematics, eds., and trans., Zachary Luke Fraser and Tzuchien Tho (Melbourne: Re-press, 2007), I.i..

atemporal and universal truth.

In a similar way, subjects faithful to the new technologies of Boolean logic and consequently information technologies were forged from the logic of set theory, and it is this to which we turn to illustrate Badiou's fidelity to the *Cantor Event*. Rebecca Goldstein (2005) summarizes fidelity to the event as the move to an "axiomatic system divested of all appeals to intuition"[37]. Truth then, in the formal system, becomes stripped of its "meaning," i.e. of its content. Such a system, devoid of intuitive appeals to truth, remains wholly mechanistic and algorithmic. This is why Badiou thinks that technology is not a real concept, but is merely a journalistic debate. As such it is not a serious question for philosophy. The question of technology should only arise within the truth-procedure of political spheres (or science, art, or love). In other words, politics is a space where truth may emerge. There are no technological problems *per se*, only techno–political problems. In determining the political, the technological question is exhausted.[38]

In my view, Badiou's ontology provides a powerful account of computer technology, with its set-theoretical underpinnings, but cannot, on its own, ever truly escape the *status quo* of the state of its situation. Although modern technology admits to a community of subjects faithful to the event (for example, using the internet and its supporting interfaces), while we live and remain in the situation (i.e., IT revolution), the very possibility of naming the event is foreclosed. We do not know where the technology will lead. Indeed it is only now that the true potential of the printed word (15th Century) is becoming evident, such that the printed word has morphed into 3D printing. Through the use of 3D printing techniques, designers are developing works of art that are completely immersive. Because we do not yet have the temporal distance for the naming, immersive technologies they are still revolutionary. But this also means that we must think through to the end of these inventions so that in naming them we are also incorporating a political and social truth procedure. This means that we must not leave technology to its purely formal mathematical origins

37 Rebecca Goldstein, *Incompleteness: The Proof and Paradox of Kurt Gödel* (New York: W.W. Norton 2005), 129.
38 Alain Badiou in an Open Lecture *On The Truth-Process*, August 2002.

and wait to assign value and make critical judgments until technology is absorbed into the meaning-making activities of science, politics, art, and love. Feenberg is right here to insist on the way technologies have political agency but we also need to extend Feenberg's democratization of technology to include the naming process of those inventions to subvert the scientific tendency to reify objects we use. For if our technologies are reified, so too are the relations that develop using those technologies. We can destabilize these tendencies when we begin to understand technology in terms of time. Praxical time is a time of building up and working out of a culture. This is not meant as constructing but rather transforming what is already given, and being attuned to the possibilities of what the new world order can offer. This paper points to a speculative approach in the design process, using a truth procedure that requires hypothesizing about the possible ends of technologies before they are created. In a Heideggerian retrieval of attunement to language, this also demands attention to naming such technology.

Conclusion

This paper has argued that an integration of speculative ontology and hermeneutical phenomenology is essential for the advancement of critical theory, specifically relating to technology as outlined by Feenberg. Modern internet technologies are grounded in a theory of absolute truth. They depend on a rationally ordered system encased within an algorithm of finite instructions. This notion of truth contrasts with Feenberg's secondary instrumentalization and Heidegger's dwelling-in-the-world as alētheia, which is always in a process of disclosure. The latter is a tension that arises from the multistability of things ready-to-hand, within the context of the present-at-hand, history, and our involvement in the world as a state of progress and change that is always in conflict, a *praxical* time. *Praxical* time (revolutionary time), is what constitutes a genuine active participation in the making of and working out of a culture. Internal to revolutionary time, human beings find a place to dwell, a place that is familiar. The site of familiarity, for much of Western society, constitutes the virtual world of online relations.

In this time of revolution (praxical time), we need to seek ways to think beyond the logic of information technology to include its social and political context. This paper argues that when we anticipate future technologies we can embed the ethical and political *prior* to production. As has been shown, this can only be understood in light of a serious reflection on the metaphysical consciousness of humanity, and not merely on immediate and discrete technologies. Once we understand technology in its own terms as a movement of consciousness within the prevailing philosophical structures, we can predict with some degree of accuracy the consequences of developing certain technologies. Concurrent with recent innovations, we must also take the naming of our technologies as seriously as the technologies we create. By integrating speculative ontology and hermeneutical phenomenology, critical theory can chart a course that integrates the entire spectrum of actors to build a culture that embraces immersive technologies such that relationships are not forged from the commodity market. This can only happen if this change is not left to the technical team that develop the software, but is open to a democratic process.

Bibliography

Badiou, A. (2002, August). On the Truth-Process. *Open Lecture.*

Badiou, A. (2005). *Being and Event.* (O. Feltham, Trans.) London, New York: Continuum.

Badiou, A. (2007). *Concept of Model: An Introduction to the Materialist Epistemology of Mathematics.* (Z. L. Fraser, T. Tho, Eds., Z. L. Fraser, & T. Tho, Trans.) Melbourne: Re-press.

Feenberg, A. (1991). *Critical Theory of Technology* . New York, Oxford: Oxford University Press.

Feenberg, A. (1992, July 20). Subversive Rationalization: Technology, Power and Democracy. *Inquiry*, 301–322.

Feenberg, A. (1999). *Questioning Technology*. London, New York: Routledge.

Goldstein, R. (2005). *Incompleteness: The Proof and Paradox of Kurt Godel.* New York: W.W. Norton.

Heidegger, M. (1971). The Thing. In M. Heidegger, *Poetry, Language, Thought* (A. Hofstadter, Trans., pp. 165 - 187). New York: Harper & Row.

Heidegger, M. (1982). *The Basic Problems of Phenomenology.* (A. Hofstadter, Trans.) Bloomington: Indiana University Press.

Heidegger, M. (1993). Building, Dwelling, Thinking . In M. Heidegger, *Basic Writings* (pp. 343-365). London, New York: Routledge.

Heidegger, M. (1993). The Question Concerning Technology. In M. Heidegger, *Basic Writings From Being and Time (1927) to The Task of Thinking (1964)* (pp. 307 - 343). London, New York: Routledge.

Heidegger, M. (1999). *Contributions to Philosophy (From Enowing).* (P. Emad, & K. Maly, Trans.) Bloomingtion,

Indianapolis: Indiana University Press.

Heidegger, M. (2000). *An Introduction to Metaphysics*. (G. Fried, & R. Polt, Trans.) New Haven : Yale University Press.

Heidegger, M. (2002). Time and Being. In M. Heidegger, *On Time and Being* (J. Stambaugh, Trans.). Chicago: University of Chicago Press.

Heidegger, M. (2009). *Phenomenological Interpretations of Aristotle. Initiation into Phenomenological Research*. (R. Rojcewicz, Trans.) Bloomington, Indianapolis: Indiana University Press.

Heidegger, M. (2010). *Being and Time*. (J. Staumbough, Trans.) Albany: State University of New York Press.

Heidegger, M. (n.d.). *Introduction to "What is Metaphysics"*. (W. Kaufmann, Trans.)

Kant, I. (1960 (1934)). *Religion within the Limits of Reason Alone*. (T. M. Greene, & H. H. Hudson, Trans.) New York: Harper Torchbooks.

Lukács, G. (1971). *History of Class Consciousness Studies in Marxist Dialectics*. (R. Livingstone, Trans.) Cambridge, Massachusetts: The MIT Press.

Marcuse, H. (1964). *One-Dimensional Man*. Boston: Beacon.

Mitcham, C. (1994). *Thinking Through Technology The Path Between Engineering and Philosophy*. London, Chicago: Chicago University Press.

Snow, A. (2016, 7 13). *Welcome to Oculus XXX: In-Your-Face 3D is the Future of Porn*. Retrieved from The Daily Beast: http://www.thedailybeast.com/articles/2016/05/31/smart-car-meet-the-smart-city.html

Winner, L. (1986). *The Whale and the Reactor: A Search for Limits in an Age of High Technology*. Chicago: University of Chicago Press.

The Terror of Annihilation: A Phenomenology of Shame

Andrew Nutt, MA

Abstract

This paper outlines how shame is created and absolved. Contrasted with drive theory there is a movement within psychoanalysis toward an intersubjective approach that views identity as the sum amalgamation of one's relationships. Intersubjective theory argues that shame is a result of a breakdown in the interpersonal field. This parallels recent interpersonal neurobiology (IPNB) discoveries that demonstrate the centrality of relationships for psychological health and flourishing. The research in both of these fields points toward a relational ontology that emerges from connections with other subjects. Threatened relationships are experienced as a threatened sense of self. Shame is the terror of annihilation that comes as a result of a perceived powerlessness to relationally connect with others. Though shame is ubiquitous and pervasive, the antidote is found through mutual recognition and empathetic attunement which transforms private alienation into shared grief. It is ultimately through relationships that shame is both created and healed.

Interpersonal Neurobiology

Interpersonal neurobiology studies the social and biological feedback loop of consciousness. In the early 1990's, at the beginning of what is known as the "decade of the brain," Daniel Siegel invited approximately 40 scientists from diverse disciplines to answer the question: what is the connection between the mind and the brain? (Siegel, 2012, p. xx). Louis Cozolino (2006) explains how Interpersonal Neurobiology (IPNB) currently engages the study of consciousness:

> Interpersonal neurobiology assumes that the brain is a social organ that is built through experience. Through interdisciplinary exploration it seeks to discover the workings of experience – dependent plasticity, or the ways in which the brain is constructed by experience. At the core of interpersonal neurobiology is a focus on the neural systems that shape attachment. And, in turn, interpersonal neurobiology considers how these systems are shaped by relationships. (p. 7)

The emphasis on relationships within IPNB expands the historic paradox of a mind and body dualism.

Daniel Siegel (2012) outlines a simple and helpful trifold model of consciousness. First, "The brain is the mechanism of energy and information flow throughout the extended nervous system" (p. F-7). The brain is the nonconscious physical organ that receives sensory data through the five senses. The brain also produces chemicals that control energy and emotion in the body. Pharmaceutical drugs alter a person's state of being by engaging the physical mechanism of the brain as it produces and distributes electrical signals and chemicals.

Second, "The mind is the embodied relational process that regulates the flow of energy and information" (Siegel, 2012, p. F-7). The mind receives the sensory data from the brain and interprets it into meaningful patterns or narratives. The mind is both a conscious and nonconscious hermeneutical center that tells the brain what chemicals need to be released to create the appropriate emotion or reaction. The guilt versus shame perspective is one example of this process. When a negative event happens, it is relayed through the senses to the brain. The mind then interprets the data as either guilt (I have done bad) or shame (I am bad.) Depending on which way the interpretation goes, the brain will release the appropriate chemicals which cause the coinciding emotional affect. The mind has existential and immaterial properties unlike the brain's physical properties.

Third, "When we communicate with one another, we share energy and information flow. Relationships are built from patterns of communication, which are really patterns of sharing energy and information flow" (Siegel, 2012, p. 28-5). Our minds hermeneutic is situated within a relational history. Patterns of being otherwise known as attachment structures are formed from early relationships with primary caregivers. "Emotion lies in the middle of the triangle and are the: Ever-changing states of integration within and between people" (Siegel, 2012, p. 32-7). Emotion is the product of biology, volition, and relationships and is the varying affective experience of being in the world.

The flight of an airplane illustrates the triangle of consciousness. The physical brain is like the physical plane. If a person suffers a traumatic brain injury or a plane loses an engine the flight will not be smooth. The mind is the pilot. If harmful choices are made, or there is a pilot error, a perfectly sturdy plane may experience significant problems or crash. Relationships offer patterns or schemas of how to navigate the world like a flight plan. Even with a reliable pilot and a sturdy aircraft the flight can experience difficulties if the flight data is processed through faulty equations.

It is important to note the absence of the Cartesian split between thought (mind) and matter (brain) in this model. It is also intriguing to note that medical sciences, such as IPNB, are making a shift toward recognizing humankind's complexity, a perspective typically left to the humanities. Relationships are foundational to consciousness and are critical to the formation, existence and maintenance of health. The next section examines the relational corner of the triangle in more depth.

The caregiver's response to a child's need sets the basic attachment structure of the child. An attuned caregiver is able to offer their regulated brain state to an infant who is dysregulated, bringing the infant to a place of regulation (Siegel, 2015). If a pattern of misattunement develops the child will have an insecure attachment. Within IPNB literature, shame is closely related with insecure attachment (DeYoung, 2015). The core concept of shame is an inability to relationally connect. When a child has a significant emotional affect, either good or bad, and is not met with resonance by the parent, the child experiences disconnection which leads to feelings of alienation and shame. This is exponentially more significant if the emotion causes dysregulation or even flooding and is not met with attunement.

When this inability to connect happens repeatedly, shame goes from a present emotional phenomenon to a deeply ingrained nonconscious structure that often retains no emotional affect.

Infants find emotional regulation through the responding face and gaze of the caregiver. When infants are confronted with a blank or unattuned face of a caregiver the infant becomes panicked and tries to restore the gaze (DiCorcia, Snidman, Sravish & Tronick, 2016). Infants usually mitigate the experience of shame through withdrawing or anxiously acting out which sets their basic attachment structure.

Sartre (1992) proposes the freedom of being-for-itself is removed through the gaze of the other leaving an objectified being-in-itself. This is the same objectification that happens with a caregiver's unresponsive face or lack of gaze. The infant is perceived as a being-in-itself not as another subject to be relationally connected to with reciprocal impact. The yielding and responsive caregiver's gaze does not objectify or force a being-in-itself upon the infant; it approaches with a sense of wonder and curiosity allowing the infant freedom of feeling and expression without the risk of objectification through non-attunement. It is important to distinguish the attuning, non-directive, life giving gaze of the other from the objectifying, being-in-itself gaze (or lack of gaze) of the other.

The infant is in a vulnerable position because he cannot restore his mother's gaze on his own. The desire for engagement from the absent or dysregulated caregiver is interpreted by the infant as being a fault within himself. The child feels like he is bad for having need. Children quickly learn to show "only those parts of themselves that can get along with the range of affective responses that are available to them from important others." (DeYoung, 2015, p. 22) For the sake of stability, it is more important for the infant to internalize everything negative in the relationship and maintain the dyadic connection sacrificing his belief in his own competency or goodness.

Research on shame and infants done by IPNB displays the startling reality that when presented with the data of a misattuned caregiver the infant unconsciously blames himself rather than face the reality that he has been abandoned. For the infant, isolation is the greatest danger to avoid. Siegel (2012) explains, "Shame is an adaptive response to a negative life situation. By maintaining the important attachment figure as good and competent, the dependent young infant or child maintains an inner sense that someone in the world is able to protect them" (p. 24-3). Infants always choose the narrative of dysregulation not disconnection. The infant blames himself which leaves him still "connected" in the dyad but dysregulated. It seems that the infant perceives disconnection as the greatest threat to safety and wellbeing. It is important to note that infants lack a frame of reference to comprehend the possibility that their parents are fallible which means they are forced into creating a narrative of personal failure. Similarly, survivors of intrafamilial trauma like domestic violence and sexual abuse often choose self-hatred and self-blame over abandonment. In overt and subtle ways, survivors and infants both naturally hold themselves and their bodies responsible for their trauma. This points to personal failure as a less devastating option than disconnection or abandonment.

Misattunement and dysregulation are small "t" traumas that

over time can have just as much life altering impact as capitol "T" traumas, such as abuse or interpersonal physical violence. Misattunement over time cements the messages of shame into the brain of the infant confirming the saying: "neurons that fire together wire together" (Shatz, 1992, p.64). These structures or ways of being in the world get played out for the rest of the person's life. Drawing from these nonconscious schemas of shame, many adults avoid situations and kill desires that remind them of misattunement from their caregiver (DeYoung, 2015, p.44). The betrayal of past abandonments lead to the hopelessness of future security. Most people feel like it's better to remain "connected" and not really known in relationships than to show up and have to face the possibility of abandonment.

Shame is a way of being in the world that wears many different emotional hats. As the infant matures, coping mechanisms help keep the haunting sense of "bad" at bay by hiding, blaming and projecting. Commitments are formed such as: "I will never allow myself to be vulnerable" or "I will never be in a relationship where the other person has needs I can't meet."

Intersubjectivity

There is a broad movement within psychoanalysis toward a relational orientation and away from drive theory. Stephen Mitchell, Jessica Benjamin and Lew Aron write about the mutual encounter and the therapeutic process while George Atwood, Donna Orange and Robert Stolorow tend to focus more on systems theory. The following section will be primarily engaging the work of the latter theoreticians. A few core concepts of intersubjectivity are as follows:

First, there is a rejection of the isolated Cartesian mind. Second, there is a move away from drive theory toward affect theory (Hill, 2015) in that intersubjective theory does not have central organizing intrapsychic principles like the Oedipus complex, or depressive and schizoid positions. Third, the psychoanalytic stance is one of phenomenological contextualism. Atwood and Stolorow (1984) elaborate, "Psychological phenomena cannot be understood apart from the intersubjective contexts in which they take form" (p. 64). Fourth, the intrapsychic is always found within the interpersonal (Stolorow, Atwood, & Brandchaft, 1994). Fifth, "An intersubjective field is a system of reciprocal mutual influence" (Stolorow & Atwood, 1992, p.3). Subjectivity arises out of mutual recognition. Jessica Benjamin (1988) proposes that subjectivity begets subjectivity and only as the infant loses his omnipotent objectification of his mother is his own subjectivity realized. Sixth, the definition of intersubjectivity is any "psychological field formed by interacting worlds of experience, at whatever developmental level these worlds may be organized" (Atwood & Stolorow, 1992, p.3). Intersubjective theory helps to fill out a philosophical and psychoanalytical perspective of shame.

Shame deals with one's perceived sense of self which is formed at the intersections of relational fields. Our ever-changing identity is navigated in a similar way to the sonar navigational systems of a bat or dolphin. We come to know who we are by bumping into others and their relational configurations. The self is an approximation created out of the manifold experiences of being in the world with other people. Atwood and Stolorow (1996) elaborate, "An individual mind or psyche is itself a psychological product crystallizing from within a nexus of intersubjective relatedness" (p. 182). The concept of self is a crystallization of past and present relational exchanges.

When a caregiver repeatedly meets an infant with an objectifying, unattuned or unavailable blank face in a time of emotional affect (either good or bad,) pathological structures are formed (Atwood, Brandchaft and Stolorow, 1994.) Harmful relational interactions form the soft clay of the infant's subjectivity and can be devastating when there are no other healthy relationships available to the infant. Misattunement over time will cause a shift in an infant's way of being in the world. Atwood and Stolorow (2014) explain, "When the psychological organization of the parent cannot sufficiently accommodate to the changing, phase specific needs of the developing child, then the more malleable and vulnerable psychological structure of the child will accommodate to what is available" (p. 55). If this type of interaction continues without repair, it will be crystallized into pre-conscious styles of relating marked by defensive measures (Atwood, Stolorow, and Brandchaft, 1994). Continual experiences of shame become solidified into intrapsychic schema that carry no emotional affect.

Using Hegel's dialectic philosophy, Aron and Starr (2013) propose that identity and therefore shame are largely held by the other. "The self is only a self by virtue of being defined as such by the other. Selfhood is always a social phenomenon, dependent on the social bond with others and at risk when the self is not recognized" (p. 58). A lack of recognition can trigger the anxiety of a jeopardized self. Melvin Lansky (1992) poignantly explains what shame tells us about our place in the world:

> The master regulatory emotion signaling threat to that bonding to others, which empowers the sense of self, is shame. Shame is either a signal of danger to the bond or that end stage affect signaling loss of the bond. Shame may denote either the affect itself or the social component aimed at avoiding the threat to the bond. (p. 9)

Shame is the threat or realization that relational connection with the other has been removed by them.

Synthesis

After studying both of these very different disciplines a type of relational ontology emerges. Without relationships Siegel's triangle collapses along with Atwood and Stolorow's intersubjective field. Both of these diverse disciplines argue that relationships are a critical element of intrapsychic existence while also forming what we understand of reality. The existence of relational connection is the prerequisite for the existence of the self. From a Christian perspective, existence is always bound to community through being made in the image of a triune God (Zizioulas, 1985).

Within existence, there is an implicit terror of nonexistence. Our existence or being is inherently vulnerable because our ontology is held by the other. This terror is rarely shown through amygdala hyperactivation, but rather through low grade anxiety. It shows itself as the feeling of being on guard or being watched. It haunts consciousness with questions of: "Am I pretty enough; smart enough; respected enough; powerful enough?" These questions often refer to a specific culture's standard and with enough toil can be answered positively. Consumer culture offers the perfect situation of commodities to assuage the anxiety that haunts humanity.

The vulnerability of having ontology in the hands of another produces terror when the character or capacity of the other is called into question. The only way to never be shamed is to never be vulnerable and never give people power over you. Yet, without vulnerability you can't relationally connect. The bind of relational "darned if you do," definitely "darned if you don't" is one of the foundational aspects of being in the world. It is necessary to give people power to shame, in order to form relational connection with them.

Relational connection requires joining distinct entities without abolishing or diminishing the personhood of either. Enmeshment is the loss of personal psychic structure for the sake of connection. On the other hand, if relational connection does not in some way affect the psychic structure and trigger the release of the hormone oxytocin, there is no real relational connection. Connection requires both intrapsychic stability and vulnerability, amalgamation and individuation, diversity and unity.

The thesis of this paper is: Shame is the terror of annihilation that comes as a result of a perceived powerlessness to relationally connect with others. There are two important parts to this definition. First, shame has an initial parallel emotional affect to anxiety or fear. A social blunder triggers a fight or flight response and the release of adrenaline. A threat to relational standing causes terror because ontology is bound up in relationships. The denial of another's subjectivity is objectification, which is really a strike to the heart of their ontology. A threat to ontology is also a threat to existence. In other words, if relationships are jeopardized, so are the organizing structures that form a coherent sense of self. The loss of relationships threatens an annihilation of the sense of self. Most people avoid collapse because they have a diversity of relationships and enough positive relational equity from past relationships. This secure foundation does not change the nature of shames message which is the threat of non-existence while existing. It is the possibility of being a living dead.

The second important part of the definition deals with powerlessness. There is no way for the shamed person to restore the gaze of the other, it must be given to them. The impact of shame is linked both to the level of powerlessness a person has and their desire to relationally connect. In social economies there are many ways regain power or earn back the gaze of the other, which takes shame away. The greater the powerlessness to restore the gaze, the greater the shame.

Shame holds the perception that being authentic and allowing others to see flaws will cause rejection. This bind leaves two options which are usually answered in a largely nonconscious manner. The first option is to be authentic and isolated. The second and more common option is to be inauthentic and connected; which is really not connection because it is the presentation of a pseudo self. The powerlessness of shame removes voice and efficacy. It is impossible to restore the gaze of the other because connection requires the other's desire to attune. The powerless nature of shame often leads to hopelessness and addictive behaviors that attempt to numb and cope with broken connections rather than to fight for new connections.

Shame should be addressed through attunement. If non-existence and the removal of subjectivity are the threat, the cure must involve the gift of existence and the recognition of subjectivity. This is exactly what attunement is. It is the restoration of the gaze, the offer of recognition and connection. Siegel (2012) says attunement is the apprehension of "internal emotional and bodily states" in a way that causes the observed person to feel resonated with (p. AI-8). This resonance is accomplished through "interconnected neural regions that enable a person to tune into others and align his or her internal states with those of another person" (p. AI-69). Siegel (2015) also says, "When we track the signals of another person, we focus our attention on his communication and stay present with his changing states from moment to moment, in an open and responsive way" (p. 313). Attunement offers a secure neural integration and the willingness to take on another's dysregulated state (DeYoung, 2015.) When a person is going through a shame state, they need attunement; a being-with, being-for, and a being-through type of presence. Attunement to a person experiencing shame is a willingness to feel what they feel and traverse their personal pit of hellish emotions.

The IPNB movement has a definition of shame that is too narrow. Patricia DeYoung (2015) defines shame as: "An experience of one's felt sense of self disintegrating in relation to a dysregulating other" (p. xiii). The problem with understanding shame as dysregulation and disintegration is that it only address the affect shame brings. Shame does bring dysregulation, and a feeling of being marked or rejected, but why is this the case? Why does it matter if a person has the feeling of being marked or unable to enter into relationship? It matters because being marked or seen as not worth being attuned to is a move against the structure of human subjectivity. Feeling marked or unable to connect relationally carries weight because personhood emerges from relationships.

IPNB is limited within a system and language of biology. Fundamentally, however, humans are not only biological, but also ontological. The category of biology that IPNB operates under is far too narrow to understand the human situation in totality. The category of ontology holds within it the narrower, subcategory of biology. From an ontological standpoint, shame is the threat of non-existence which inevitably includes biological dysregulation.

In light of this distinction between ontology and biology, attunement does not just offer regulation (Siegel, 2012), but also the gift of my current temporal existence on behalf of the other. Within a framework of finitude, existence is one of the most sacred things that can be given to another human due to its finite quantity.

Attunement and kindness remove the threat of alienation and therefore annihilation within shame. They destroy the bind of not being able to be authentic in order to be connected. In the presence of kind attunement, the shamed person is able to be authentic with their flaws, while remaining relationally connected. This opens the door for them to develop a sense of being worthy to be in relationships. Attunement with relational connection reveals the trauma of being objectified which has been crystallized into nonconscious schema and allows it to be engaged instead of adsorbed or dissociated. Attunement is the key to transforming private alienation into shared grief.

Shame is always unwarranted; there is no person that deserves alienation. Interpersonally and ontologically, every person has equal standing and right for relational connection. Attunement reveals the fiction of deserved alienation that shame loudly proclaims. Within the context of attunement, the mind undergoes a hermeneutical transformation that allows data to be interpreted differently. Situations and themes that once brought shame can now be placed in the categories of trauma and guilt, freeing a person to grieve what is broken while maintaining a positive orientation toward relational connection. It is through relationships that we are most profoundly wounded and most beautifully healed.

References

Aron, L., & Starr, K. E. (2013). *A psychotherapy for the people: Toward a progressive psychoanalysis.* New York, NY: Routledge.

Atwood, G. E., & Stolorow, R. D. (1984). *Structures of subjectivity: Explorations in psychoanalytic phenomenology and contextualism.* Hillsdale, NJ: The Analytic Press.

Atwood, G. E., & Stolorow, R. D. (1992). *Contexts of being: The intersubjective foundations of psychological life.* Hillsdale, NJ: Analytic Press.

Atwood, G. E., & Stolorow, R. D. (1996). The Intersubjective Perspective. Psychoanalytic Review, 83(2), 181-194.

Atwood, G. E., & Stolorow, R. D. (2014). *Structures of subjectivity: Explorations in psychoanalytic phenomenology and contextualism.* London: Routledge.

Atwood, G. E., Stolorow, R. D., & Brandchaft, B. (Eds.). (1994). *The intersubjective perspective.* Northvale, N.J: J. Aronson.

Benjamin, J. (1988). *The bonds of love: Psychoanalysis, feminism, and the problem of domination.* New York, NY: Pantheon Books.

Cozolino, L. (2006). *The neuroscience of human relationships: Attachment and the developing social brain.* New York, NY: Norton.

DeYoung, P. A. (2015). *Understanding and treating chronic shame: A relational/neurobiological approach.* New York, NY, US: Routledge/Taylor & Francis Group.

Dicorcia, J. A., Snidman, N., Sravish A. V., & Tronick, E. (2016). "Evaluating the nature of the still-face effect in the double face-to-face still-face paradigm using different comparison groups. *Infancy, 21*(3), 332-52.

Hill, D. (2015). *Affect regulation theory: A clinical model.* New York, NY: W. W. Norton & Company.

Lansky, M. R. (1992). *Fathers who fail: Shame and psychopathology in the family system.* Hillsdale, NJ: Analytic Press.

Sartre, J. P. and Hazel, E. (1992) *Being and nothingness: A phenomenological essay on ontology.* New York, NY: Washington Square Press.

Siegel, D. (2012). *Pocket guide to interpersonal neurobiology: An integrative handbook of the mind.* New York, NY: W.W. Norton.

Siegel, D. (2015). *The developing mind: How relationships and the brain interact to shape who we are.* (2nd ed.). New York, NY: The Guilford Press.

Zizioulas, J. (1985). *Being as communion: Studies in personhood and the church.* Crestwood, NY: St. Vladimir's Seminary.

Why do "they" hate us so?

Michel Valentin, PhD

"What a terrible time than where idiots are leading the blind."
William Shakespeare.[1]

It is very difficult to stay clear-headed in a very complicated world which seems to have lost its balance (a state called *koyaanisqatsi* by Hopi wisdom);[2] especially when confronted by a constant environment of violence of all sorts (named *naqoyqatsi* according to the same wisdom), and its Media spectacular rendition which blurs all differences and confuses issues.[3] In the world we "have" now, violence contends with hope for peaceful change, and the outcome is uncertain.

Sixteen years after the United States declared "war on terrorism," there is no victory in sight. In fact, across the globe, the toll in death and wounded, as well as the loss of economic assets (amounting to $52 billion caused by terrorism, are worse than ever.

Why so much radical, fatal, unrelenting hate? It seems that only the Sphinx, or God, could provide answers. Common-sense points at "their" murderous jealousy (of our consumerism), "their" hateful resentment (of our "obscene enjoyment"), or Medieval-like intolerance (of our beliefs and life-style).

Maybe, instead, we should re-phrase the question as such: "What, in our society, triggers the murderous rage and extremist violence of terrorists claiming fundamentalist religious allegiance?"

To begin to understand and try to propose answers and solutions, we should first make use of the tools provided by Postmodern Critical and Textual theory that Anglo-Saxon/British Analytical Philosophy (and pragmatism) calls Continental Theory, and apply them to fundamentalist terrorism as if it was a text. We should especially acquaint ourselves with theoretical concepts such as, on the one hand, social/individual "de-territorialization" (term belonging to Deleuzian socio-philosophy out of Guattari's anti-psychoanalytic movement), and on the other, the fundamental, intimate, intersubjective and intrasubjective intertwining of the subject/other dyad, unconsciously linked to the Other's *jouissance* (term belonging to Slavoj Zizek's socio-psychoanalytic conceptualization taken straight out of Lacanian theory). Both can help explain fundamentalist religions' violent appeal, at the inter-personal and intra-personal levels.

At the interpersonal level, in order to understand the causal explanations and roots of fundamentalist terrorism, this essay attaches a fundamental role to the socio-economic sphere and conditions, to politics and history, and not to what the neo-con political scientist Francis Fukuyama, for instance, has called "the clash of civilizations" in *The End of History and the Last Man* (1992).[4]

At the intrapersonal level (the "terrorist psyche" so to speak), this essay minimizes the Anglo-Saxon tendency of privileging cognitivism, brain mapping (dysfunctional or abnormal brain electro-chemical functioning producing criminal or pathological/anti-social behavior for instance), and heredity (genes). We believe that human perversity, pathological and even psychotic behavior are fathomable and can be relatively well understood using Sigmund Freud's theories [made more relevant to the postmodern world by post-structuralist work—especially the "return to Freud" done by Jacques Lacan psychoanalysis (the famous "Cause Freudienne") and his cultural follower, Slavoj Zizek...[5] What we are trying to show is that Islamist terrorism is more a symptom of the West, of globalization and hyper-virtuality (hyper-realism) and neo-capitalism, in so far as the Occident/West spearheads and imposes globalization, than a symptom of Islam itself, of Islam considered in isolation. Globalization can be considered as the third wave of colonialism, according to Michael Hardt and Toni Negri's *Empire*, or postmodern capital as "the dialectical third stage of capitalism" as Fredric Jameson calls it.

Basically, before we engage the "big guns" of theory, the whole postmodern problematic of violence and otherness boils down to one main thing: death—this Tarot card that terrorists wage back/engage back so violently in their own game of life and death that they impose on us, according to their own rules. The "trump card" that the Occident wants to make disappear from its Symbolic system, as Jean Baudrillard explains in "*Symbolic Exchange and Death*."[6] Fundamentalist terrorism would then appear as the desperate, last resort, nihilistic attempt at stamping out the Western triumph of the semiotic commodity (materialism as the circulation of goods and merchandises...) over the "symbolic exchange" characterizing traditional societies based on the *gift* (Marcel Mauss's concept)—hence the recourse to death in the "equation." The (fatal) mistake of fundamental terrorism is not to be able to realize that capitalism has already subsumed the semiotic dimension of the commodity under the prevalence of the abstract, hyper-reality of the sign. The green crescent upheld by the materiality of bombs, guns, blood and knives, cannot do anything against the virtuality of the $ sign as floating-signifier.

That is to say that death, as the fundamental goal of all life, epitomizing the tragic and agonistic dimension of humanity, is the forgotten, hidden, common denominator of the ideology of "our" capitalist System. It is the invisible reminder that the Western capitalist mode of production and enjoyment tries to erase, escape, or ignore, and which comes back, unannounced, seemingly unwarranted, through the repressed dimension of our consumerist societies which prefer not to think that they (and we) have an unconscious. Of course, what is forgotten or repressed comes back from the unwanted, negative, or unconscionable side of things, French surrealist playwright Antonin Artaud would have said.

This willful, innocent, convenient or ingenuous omission (who really knows) is the fatal flaw in our little "socio-cosmology"—the more so because it makes us loudly protest and cry "unfair" when we are hit, as if we were innocent; as if we did not have it coming, like General Custer at the battle of the Little Big Horn River (1876). As if our actions and reactions were only/mostly motivated by the common good. Something often re-iterated, now and then, especially during times of crisis, of national doubt (when "The Real," to borrow from Lacanian Borromean knot topology, touches ground, or brushes our faces with its lethal sweep,) by American Presidents stressing that Americans are a good and generous people; that "we" represent the good and "the others," i.e. those which do not espouse our values, Human Rights..., who do not play fair, or by the/our rules, are "bad." As if we had nothing to do in the making of any Evil Empires, Axis of Evil, or terrorists.

The Absolutism of Terrorism

What is new with postmodern fundamentalism is that it manipulates the postmodern state of simulation and hyper-reality/hyper-virtuality.[7] As all fundamentalism, it does not tolerate nuances, and it refuses dialogue. Oriented by conservative or reactionary family values, extreme Islamists repudiate what they consider to be immoral Western permissiveness and consumerist culture, which explains the categories of ethical purity found in the religion they espouse. The violation of human rights perpetrated by ISIS on a daily basis is partly explained by the postmodern totalitarian dimension of globalization which leaves no room for relativism, and the way globalization positions itself ontologically—which explains the absolutist dimension of its vengeance. Moral rectitude used to require rhetorical violence; not any more: this violence has become physical, total and in complete contradiction with its own principles, although as we have briefly seen, in keeping with apocalyptic Islamic beliefs. Akin to the character of Linguère Ramatou in Djibril Diop Mambety's *The Hyena's Last Laugh* (1992), ISIS returns with a vengeance to punish the (Islamic or Christian) community collectively. Radical Islamists/Jihadists position themselves on God's side. The terrorist's violence is the weapon of absolute refusal, destructive of others and self-destructive. It distributes God's justice apocalyptically (instrument of the will of the Big Other in Lacanian theory as we will explain later). It also distributes a certain form of Muslim revenge, i.e. to give others (Westerners) a taste of what Maghrebin, Near-East and Middle-East Muslims had to suffer for decades.

Globalization and Terrorism

Western civilization's global reach, its hyper-technological power, its imperial world domination, its overwhelming universal propaganda and consumerism, its fundamental individualism, the particular way it objectifies everything via the economy (pensée unique), its self-righteousness and obsession with linear progress (ideology), have become unbearable for many.[8] This triumphant ideology and practice inflect in many a sense of deep injustice, a sense of inferiority, of inadequacy and void (ontological despair), and, aggravating circumstance, a realization of utter impotency. This may provoke in many a deep-seated sense of rage (made worse by possible trauma—meaning that trauma and frustration will energize each other) and a definitive refusal. The radicalism of this refusal can turn absolute depending on the ways individuals, groups internalize the rejection. Poverty, unemployment, racism, racial profiling..., all conjugate their effects, re-enforcing a sense of total alienation; coming back as daily reminders of being from nowhere, of non-belongingness. Many individuals cannot process, internalize or sublimate the paradigms of this marginalization and become literally mentally fractured. But all this is not enough to turn dis-enfranchised young people into calculating, cold-blooded assassins. To make a fundamentalist a terrorist, something must go far beyond the hatred of the disinherited and exploited for the dominant ideology and economy, *"those who.... ended up on the wrong side of the global order."*[9] What makes them opt for a more terrible/exacting "Master," asking for cleansing and purification by bloodbath and death, than the capitalist Western society?

The concentration of power which monopolizes and condenses everything into a technocratic/hyper-technological and informational machinery/network preempting any alternative forms of thinking creates the objective conditions for systemic violence and brutal retaliation. The overreaching form of globalization explains the overarching reach of terrorism which takes the whole world as its enemy, since the enemy is everywhere, present in everybody. Globalization implies a global body. The universal system of generalized exchange (everything/everybody can be bought/sold/traded) implies the death of many cultures, societies, animal species. Paradoxically, this global system of generalized exchange excludes death—at least officially. On the contrary, fundamentalist terrorism focuses on a singular exchange with death; Baudrillard would say an ecstatic interfacing with death.[10] That is to say that the universal system of exchange which postures a pro-life concern, brings about an avenging response through precisely what cannot enter, or what is factored out from the Symbolic exchange, i.e. death; or more precisely, its one-directional relation with death—hence the US military strategy aiming at zero-American casualty. This explains the heavy reliance on High-Tech weapons, and "Shock and Awe" types of military operations—which is a form of "State Terrorism "(Bagdad Bombing, August 28 2009.)[11] On the contrary, fundamentalist terrorism focuses on a singular exchange with death. Pre-empting/hyper-virtualizing history, politics and ideology (class-struggle), postmodernist capitalism transforms the world at maximum speed (Paul Virilio-[12]-) as if in a race for survival, a race against (its own?) death. Late capitalism transforms the world by force. Terrorism radicalizes it by the sacrifice (its own and the one of others). This corresponds to what Jean Baudrillard calls a "*terroristic situational transfer.*" [13]Hegemonic power generates its own anti-bodies.

The flows of postmodern, late, or neo-capitalism distribute all over the world (globalization) amounts more, as the title of one of the last books of the Slovanian critic Slavoj Zizek indicates, *Trouble in Paradise*, than mere middle-class build-ups, lifting up of masses out of poverty, beneficial progress, and comfort enhancement. These flows and fluxes are materialized by merchandises, finances, travelers, information..., and can be characterized as "primary" (Freudian and Lacanian notion) because they work against the Symbolic system, destabilizing/eroding/bypassing it, making it irrelevant—and, also, because of what is put into circulation.

Undercurrent to these fluxes of money, people and commodities, sustaining them paradoxically, parasitizing them like flotsam accordingly, or paralleling them clockwise or counter-clockwise, are five main flows:

0. the triple distributive flows of drug trafficking (which,

for instance, fed Miami' s booming economy in the 80s and 90s);

a. illicit financial trafficking (tax evasions and offshore accounts epitomized by the "Panama Scandal");

b. human trafficking (emigration—65 million emigrants in today's world, child labor, workers slavery—sex workers included...);

c. the flow of troops and military aid which guarantees the "safety of the Empire;"

d. the flow of fundamentalist terrorism which, itself, intensifies the precedent one, i.e. the flow of arms and soldiers from the Occident to Africa and the Orient.

These more or less secretive flows (except for the fourth one) correspond to the other side of the coin of the generalized exchange of postmodern capital. They are the obfuscated side of "global leadership," to borrow a title from a University of Montana curricular initiative. These five flows are not due to isolated or local forces produced by the effects inherent to a local specific playing field. They are part of the fundamental picture of postmodern capital. Not only is Islamist fundamentalism a product of globalization, like emigration, it directly feeds, follows, uses, and parasitizes the flows and fluxes of capital. For instance, Wahabbism is globalized by petro-dollars, while ISIS profits from crude oil and antiquities trafficking. That is to say that fundamentalist terrorism is the logical by-product of neo-capitalism, its dialectical reversal:

"What is called religion today (in a variety of forms, from left to right) is really politics under a different name. (Indeed, maybe religion has always been that.) What is called religious fundamentalism is then a political option, which is embraced when other political options have been shut down: most notably, left politics and communist parties all over the Islamic world, if not the third world generally... Instead, we have to enlarge our historical perspective to include the wholesale massacres of the Left systematically encouraged and directed by Americans in a period that stretches back virtually to the beginnings of the cold war... Yet the physical extermination of the Iraqi and Indonesian

communist parties, although now virtually forgotten, were crimes as abominable as any contemporary genocide. These are instances in which assassination and the wholesale murder of your opponents are preeminently successful in the short run; but whose unexpected consequences are far more ambiguous historically...But this simply means that a left alternative for popular resistance and revolt has been closed off. The so-called fundamentalist religious option then becomes the only recourse and the only available form of a politics of opposition; and this is clearly the case of bin Laden's movement, however limited it may be to intellectuals and activists."[14]

As Jean Baudrillard wrote, the unrestricted world market—globalization—brings about its own shadow.[15]

As its name indicates, globalization works all over the world redefining nations and societies, humans and eco-systems, leaving no stone unturned.[16] The world has become a fluid terrain of multiple lines of fluxes and flight of capital, goods, people..., hierarchized areas of accumulation, as well as shifting zones of intensities and forces; conflicts marked by signs and indicators pointing to all possible directions and forms of transits or dereliction—from nations in the process of economical hyper-development, or accelerated development, and "democracy-building," to wrecked nations (failed states), illegal trafficking of all sorts, and pauperized states. Capital fluxes de-territorialize ethnic groups, forcing populations and citizens to move away from regions, areas and physical habitats—rural exodus due to industrialization, or emigration due to lack of industrialization, or rampant, endemic poverty.[17] These fluxes conjugating flows of money, energy and high-tech solutions also de-territorialize people away from habits and customs, cultural habitats, mores and traditional values. To use a Deleuzian terminology, globalization prepares bodies and minds for an alignment conducive to capitalism's extension. They streamline bodies and mentalities, transform or fracture the traditional behavior of citizens, nationals, tribal members who then become consumers, trans-nationals (paupers and migrants), individuals (called modernization), or, in the worst cases, victims rendered nomadic (refugees); i.e. (ex-)political masses turned into multitudes of broken individuals. All this partly explains the general aggravation of the mental fragility of the population at large. When global capital cannot smooth out the striated/heterogeneous body of a society/country, its implacable logic can bring about a violent de-territorialization, an up-rooting of populations (military fluxes or interventions) provoking violent emigrations of populations. In the worst case, de-territorialization brings about violent emigration, which can be mental and internal, or physical and external. The mental and internal emigration may produce terrorism (Kristeva's "*the stranger in ourselves*," or "the self violently migrating from ego to super-ego"). The physical and external emigration brings about hordes/waves of displaced people, terrified refugees fleeing for their lives towards the "First World", i.e. the economic heart of the Empire.[18]

These emigration flows follow the fluxes of capital towards its areas of accumulation (North America, Australian, Western Europe—especially Germany), or flee away from its areas of rupture/resistance (capitalist obsolescence, i.e. the Maghreb and the Near- and Middle-East—the Emirates excluded), where the legacy of history (colonialism), and postcolonialism clashing with the demands of postmodernity, negatively over-determines the socio-political situation.[19] One such area being the Orient, where the Eastern Maghreb and the Middle-East are undergoing extreme convulsions due to the contradictions between the different democratic movements, Islamist fundamentalism, and the pressure exerted by Western consumerism (American-based/initiated nation-building).

"Lift your eyes to the horizons of business, and with the inspiration of the thought that you are Americans and are means to carry liberty and justice and the principles of humanity wherever you go, go out and sell goods that will make the world more comfortable and more happy, and convert them to the principles of America."[20]

Overall, in spite of isolationist periods, America has always tried to equate the needs of capital with her political and military leadership, by creating a U.S.-led world-order, where the global capitalist system and the projection of U.S. national power are in synchronicity. This has involved America into imposing its economic hegemony and the radical change of different peoples' forms of social life.

Both terrorism and emigration are two faces of the same coin. They are both symptoms of radical de-territorialization.

The Spirit of Terrorism: A Collective Psychosis?[21]

May we like it or not, terrorism participates in the general exchange of words and things (politics, economy, culture), as well as the general exchange of what Marxists, and Gramsci especially, intuitively understood, and tentatively called "*structures of feeling*," or what J.F. Lyotard calls "libidinal economy",[22] i.e. the intra-subjective and inter-subjective circulation of all that constitutes the emotional and mental life, investments and reactions at the conscious and unconscious level: energies, concerns, desires, anxieties, pleasures, revulsions, and phobias. Why such a total, all-inclusive understanding of desire and exchange? It is because desire is linked to exchange (and trade), from the prohibition of incest to the exchange of symbols, merchandises, signs, objects. Exchanges impose a symbolic value on objects as Lyotard explains.[23]

The pleasure principle (and its correlate, libidinality) and the way it circulates in the political and mercantile economy is linked to consciously and unconsciously motivated forms of attraction, affection and alliance, aggression, destruction, and the violence of lethal consumption/addiction (what Lacanian psychoanalysis calls the unconscious). They form the psychological part of the ego and the basis of identification (the part of the self, psyche, and emotional life targeted by American ego-psychology), as well as the unconscious underpinnings of the Subject—$, (symptoms and pathologies) which are beyond the access of the ego, consciousness (and ego-psychology). They are used and "sedimented" in the human psyche by the System, since they are at once mobile and static, helping to shape individual and collective ideology. Advertising, techniques of mass-manipulation, propaganda, consumer-related research, the entertainment industry..., all have learned how to manipulate "the libidinal economy," as well as being a fundamental part of it. Thinkers have often declared that the fundamental force of late-capitalism was its power and savvy to know how to directly plug into the primary/secondary mental life of the subject, his/her emotions and unconscious drives.

The way libidinal economy works (as defined by Jean-François Lyotard—[24]), more or less corresponds to the tracings of desire or molecular lines (as defined by Gilles Deleuze—[25]) which reconfigurate individuals' behavior and the micro-politics of the body-politic, as well as the socius. To each socio-economico-political system corresponds a particular libidinal economy, i.e. a specific libidinal investment. The libidinal economy of an agrarian society is obviously not the same as the one of an advanced capitalist society. Tagging, theft, vandalism used to be expressions of revolt. They still are; but something is different. The game has changed because the Symbolic system has changed.

The new, neo-liberal (European meaning), libidinal economy corresponds to the way postmodern capitalism has re-arranged, re-distributed desire, its intensity, and identification (their condensation and displacement), and the complex relationship between sexuality and the unconscious, or what Deleuze calls de-territorialization. Postmodern, as well as fundamentalist terrorism, which according to our understanding, is a by-product, a spin-off of late-capitalism, are part of the grand scheme of things consciously and unconsciously generated/organized by a totally overwhelmed Symbolic system in crisis (there is simply no exchange without a Symbolic system) and its Imaginary excess (Lacanian meaning),. The Symbolic system now coincides less and less with the configurations of globalization, or better, globalization dictates to the Symbolic new forms, configurations and actualizations of desire, a new modus operandi, which in many instances, destroys older Symbolic forms and functions, freeing the Imaginary up to one point from the Symbolic's strictures and structures. That is to say that love and hate participate in this exchange system, not perhaps equally, and certainly not with the same equanimity, but they do. As Jean Baudrillard used to say, there is no good without bad, or love without hate. Of course, hate may be, in certain different configurations, in its concrete manifestations, the product of a different logic, i.e. a different relation between what Lacanian topology has called the Borromean rings—and this is where fundamentalist terrorism lurks. Fundamentalist terrorism shows how globalization induces psychotic behavior.

The postmodern terrorist responds ironically and directly to the industrial or technological metaphor with which Deleuze, with his "libidinal materialist" theory, describes humans as "desiring-machines" who produce the social out of desire. Aren't terrorists "celibatory machines" who do not want to produce any social dimension—except the Caliphate perhaps, but one wonders if it is not an excuse, all things considered. In fact with their closed-in language (cyphers and encryption), their peculiar practice of "truth" (hermetic and non-communicative) does not need to disclose anything (except "the terminal act" at the end or killing/suicide redemption).Why? Because there is nothing to disclose/discuss/reveal at the level of the doxa, political system, or even mysticism. In their manicheistic system, there is no allusion to any authority, logic, tradition, politics to ground and justify their beliefs and actions, except the illusion of an incommunicado God (or deigning to speak only through a radical imam). Hence, also their indifference to any kind of persuading technique or propaganda to reach out towards the Infidels (the West).The only tool of recruitment they use is the Internet/Web, i.e. the social Media network where one can have hundreds of friends or contacts without having to face anybody in the flesh/in person, or even hear their voices if one does not want. They are the perfect incarnation of the "*machine célibataire*," "male celibate automaton," living alone, or with their mother, or in seclusion, self-sufficient, tele-guided from the outside—or the outside in them (Lacanian notion of *extémité* which we will visit later).[26] They blend machines (High-Tech), hyper-real nervous systems (Web and social Media), and weapons incarnating the death-drive (automatic guns, explosives). Their logic is the cold logic of the Cartesian machine-body. They are little cyborgs where bodies and death are directly interfaced/linked (the body as "*machine infernale*"—bomb), cybernetic organisms, drugged-up biological "machines of suffering" bent on inflicting the greatest possible harm, with chemical shoes, underwear, wired chest jackets (the Brussels and Istanbul Airport attacks).

They are without any female language—except the non-referential, unconscious, primary voice of the incestuous M(o) ther, something we will consider later. This partly explains why the fundamentalist terrorists seem to prefer minimalist forms of social agglutination, of *being-togetherness* (sociologist Michel Maffesoli), contrary to the inner-city gangs with their hierarchy, leaders, "wives," and their rituals such as the "symbolic castration" in parentis loco, or better, in absentia of a *name-of-the-father*, i.e. the "drive-by-shooting" group rite of initiation (passage from a Symbolic act to "an act in the Real" would a Lacanian certainly propose). They favor (security being not the main reason) small bands of "*machine célibataires*." It is interesting to notice that many jihadists/fundamentalist terrorists are brothers (the French/Algerian Said and Cherif Kourachi brothers—the January 8, 2015 *Charlie Hebdo* attack; the Chechnyan/Dagestani/Kyrgyze/Kalmykian/American Tamerlan and Dzhokhar Tsarnaev brothers—the April 18, 2001 Boston Marathon bombers). They also form a loose coalition of individuals, or cells, organized or self-generating: the British Michael Read (shoe bomber) and the Franco/Moroccan Omar Massaoui (a member of the 9/11 terrorist-cell) met through the radical Brixton Mosque in London, where the local al-Muhajiroun ("The Emigrants") gathered.

The asocial minimalism of many a terrorist is often caused or aggravated by depression and anxiety. Umar Abdulmutallab, the unsuccessful "Underwear Bomber" of Northwest Flight 253 (Amsterdam to Detroit—Christmas Day 2009) was also described as a student "*preoccupied by university admissions and English soccer clubs..., apparently lonely and conflicted.*"[27] The German-Iranian shooter of Munich (July 23, 2006) was a depressed, solitary young man (a withdrawn loner), who had been bullied in school, and spent time playing "violent video games." He also suffered from panic attacks for which he received psychiatric help. Mohammad D., the Syrian immigrant who blew himself up in the crowd at Ansbach (Germany) on July 24, 2016, was supposed to be deported. But his suicidal tendencies and his mental state which necessitated psychiatric care, suspended his deportation. Mohammad Atta (9/11 cell), who came from an Egyptian well-to-do family, was described by other students in the University Centrumraum in Hamburg as living in a "complete, almost aggressive insularity."

What is also typical of many of these terrorists is their nomadism (again–de-territorialization), their delinquent behavior (many were petty criminals, little dealers or thieves, known from the local police where they lived), their anti-social, violent behavior, and their poverty (with the exception of Mohammed Atta, who came from a well-to-do stable family, and Umar Farouk Abdulmutallab, son of a Nigerian wealthy banker). The Franco-Algerian G.I.A. terrorist Khaled Kelkal, involved in terrorist bombings in France in 1995, was a top-of-his class student, who became a delinquent with his brother. Omar Moussaoui was born with three siblings in a milieu of domestic violence (abusive father who deserted the family) and poverty. The Moroccan/Algerian/French Salah Abdeslam—involved in the Paris mass attack of November 18, 2015, was a petty criminal living in the Molenbeeck district of Brussels. The Moroccan Ayoub El Khazzani –the Thalys train shooter (subdued by three American and one British passengers) was living homeless in Brussels. Most came from poor, dysfunctional emigrant families.

That is to say that they carry with them their symptoms, until these can be discharged unto the Cause, the ready-made, awaiting ideological recipient—which is not surprising, since these symptoms often come from their childhood and correspond to residual unsolved trauma (racism and rejection in Moussaoui's case). These trauma are, of course, aggravated by their being unwanted, marginalized, rejected situation.

The Other (Lacanian big Other), and this is important, is out of fundamentalist terrorists's psychic structure; it is certainly foreclosed—which would give their language and actions a quasi-psychotic dimension. As for any good "celibate machines," pure exteriority takes the place of the *name-of-the-father*, which makes them vulnerable to any sublation (a tragic, ironic, or pathetic—accordingly, version of the Hegelian *Aufhebung)* by an external cause which is then internalized. Of course, this internalization of an externality has to be grounded by a locality or dislocation of locality, an absence or non-lieu allied to a phobia (ambivalent homophobia in Omar Mateen's case—who killed more than 50 clients of Orlando's Gay Club Pulse, on June 12, 2016), hatred of the *banlieue* for the *beurs*, the ghetto, decayed inner-city, or project for American black youth, the traumatic loss of the homeland, the killings of Muslims by Americans and their allies in North-Africa and the Orient... This is where the postmodern, capitalist de-territorialization espoused/extolled by Deleuze meets head on the physical de-territorialization of the youth or would-be terrorists. They reinforce each other.

In more ways than one, the terrorist is literally "beside himself." In this lost/confused situation, Islam may come only a posteriori, as a fill-up, or desperate, last minute motivation to justify the terrorist act (libidinally oriented of course by the obfuscation/trauma of the origins—probably Omar Mateen's case). Since they have no interiority, but the confused and confusing arcane of a private world/hell without *name-of-the-father* to point towards the way out, and to help ground an identity, a subjectivity and interiority, jihadists cannot be mystics. The exteriority of God has never shone in them through any mirroring interiority: the soul (representation of identity and transcendental subjectivity). This is why their passion has no compassion. Fundamentalist terrorists have refused the title/function of "son" in search of a super image of the father, which then lives in them in a way that Lacan calls "*extimate.*" Since their *jouissance* is heavily marked by death (it is the Big Other which puts a damper or limit on *jouissance*—the limit being called pleasure), suicide is the logical outcome of their enterprise: the fusion with (the) God (of wrath). This is why the terrorist's apparatus is replete with the paraphilia of a death-yielding-machinery (juvenile, fetishistic obsession): black Kalashnikovs, black Ninja clothing, grenades, bombs, knives, and especially the shining-like blade of the sword (scimitar) which delivers a "fast and clean-like popular-type of justice" (aka the guillotine) with no compensation and no recourse (absolute), and with the smoothness of the perfect execution and/or suicide, since they are in inverted position to each other in Jihadists' minds—the sword was the preferred weapon of the Samurais and the "art of *seppuku*." The justice-yielding sword is also the mediatic and "Hollywoodianally medievalist" tool par excellence, whose symbolic dimension makes way for a world with no alterity—a terrifying world under the black sun of Allah, their own version of a God with no actual mothers or fathers (the only women allowed besides the supernumerary virgins awaiting the warriors in Paradise are the concubines and wives of forced marriages—the infamous *repos du guerrier*).

As if following the inclinations of their libidinal economy, Jihadists, on the contrary, aggressively affirm the instantaneous nature or ephemerality of desire. As if following Lyotard's understanding of desire ("after the letter," so to speak), they do not create anything other than a "happening," as if terrorists had no other purpose but to produce a response of the highest intensity. Fundamentalist terrorism incarnates the form of desire bent on pointless pleasure which does not seek any particular needs except the totalitarian vow to exact tribute. This explains that the terrorist act has both an "event status" as a malevolent, political and even "cultural" event (to strike terror and provoke/precipitate a schism, a conflict, a civil war) and a "representational one" (amplified by the Media).[28] It is an in-site happening centered on a death-type-of-art-piece, a sacrifice of postmodernity to postmodernity, targeting the happiness, *jouissance*, well-being, pleasure, of the West via a vengeance, a revenge, a phantasmatic strike of God (we will come back on this aspect).

If postmodernism, according to J.F. Lyotard, denies good form and value by setting the non-representable in representation itself, not via symbolization because symbolization is exteriorization, then jihadist terrorism is a postmodern form—albeit eruptive, violent of course, and total. It brings the inside of the symptomatic other at war, in turmoil, or in agony, into the inside of the subject at peace via the event. It is not metaphoric since it does not transport the subject to the outside meaning of an event, in order to convince him/her, by opening his/her interiority to his (the terrorist's). They bring the "event" on a plateau, like Saint John the Baptist's head on a charger (flat dish), to Salome after her "seven veil dance" at the court of Herod and Herodias in the New Testament, as spiteful revenge. The fundamentalist terrorist act is totalitarian because it reduces everything and subsumes all contingencies to the totality of a revenge. The type of absolute revolt it incarnates has no revolutionary dimension as such since it is not concerned by any objective necessity of History and has no self-consciousness of history necessity. It is a peculiar form of desire, of *jouissance* directly produced by social. Although terrorists try to give an overarching purpose to their *jouissance*, the anomies of terrorists are directly plugged into the antinomies of the body politic. Their pitiless, unrelenting, undaunted, "on a mission-like" behavior is fueled by the *jouissance* of the death drive—something very postmodern and illustrated by Kroenenberg's Crash (1996)—where *jouissance* comes out of the "planned happening" of a car accident followed by the enjoyment of scared/maimed bodies, giving to the "*petite mort*" (French for orgasm) a Real dimension (Lacanian meaning). Furthermore the terrorist's desire inscribes itself in a harsh, horrific reality, the one of a mangled, dismembered, fragmented or exploded body—the body-politic of the West and its socius. All this points towards a tragic re-enactment of the fear and doubting absence of origins in the terrorist's psyche. The loss or absence of the father as big Other (guaranteeing the consistency of the Symbolic system, of the cultural realm), provokes an identification of the terrorist, at the level of the *imago* (Lacanian concept of the mirror stage first theorized in 1949), with an image of his own fragmented body, i.e. an image of castration expressing the subject's total lack of any substantial, coherent unity, provoking extreme anxiety, and even desperate violence to the point of affecting his actual body, symptomizing it, or arousing fantasy-projections of this violence onto the other's body.[29] In fact, the historical changes within the economy (libidinal and other) of the family structure plays a key-role in the narrativization and display of sexuality and violence. New research links the appearance of' "terrorism" as a category of modern political action, towards the end of the 18th century (The French Terror period), to the growth of what was called in England "terror fiction" or " terrorist novel writing" (1797),[30] a genre now known as "Gothic," and to conspiracy theory.[31] It is interesting to notice how, in the Gothic or "terrorist" narrative, supernatural agents avenge those who have suffered too much in a world without justice, as if the Judeo-Christian motto had turned around: "do upon others what others have done upon you, or 'your people'."

The terrorist is an anti-romantic figure (despite the aura projected by the in/famous Carlos), investing energy away from the traditional family (many left children and family behind), de-coding desire, hi-jacking it via the "molar lines" of the Web, in order to over-code it along a frozen interpretation, an old reading of Koranic lines, re-investing it in the tribe/ gang, or a fantasy of the primal group, à la *Lord of the Flies*,[32] ironically following the new "nomadology" favored/initiated by postmodern capital. These Jihadists function as "celibatory machines" (Tausk) for whom women are but the "*repos du Guerrier.*" They are autopoietic machines of unconscious investment—meaning that their unconscious orientations pre-determine/ favor their libidinal energetic investment in the cause as ultimate revenge and defiance. Many terrorists behave as if they were the a-social product of a "molecular unconscious" (à la Deleuze and Guattari) that would only know energy parameters and energy functions, like the "de-Oedipalized" street-gangs (most of them have no father or have an "obscene father") of inner-city ghettoes' marginalized youth (they are examples of Deleuzian '*Anti-Oedipuses*' alright!). Phenomenologically, their "fatherland" (and "motherland") is the "no man's land" of the *banlieue* ("banishment place" out of the city-walls defining the security of the locus and the community in Medieval France); i.e. a zone of non sequitur logic and non-lieu status (both in the meaning of "nonsuit" and "no man's land," where today the police (or its militarized version, the C.R.S.) only ventures when riots explode.) The neo-con analyst Kaplan already pre-figured the descent into dystopianism of future megalopolises in *The Coming Anarchy*. The ontic situation of the terrorist can be metaphorized by two images: the one illustrated by Scorcese's film *The Wolf of Wall Street*,[33] and the numerous images of "lone-wolf-terrorists"—meaning that the financial predator goes hand in hand with the lone mass-killer.

Muslim fundamentalists are not so much "sick-unto-God" as they are "sick-unto-the-father."

Psychotic Logic of ISIS[34]

Sometimes God has to be reminded of his duty toward mankind.[35]

ISIS via men reminds God to respect the order of the universe, i.e. to play God. ISIS put God back in its place, in its godly place—a universe displaced by Satan (modernity and its symbol, America), put out of order by the Infidels, the West, and Christianity who let the universe escape God. This reminder can be very violent and extreme as if Muslim fundamentalists were angry against God for having given free rein to the infidels. ISIS violently reminds God of his task/duty towards mankind. ISIS is the instrument of this task, of this Revival in "the Real" (Lacanian terminology):

"There are still religious associations that are bound together by a practice of crime—crime in which their members know how to find anew the superhuman presences that ensure destruction in order to keep the Universe in balance."[36]

ISIS's *jouissance* is to be the arm of God by assuming the role/place of the ultimate paternal metaphor, the Lacanian big Other. ISIS is not playing the role of a mediator listening to an angel, or the Virgin Mary (intercessor between God and Man), or even a facilitator listening to God via his archangels, like Joan of Arc. They express the direct wrath of God. They are the arm of his vengeance. This what makes fundamentalist terrorists psychotics. Ironically, and very logically, it is because they are missing the presence of this paternal metaphor themselves, originating for the most part from broken, dysfunctional families, with absent fathers, and places of ultimate de-territorialization (French *banlieues*), that DAECH/ISIS terrorists reclaim this absence at another level, from another perspective. Since they were not given the means to assume this fundamental absence, or in Deleuzian terms, to re-territorialize themselves (something they more or less rightfully blame on the host country—France, for instance), they defend the paternal metaphor against itself, against all odds (Jihad). Fundamentalist terrorists (all young) function in many ways like groups of young men of American inner-cities' gangs. The gang offers solace, shelter, and identification in exchange for total submission.

They therefore become more Muslims than the Muslims themselves, since religion is of crucial importance in fundamentalist terrorism. The problem is that there are many divergent interpretations of religion, as the history of religions easily show. Contrary to what many critics assert, who want to deflect terrorists' acts away from religion, in order to safeguard it, fundamentalist terrorists are religious.

"Nature is a slave of its own laws...; the only way to create something effectively new is therefore an absolute Crime... It is therein that Lacan locates the link between sublimation and the death-drive: sublimation equates to creation ex-nihilo, on the basis of annihilation of the preceding Tradition. It is not difficult to see how all radical revolutionary projects, Khmer Rouge included, rely on this same fantasy of a radical annihilation of Tradition and of the creation ex nihilo of a new (sublime) Man, delivered from the corruption of previous history." [37]

By fighting off Western oppression, and rejecting any reign of law, the fundamentalist terrorist puts himself at the mercy (under the sway) of the M(o)ther (the "primordial Other" fantazised as being one with the infant—the *id*) who appears later as the specter of total Omnipotence. Since he desperately yearns for the desire of this foreclosed big Other (or father), whose love/guidance/acceptance he unconsciously craves, and since this *name-of-the-father* is not accessible, the big Other is replaced by the "Primordial Other," this "impossible symmetric other" of the big Other or *name-of-the-father*. It is an "Other" without any lack and beyond/before any law (i.e. the "incestuous M(o)ther") upon whom the subject becomes unconsciously totally dependent, submitted, and subservient. It is interesting that ISIS' war flags are made of black cloth inscribed with white Arabic sentences—black as the color of the sun of the foreclosed *name-of-the father* coming back under the guise of incestuous M(o)ther. Paradoxically the freedom of the fundamentalist terrorist by identifying with the absolute/unbound desire of the "primordial Other" becomes totally alienated. Aby Musab al-Zarqawi, the son of an impoverished Palestinian family resettled in Jordan, also a high-school dropout and petty criminal in his youth (he was killed in 2006 by two American guided bombs dropped from two jets while in a "safe-house" in Iraq), whose nickname was "Shaykh of the Slaughterers," wanted to turn Islam into a weapon to crush the West by creating a constant existential threat. In a way, one can speak of a hijacking of Islam, in the same way as Al-Qaeda masterminds of 9/11 have hijacked the Western vectors of transport, travel and communication and turn them into missiles of destruction/annihilation. It is therefore wrong to associate Jihadists with the worst kind of male, sexist, and patriarchal behavior, because the paternal metaphor of ISIS is foreclosed. Its void was filled by the M(o)ther-of-all-otherness: the phallic m(o)ther who haunts the intersectional "space" of the Imaginary and the Real, and who does not know any boundaries.

Terrorists' Split Personalities

The projection of hatred and self-disgust which typifies fundamentalist terrorists's mentalities starts when emigration fails or has failed. There is a "non-lieu", as we have analyzed before, in the execution of the emigration movement. This failure of emigration migrates into the self and splits it into two. The terrorist feels as an abject object, only worthy in ethnic- and class-terms of the West worst place of exclusion besides the prisons (the *banlieues* or ghettoes) where the abject of the West, its "lumpen proletariat" is dumped. The ethics of space and movement have affected the terrorist directly in a negative way. The physical marginalization incarnated in the *bidonville/ banlieue*/ghetto/transit city (Calais's *jungle*)/refugee camps, rotten inner-cities epitomizes the social devaluation and stereotyping. The breeding ground for jihadists is the physical and mental transitory state of poverty and indifference between two worlds from which one cannot escape: one unwelcoming or rejecting; the other inaccessible because locked in the parental past. A geomorphy or even geomorphological analogy explains the dilemma, who, like a situational differential cannot gear up. The transitionary state turns into a permanent hiatus, crack, or fall where two conflicting domains clash like two tectonic plates, one subsumed, the other lifted up—hence the volcanic eruptions. The interstitial, the libidinal, the molecular, and the fragmented, all in their own ways, symbolize the different conceptual approaches to explain the fundamentalist terrorism phenomenon phenomenologically. The impossibility of hybridity within a totally de-territorialized status where the self has no place to go, and where the right to difference turns into public indifference and/or anxiety about the other's *jouissance* (by-product of multiculturalism and communitarianism).

The target-recipient of terroristic violence is really of no importance (race, sex, age, proximity) since everybody is collectively guilty, although those deemed directly responsible are first targeted (Americans, Europeans...). The target is chosen in function of its symbolic dimension (places and nexuses of traffic, flows and exchange) and Mediatic importance (Pentagon, Twin Towers, the White House, international hubs such as airports), places of entertainment (Western *jouissance* seen as debauchery) such as Paris's night life places, restaurants or night-clubs, heterodox mosques (in Muslim countries), monuments (considered as places of idolatry), etc.

The ego-ideal (Freudian secondary dimension) is absorbed or recovered by the ideal-ego (Freudian primary dimension) since the name-of-the-father is absent, inexistent, obscene or impotent. This is important since it explains the "high" reached by the terrorists (remember the shoe-bomber's extreme frustration when he was not able to carry on his plans—passengers were forced to restrain him for the duration of the flight) and the intense narcissism inherent to the terrorist *passage à l'acte* (acting out) which implies a glorifying self-sacrifice for a cause larger than the individual/subject. The ideal-ego is projected on the act and the cause. Here the Imaginary and the Real are directly inter-connected imposing another logic on the Symbolic, or simply by-passing it. The ego-ideal generally develops love and objects of love attached to other persons, while the ideal-ego develops grandiosity, delusion and extreme narcissism.

Terrorism Paradoxical Inversions

The Occident and the Orient (or, at least, its most tragically affected regions) now exchange missiles and missives of radical ideas (*letters* of hatred), terrifyingly exhibitionist images, i.e. a generalized rhetoric of escalating violent behavior which vies for the control of minds and bodies of whole populations. The "weird game" of this fatal logic played by the terrorists not only works "tit for tat," but also inverts the "benevolently utilitarian" and "pacifying" image the West wants to project to the world which invokes an eternal and universal conscience of the Rights of Man.

Why this paradoxical and peculiar inversion? For four main, interconnected reasons.

- Because the Western mode of total development and its only existing challenge, i.e. the terrorist, fundamentalist, total rejection, both pursue immortality and the negation of time, but from opposite directions.

- Because collectivities cannot sustain themselves on mere humanitarianism (human rights, and so on), on what Slavoj Zizek calls the "collective links of love" without any support in the big Other (God). A disappearance of the big Other brings about another logic, another reality, another binary system.

- "The transgression of the code is the reversion of opposite terms, and therefore of the calculated differences through which the dominance of one term over the over is established."[38]

- Because, as the following quote from Slavoj Zizek indicates, the logic of Lacanian psychoanalysis applied to communication explains why the message (if we may say so) sent by fundamental terrorism is inverted:

- "According to Lacan's definition of successful communication, I get back from the other my own message in its inverted form, which is to say with its true meaning, the truth about myself that I had repressed. Is today's Western capitalism getting back from the Islamist fundamentalists its own message but in its inverted true form? In other words, is Muslim fundamentalism the symptom of capitalist globalization and liberal tolerance? Is the exploding in fury against liberal corruption the very figure who enables the liberal to encounter the truth behind

> his own hypocrisy? Perhaps we should learn from the most popular song about Kansas, and look for our allies somewhere over the rainbow: beyond the "rainbow coalition" of radical liberals and their single-issue struggles, and towards those who they see as their enemy."[39]

Secular, Western rationality (under its hard or soft forms—atheism, or "temperate" religiosity) is answered with religious Medieval fanaticism;[40] progressive and liberal tolerance with transgressive and "barbarian" provocations; Western Humanism ("human rights," "normality," quality of life,"..., or what Jean Baudrillard calls "*the vissicitudes of profitability*") with inhuman acts;[41] the capitalist privatization of all space with a nomadic-type of communal, neo-tribal space; the Media hyper-virtual manipulation/simulation of reality (from TV-reality to survivor shows) with "live" videos of raw, bloody, "real" public executions. The Social Media become a-social: Facebook is defaced: instead of hundreds of friends, hundreds of terrorists.

Commercial advertising is countered by religious propaganda; the West's drones and smart bombs by cleverly hidden explosives smuggled on-board jet-planes; the US-led coalition of neo-crusaders by a new "*Internationale*" of radicalized, Muslim jihadists (the new form of "International Brigades" is made up of 100,000 to 200,000 jihadists according to Western intelligence, American nation-building by the Caliphate; the Founding Fathers' model legacy by the Prophet's voice; Political Correctness and Western-cloned democracies by a literal and reactionary interpretation of the Koran; the subordination of egotism to the self-reproduction of Capital by the subordination of individualism to the Sharia, etc.

The Western exhibitionist, ubiquitous gaze which wants to make everything visible and transparent is opposed by black veils and djellabas which cloak faces and bodies, blocking the introspecting gaze; to Western pornography, prurient nakedness, and promiscuous bodies (especially women's) the response is a veiled female dimension and a de-eroticized male presence (bushy beards and hair, unkempt appearance, loose djellabas...). The Western crass-materialism is answered by the crass ideology of mentally/morally desperate people—sons and daughters of failed nation-states, war-ravaged countries, or neo-colonized states. To the nothingness and vacuity of Western individualism and reification answers the fullness of a hypostatized and hystericized Islam. To the rhizome-like proliferation of capital answers the viral-like propagation of terrorism. To the viral dimension of globalization's High-Tech network of interconnection in real time propagating the information/data necessary to the life of capitalism, answers the viral, encrypted messages bringing about death and mayhem.

The fundamentalist, ideological propaganda even reaches into the heart of the West, addressing its inner contradictions, i.e. the ethnically and culturally alienated youth (the hybrid, impoverished, and marginalized "suburbanites" of large European cities, the poor and marginalized of American "ghettos"...) and, something new, the "estranged/alienated" youth of the relatively affluent Western middle-class (now "courted" by ISIL).

Emigration

Terrorism and emigration form two sides of the same coin.

From what we know of recorded history and what we can deduct from prehistory, insect, animal and human emigrations have always been part of life on this planet (at least). The annual migration of the monarch butterfly is called by biologists one of nature's miracles. Early on, for reasons still unknown, humans migrated from Africa, generating the different races we know. Climate changes, push from other migrating people (such as the Huns who pushed Germanic tribes Westward), socio-political upheavals, poverty and persecutions are the key reasons for emigration. A combination of unemployment, famine and religious persecution drove more than 30 million European immigrants to the United States in the 19th and early 20th centuries. The first major wave of immigration to the U.S. occurred between 1820 and 1870, when a famine in Ireland and Northern Europe and economic troubles in Germany brought more than 7 million immigrants to America. But the height of immigration was between 1880 and 1920, when more than 20 million immigrants from Central, Eastern and Southern Europe, including millions of Russian Jews fleeing religious persecution, came to the U.S. The open door immigration policy ended with the passage of the Emergency Quota Act in 1921 which set quotas according to nationality.

So what is new with the postmodern emigration due to globalization?

Globalization exemplifies and exacerbates, by bringing out into the open the uncertainty and fragility of the identity attached to the Subject, by re-ifying the Subject's desire (consumer's society) along certain socio-political lines which are not all-inclusive (since the System's "gratuities" are based on competition, rivalry, merit, work, etc.), by bringing to the Subject's proximity the *jouissance* of the other, therefore threatening the integrity of the Subject's desire, by de-stabilizing the fragile balance of the subject, by bringing out the movement of transit inherent to the group and the individual (question of geo-psychoanalysis.) Transit between the inside and outside, in ourselves and out of ourselves, between the ego, the subject and otherness: "*we are all in the process of becoming foreigners in a universe that is being widened more than ever, that is more than ever heterogeneous beneath its apparent scientific and media-inspired unity.*"[42]

What defines globalization is massive circulation, immigration/emigration.

Emigration and terrorism imply the highest development of the panoptical apparatus and technological procedures. Emigration obeys subordination. Terrorism terrorizes subordination, in its will to counter the police action extended by Western civilization to the entire world. Although emigration plays an important role in the socio-economic dimension of the world, it goes beyond its limits and brings about racial fantasy into the heart of the postmodern Empire.

The Roman (as pre-Modern or Modernist) Empire's demise according to many historians was partly caused by the inability of Rome to accommodate the constant trickling down of immigrants (called barbarians by the Romans).

The cultural and societal disintegration (High-Tech and consumerism), and the fluxes of identity that postmodernism effectuates/generates on individuals and societies cannot be faced; the disintegration of one's reality is always frightening—hence the necessity to find a scapegoat. "*The ear is receptive to conflicts only if the body loses its footing.*"[43]

The emigrants are the ready-made scapegoats, because:

1. The sudden and massive intrusion of the other brings in the rigid persona (i.e. the self-correct and self-correcting positioning keeping the footing of the Subject on the bedrock of what s/he perceives as his/her own authenticity, identity and coherence. It is rigid because it is a shield against fragmentation, insanity and cultural disintegration, and the violent reactions against disintegration, which can bring about hysteria. Hysteria fuses together enjoyment, horror and disavowal and can induce hallucinations. The big Other is the only means through which the subject is made thinkable, possible. The irruption of otherness (emigrants) may arouse in rigid personae mechanisms of primary narcissism accompanied by coercive appeals to defensive dimensions of destruction and aggression. These mental/a-cultural phenomena can sediment into collective formations such as those that characterize postmodern populist reactions to the sudden intrusion of otherness.

2. Ideology makes sure that the boundaries of the self join with (or coincide with) the boundaries of a nation—uniting the collective and the individual. On the border, the individual and the collective meet as Orson Welles' s *Touch of Evil* illustrates.

    - The intrusion of illegal, speechless, generally poor immigrants without any status and standing, arouse sadomasochistic exchanges between immigrants and nation-state civil-servants [Hungarian police (women officers included) beating immigrants with belts for instance]. Sadism is the logic of an institutional, bureaucracy under siege. The tormenting of helpless victims redoubled by the obscene superegoic sadistic injunctions of the Law, form the underside of any governmental system.

- Emigrants/immigrants represent, in spite of themselves, a dialectical force of presence and absence which brings to the fore in each citizen, the gap between the core of the personality of the individual, and the symbolic narrative in which the individual lives.

- The spectacle of anarchic and obscene *jouissance* generally arouses the "punitive ego" in the by-stander or the citizen.

- What is at stake in immigration is the fear of fragmentation in "nation-staters" or sedentary citizens. The flood-like fluidity, and the heterogeneous over-flow that immigrants incarnate make citizens uneasy.

The immigrant represents this other which delineates, opposes, subverts (linguistically for instance) or complements the subjectivity of identity. In extreme cases, it becomes a symptom, i.e. a body foreign to the ego of the subject, since the symptom is always a foreign body. It arouses fears of phagocytation, of being devoured by the Other: "*For the foreigner perceived as an invader reveals a buried passion within those who are entrenched: the passion to kill the other, who had first been feared or despised, then promoted from the ranks of dregs to the status of powerful persecutor against whom a "we" solidifies in order to take revenge.*"[44]This is why the more disturbing the outsider is as immigrant, the more s/he is seen as a symptom, and is often banished as far as possible.

Emigration is not due to isolated forces produced by contradictions inherent to a local, specific playing-field, but is the result of complex interactions between the "First World" and the ex-"Third World."[45]

Endnotes

1 *Julius Caesar.*

2 Name of the first film (1982) of Godfrey Reggio's *qatsi* trilogy; the second, *Powaqqatsi* (1988), means "parasitic way of life" or "life in transition", followed by the more hyper-virtual film *Naqoyqatsi* (2002) meaning "life as war", "civilized violence", or "a life of killing each other." The sound-track music of all three films is by Philip Glass.

3 Guy Debord. *The Society of the Spectacle*. 1967. Joshua Oppenheimer's 2012 documentary *The Act of Killing* about the massacre of 2 million plus communists and leftists during the Indonesian power struggle between President Sukarno and General Suharto, dramatically illustrates the grotesque back-and forth of movement of "the spectacle" between "reality," "the trauma," "memory," the Real (Lacanian definition), the re-enactment of the historical past, and its spectral hyper-virtuality. These themes also constitute the main fray of the cinema of Alain Resnais.

4 Samuel Huntington's *Clash of Civilizations* (1993/6) and Francis Fukuyama's *The End of History and the Last Man* (1992). Fukuyama argues that the worldwide-spread of liberal democracies, Western free-market capitalism, and its lifestyle signal the end point of humanity's socio-cultural evolution and represents the final form of human government. Jean Baudrillard with his *Hystericizing the Millenium* (1994) pokes fun at Huntington and Fukuyama.

5 The École de la Cause Freudienne (ECF) was founded in 1981 to restore the original power and revolutionary effect of psychoanalysis. The ECF, with more than 300 members, organizes many ongoing courses and conferences, maintains a large library and promotes the teaching of psychoanalysis, particularly in the small "cartel" groups devised by Jacques Lacan.

6 *L'Echange Symbolique et la Mort.* 1974–translated in English in 1993.

7 See Alain Badiou whose work based on mathematics (set theory), Lacanian psychoanalysis, and Althusserian Marxism is of relevance for the analysis of postmodern violence; especially his *Ethics: an Essay on the Understanding of Evil* (1998—2001 for the English translation), in which the French philosopher articulates a strong, albeit complex, critique at the "moral terrorism" of the discourse of human rights, and particularly its US-orchestrated component, i.e. the "humanitarian" interventionism that the US tries to propagate all over as the moral compass and umbrella of globalization. Badiou's political critique of the moralization of postmodern politics (post Cold War) has been echoed by the international Marxian-Lacanian thinker Slavoj Zizek. Badiou's "principal target" is not so much Emmanuel Lévinas (Lithuanian-born, French-Jewish philosopher known for his ethics of "otherness") than the general influence of Lévinas' thought on contemporary, political and theoretical discourses. Lévinas stands in for the contemporary valorization of otherness, difference, and victimization as the grounds and stakes of a generalized ethics.

8 *We are the world* sings Bruce Springsteen. The problem is who is "we."

9 Jean Baudrillard. *The Spirit of Terrorism*. Verso. 2000. 7

10 In fact, in *The Vital Illusion*. Baudrillard writes that postmodern terror is the ecstasy of violence.

11 Shock and awe— technically known as rapid dominance, is a military doctrine based on the use of overwhelming power and spectacular displays of force to paralyze the enemy's perception of the battlefield and destroy its will to fight.

12 Paul Virilio. *Speed and Politics.* 1977—2006 in English.

13 Baudrillard. *Idem.* 8, 9.

14 Fredric Jameson. T*he Dialectics of Disaster* in *Dissent from the Homeland (Essays after September 11)*. Edited by Stanley Hauerewas and Frank Lettrichia. Duke U. Press, 2003. 59, 60.

15 "*Capitalism inherently possesses the power to derealize familiar objects, social roles, and institutions to such a degree that the so-called realistic representations can no longer evoke reality except as nostalgia or mockery.*" Jean-François Lyotard. *The Postmodern Condition*. Minneapolis: University of Minnesota Press, 1984. 74. This sentence is reminiscent of another famous one: "*everything that is solid dissolves in thin air.*" *Communist Party Manifesto*. Marx and Engels (1848).

16 3% of the earth land mass is urbanized (about 3.5 million square kilometers.

17 The journalist Robert Kaplan wrote in the *Atlantic Monthly* (February 1994) an influential article about "the new anarchy to come" in the megalopolises of the future, due to extreme income disparity and the ghettoization of the poor, while the rich live in gated communities. His Post-Cold-War thesis played a seminal importance along with the ideas of Huntington and Fukuyama, in shaping the socio-politics of the "neo-con" movement in the US.

18 According to UN statistics, in 2015, 244 million people (3.3 % of the world population) lived outside their native country. The majority crossed borders in search of better socio-economic opportunities; the others were forced to flee political crisis. The current mass movement of refugees (displaced persons) has given rise to xenophobia and identity reactions based on fear and insecurity. This has politically resulted in calls for more border-security-tightening and refugee-control policies (what is called "vetting" in the US). In Europe, this sudden mass-emigration puts into question the free circulation of citizens and the open-border policy as defined by the Schengen agreement. For capitalism, emigration is an important factor for economic development (and profits).

The seriousness of the situation forced many governments to put a high-priority on political and humanitarian issues (half of migrants are women, and many with children) for both developed and developing countries.

19 Many French jihadists are of Algerian or Berber origin, a fact which stresses the over-determination played by history (French colonialism).

20 Woodrow Wilson to American businessmen as quoted by Perry Anderson in *American Foreign Policy and its Thinkers*. Verso. 20144.

21 Inspired by Serge André's essay on psychosis: L*a Structure Psychotique de l'Ecrit*. La Muette. 2000.

22 Jean-François Lyotard. *L'Economie Libidinale* (1994—in English in 1975: *Libidinal Economy*.)

23 J. F. Lyotard. *Dispositifs Pulsionnels*. UGE-10/18. 1978. 176,177.

24 J.F. Lyotard. *Idem. Libidinal Economy.*

25 Gilles Deleuze and André Guattari. *L'Anti-Œdipe: Capitalisme et Schizophrénie*. 1972—translated into English in 1983 (University of Minnesota Press).

26 The term "*machine célibataire*" comes from Duchamp's famous *Large Glass*, or *La Machine Célibataire*, or *The Bride Stripped Bare by her Bachelors* (1913-1923)—Philadelphia Museum of Art. The uncanny alliance between machine and human, goes back to Descartes via Lamettrie, de Sade, Huyssen, the German cineaste Fritz Lang, the surrealist painter Picabia, and the critic Michel Carrouges, without forgetting the Viennese psychoanalyst Viktor Tausk who wrote "*On the Origin of the 'Influencing Machine' in Schizophrenia*" (1919), published in the journal *Internationale Zeitschrift für Psychoanalyse* and then, after translation into English by Dorian Feigenbaum, in the *Psychoanalytic Quarterly* in 1933).

27 Tracey D. Samuelson in *The Christian Science Monitor.*

28 This may explain the German composer of aleatory and musical spatialization,, serial composition and electronic music Karlheinz Stockhausen's regrettable and misunderstood comment.

29 Something mangnificently illustrated by the Chadian filmmaker Mahamat Saleh Haroun in *Abouna* (*Our Father* in English)—2002.

30 *Terrorist Novel Writing* in *The Spirit of the Public Journals.* (vol. I). Anonymous. 1797.

31 Joseph Crawford. *Gothic Fiction and the Invention of Terrorism: The Politics and Aesthetics of Fear in the Age of the Reign of Terror.* Bloomsbury. London; 2014.

32 William Golding. 1954.

33 2013

34 The Greek historian Herodotus (5th century BCE) described the Egyptian Goddess ISIS as offering initiates guidance in the afterlife and a vision or rebirth. We will not dwell on the homophony between the Egyptian Goddess and the fundamentalist radical group, especially since in traditional heuristic literary criticism, etymology was used to reveal the essential or primordial nature of things named.

35 A theme which returns with an obsessive passion in a "world abandoned by God," in the "low-brow," popular culture and the entertainment industry—such as the Cinemax TV series *Outcast* (2016) adapted from the comics of the same name by Robert Kirkman and Paul Azaceta or the TV series *Preacher* (2016) adapted by Evan Goldberg, Seth Roger and Sam Catlin for AMC, from the comic book series of the same name created by Garth Ennis and Steve Dillon (DC Comics Vertigo).

36 Lacan. *Ecrits*. Norton, 2006. 122.

37 Slavoj Zizek. *For they know not what they do: Enjoyment as a political factor*. Verso Press. 1991.

38 Jean Baudrillard. *The Ecstasy of Communication*. Verso, 2012. 66.

39 Slavoj Zizek. *The Desert of the Real*. Verso, 2013. The book's title is "a quote of a quote of a quote." It comes from an ominous, ironic sentence delivered by the character Morpheus in the first "*Matrix*" film (1999)," *Welcome to the desert of the real,*" himself quoting Jean Baudrillard's sentence in his analytical essay on societies, simulation and reality, *Simulacra and Simulation* (1981): "*If once we were able to view the Borges fable in which the cartographers of the Empire draw up a map so detailed that it ends up covering the territory exactly..., this fable has now come full circle for us, and possesses nothing but the discrete charm of second-order simulacrum... It is the real, and not the map, whose vestiges persist here and there in the deserts that are no longer those of the Empire, but ours. The desert of the real itself.*" That is to say two conceptions of the Real are conjured up via postmodern/ fundamentalist terrorism.

40 Something curiously reiterated by Pope Benedict during his visit to Turkey.

41 *Simulacra and Simulations. Jean Baudrillard, Selected Writings*. Ed. M. Poster. Stanford U. Press. 183.

42 Julia Kristeva. *Strangers to Ourelves*. Columbia U. Press, 1991. 104.

43 Julia Kristeva. *Idem*. 17.

44 Julia Kristeva. *Idem*. 20.

45 Michael Hardt and Toni Negri's *Empire*.

Adorno's Critical Theory and Psychoanalysis: The Dialectical Subject

Julian von Will, PhD

Abstract

I want to show how critical theory and psychoanalysis connect in a theoretical dialectical subject. I will sketch Adorno's concept of an individual subject through his dialectic of Kant and Freud. The clash of reason with desire, knowledge with its other, the unknown unconscious repressed, forms Adorno's notion of human subjectivity and self-consciousness. It's a dialectic built within the modern subject reconstructing it through theoretical criticism to reveal its regressive unconscious self-destruction. Adorno takes Kant's noumenal intelligible world to the Freudian unconscious to find his individual mediating mystery and misery. His subject is a field-field constellation unlocking causality through a defunct omni-consciousness struggling with material necessity. Freud preserves and thus overcomes metaphysics with the unconscious reachable through therapy, to advance the secular Self. He advanced consciousness by giving it a vast resource of unconscious content as both good and bad and beyond. He made the transcendental subject real. Freudian psychic reality is an irreducible and a powerful anti-psychologism by a logic of self-consciousness alone (I=not-I). Freudian self-consciousness is built on self-censorship detrimental to the moment, the everyday and the personal. Adorno uses Freud to spin Kant's Copernican revolution and brings Hegel's objectification of the subject to the individual. Freud is a perfect contradiction to idealism's 'lordship of the subject' and materialism's fetish with money. Kantian apriorism thinking us flows into Freudian intrapsychic division of instinct and desire mitigating object-choice and intrapersonal relation. Adorno tries to make an ontological turn through a dialectic reading of the Freudian subject. Instinct matches Kantian universals at every turn determining a logic of human consciousness. Combined with Hegel and Marx, Adorno uses psychoanalysis on societal immortality, egoism and narcissism. He uses Freudian psychology against neo-Freudian egology attacking the reduction of the unconsciousness and its reappropriated suppression to uncritical inhuman social 'standards.' Adorno uses psychoanalysis to attack the 'reality principle' as ideology. His theory is therapy and criticism construction detecting false consciousness repressing human possibility with crude materialism.

"Psychoanalysis becomes the indictment of civilization."[RP] *Adorno*

Theodor W. Adorno [1903-1969] was a key member of the Institute for Social Research and used Freudian psychoanalysis to criticize repressive social structures. He stressed the value of criticism and the importance of theory detecting fundamental contradictions in the practice of freedom, liberty and individuality. Adorno says critique is essential to democracy and theory vital for human progress. He brings these together in critical theory focusing on the dialectical relation between the individual and the social collective. In this paper I will focus on Adorno's notion of human subjectivity constellated between Kant's transcendental subject and Freud's split-subjectivity. The extreme difference between Kant and Freud captures the individual and the social through fundamental antagonisms, paradoxes and antinomies defining human subjectivity. Adorno works Kant's dialectic of reason into Freud's dialectic of desire driven by a Hegelian-Marxian dialectic illuminating essential contradictions in society's idea of individuality. Operating unconsciously, society, ego and the reality principle renounces individuality. Social practice suppresses psychology with sociology. Adorno preserves extreme propositions in Freud against socio-cultural assimilation and revision castrating the individual into a 'social therapy' and conflict free consensus of a 'healthy' ego dumbing-down reality and trivializing experience into norms and practices of consumerism. Psychological tension within the Self's character formation is unconsciously performed by society and civilization. Internalized conflicts of libidinal forces, desire perverting instinct, manifest external interpersonal relations. Adorno uses Freud to mark the 'ontological turn' in transcendental subjectivity of Kant. He clashes Kant and Hegel against Freud capturing his theoretical subject and practical individual. He combines Freudian psychology with pure idealism to reach individual materialism.

Adorno's relationship with psychoanalysis, where "nothing is true except the exaggerations", uses the concept of the divided Self to work identity and existence to individual conscious materialism. Freud is the praxis of negative dialectics bringing the theoretical subject to the individual by a dialectic of consciousness. Consciousness and Self are divided, as Kant subject is divided from ego. Freud took transcendental idealism and its proof of an irreducible consciousness to the individual by upholding the dialectic of reason forming the individual.

> "The greatness of Freud as that of all radical bourgeois thinkers consists in that he leaves such contradictions unresolved, and he scorns the pretended systematic harmony where things in themselves are torn asunder. He makes the antagonistic character of social reality apparent, as far as his theory and practice within the above-mentioned division of labor go."[RP]

Critical theory moves transcendentalism to materialism through psychoanalysis. Theory critiques practice and bridges consciousness into an objective process of knowing and Being without privileging one over the other. Adorno's criticism leads to social change by a dialectic between psychology and sociology mediated by transcendental idealism and psychoanalysis. Theory becomes practice through their tension captured in Freudian intrapsychic division, the 'inner mechanisms of the individual' and the socially constructed ideal of Self. Adorno brings Kant's constitutional subject to the Freudian individual, theory to therapy to criticize positivism in psychology, psychoanalytic revisionism and sociological identity thinking. "In the name of the reality principle, it [integrated social psychology] justifies the emotional sacrifice of the individual, without subjecting the reality principle to a rational examination."[RP] Modern subjectivity, the greatest invention where myth becomes reality and instinct turns into idea has become inhuman and alienated. Freud, a 'dark thinker' stressing hidden libido conflicts within the psyche, resists the ideology of positivism as a method and mentality shaping the collective. "That one is to speak from the bright and not from the dark side of individual and society, suits exactly the official and acceptable and respectable ideology."[RP] Freud takes the mind to instinct to show how desire perverts everyday human interaction. Desire opens to the unconscious repressed arbitrating Kantian faculties of perception, imagination and the understanding with 'deluded' wishfulfillment. Kant's blueprint of conscious reality and sufficient reason unified by subjective thinking is mutilated by desire. Freud brings metaphysics to materialism and the universal subject to individual person revealing the Self as Other found in unconscious thoughts and acts. according to Adorno, Freud offers criticism of dominate social forces of late modern capitalism, exposing social unity, warmth and well-Being for profit taking. Like Kant's advance of epistemology over metaphysics in order then to limit reason to make room for faith, Freud "tracked down conscious actions materialistically to their unconscious instinctual basis, but at the same time concurred with the bourgeois contempt of instinct which is itself a product of precisely the rationalizations that he dismantled."[MM]

Adorno uses Freudian theory to de-center the 'lordship of the subject' running both abstract theory and social ego as inhuman and disseminates positivistic method as restrictive and repressive. Freud takes the philosophical dimension of the unconscious to praxis through psychology by dialectical negation (determinate negation) of the unconscious capturing a dynamic subject mediating the individual and the social. Freud's model of intrapsychic division, split-subjectivity exposes societal unconscious processes running appearances. Adorno's immanent critique uses the unconscious repressed to demystify the transcendental and substantiate the empirical maintaining complexity in the subject's relations. Critical theory advances philosophical reflection on the dialectic and ontological difference of thinking and Being into psychological mediation of pleasure and pain. For Adorno, pain is the necessary and sufficient reason to find agreement, the "need to let suffering speak is a condition of all truth. For suffering is objectivity that weighs upon the subject."[ND] Metaphysical divergence between idea and reality ties into individual Being and ideological manipulation of this relation is central for Adorno's criticism. The Freudian subject inverts the Self as a product of society casting epistemology into wishfulfillment. The secular pillar of predictable conscious logic and controllable behavior is negated by its own identity and behavior mutated by hidden desire. Human subjectivity of reason is divided by contrary desires. The 'Self' is a contradiction of myth and reality. Adorno brings Kant's analytic subject of knowledge to delusion, split-personality and self-censorship. Kant's reality principle is made real, personal and destructive by the untruth of wishful thinking. Adorno breaks false reconciled subjectivity found in popular psychology and ideology by denying consciousness the whole of reality and reality a principle of domination over individuality. The Self as Other, identity shaped by contradiction and behavior punctuated by unknown drives factures the ideal Self representing dominate socio-cultural manifestations.

Adorno's critique of modernity and its social manifestation utilizes Freud against the status quo dominated by an analytic understanding conforming to the market, imprisoned by the money changers, locked in a diminishing materialism. Adorno says society runs not in spite of its contradictions but by means of them. Habermas calls them 'performative contradictions' driving appearances and practices. Adorno traverses Kant and Freud to show how myth becomes reality and how literalism self-destructs by unconscious oversight. Divided by desire, the unconscious mediates self-consciousness between freedom and determinism. Id thinks ego inverting practical reason and common sense. The radical hypothesis of Freud is that society functions on individual intrapsychic division where reason is compromised by desire and interpersonal relation is mitigated by fiction. Freudian theory grasped the paradox of civilization and illusion of progress. As Kant limits reason to nature Freud ties it to self-preservation, desire and domination revealing how the successful manipulation of nature is ironically destroying it. "There is a universal feeling, a universal fear, that our progress in controlling nature may increasing help to weave the very calamity it is supposed to protect us from, that it may be weaving that second nature into which society has rankly grown." [ND] The unconscious holds the fate of progress to self-deception by a lack of critical reflection.

Freud's dialectic of sex and death turns metaphysics into reality by showing how mind and body related through contradiction, by the impasse between possible and actual reality. Metaphysical dualism is personalized. Reason is matched by desire becoming part of the transcendental subject that knows no limits but those imposed by and on the Self. The transcendental of Kant is transcended by Freud and the secrete mechanism of the soul refracted in the unconscious repressed. Freudian theory turns epistemology into a wishfulfillment. Freud takes Kant's unattainable realism to the living room, and brings universal determinates to particularity, self-limiting reason to unconscious self-censorship. Psychoanalysis brought the transcendental to the individual by a breakdown in consciousness, a failure in thinking, revealing the unconscious thinking us. Desire evades naturalistic and spiritualistic interpretations. The unconscious is nonidentity mediating consciousness as a dialectical construct rejecting first principles and immediate data. The Self as Other of unconscious repressed solidifies nonidentity for Adorno in that it gets to the individual through the disappearance of thought and mediating facts. The Self does not belong to the individual as sex does not belong to the individual but to the species (Freud). Adorno's 'logic of disintegration' works the antinomies of reason to the 'forgetfulness,' blackouts and self-mutilation of desire. Freud's theory of intrapsychic division appears in the fractures of consciousness as parapraxis, dreams and psychoneuroses. The connection between the Kantian subject of time through logic is mutated through the subject of desire in timeless unconsciousness. A critical balancing act between idea and desire, works both object and instinct into a Self by their tension.

In the critique of mind, Freudian psychoanalysis preserves it and consciousness against naturalism, positivism and sociological appearance and status quo. Instinct demented by desire and imagination distorting perception withholds thinking from existence and existence from knowledge forming a false and forced unity of Self. The idea of a well-integrated personality is deconstructed as ideology, and psychophysical parallelism is checked. Freudian psychoanalysis is an indictment of civilization's self-deceptive consciousness reducing individual diversity to collective indifference. Adorno says that "human consciousness has limped behind, leaving the order of human affairs irrational."[ND] For him and Horkheimer, the "Enlightenment has extinguished any trace of its own self-consciousness... put aside the classic requirement of thinking about thought."[DE] Demythologicalization of reality turns metaphysics and the way things ought to be to an ideology of the way things are, stuck in things as they. "For while the mind extricated itself from a theological-feudal tutelage, it has fallen increasingly under the anonymous sway of the status quo."[P] Collective identity has reduced the individual to stereotype and commodity. Late modernity has made "existence itself a substitute for meaning and right". [DE] "Today, however, the definition of consciousness in terms of being has become a means of dispensing with all consciousness which does not conform to existence."[P] In the secular advance of the modern subject, Adorno argues, "metaphysics has merged with culture." [ND] "Metaphysics has slipped into material existence" silencing critical self-reflection with ornamented self-preservation. [AM] The unconscious conformity to the status quo is liquidating progress, cementing human potential to mundane consumerism. Adorno attacks the reality principle dominating contemporary social thought as apathy for anything reflective and introspective. Metaphysical is replaced by indifference. "Now that depth-psychology, has delved into the deepest recesses, people's last possibility of experiencing themselves has been cut off by organized culture... Terror before the abyss of the self is removed by the consciousness of being concerned with nothing so very different from arthritis or sinus trouble. Thus conflicts lose their menace. They are accepted, but by no means cured, being merely fitted as an unavoidable component into the surface of standardized life."[MM] Dominate materialism and capitalism subtract the subject by enslaving thought to existence no longer worth living. Rationalized society justifies the "injustice of what exists" and its "rationality is tainted with irrationalism." "Today self-consciousness no longer means anything but reflection on the ego as embarrassment, as realization of impotence: knowing that one is nothing."[MM] The modern subject is reduced to power relations, profit margins and debt. The understanding and the individual is trivialized into instrumental computations and subjectivity is subtracted from objectivity as a reside theory of truth.

Adorno constellates the Kantian subject with the Freudian subject forming his concept of the individual. Early in his career, he focused on their theoretical relation in his dissertation entitled: The Concept of the Unconscious in the Transcendental Theory of the Psyche. In this 1927 text, Adorno tries to work a relation between Kantian "I think" of subjective representation, self-limiting reason and 'thing-in-itself' to the Freudian unconscious with its elaborate defensives and innate drive theory determining the "I am" of individual consciousness. Adorno tries to bridge metaphysics, epistemology and mind to the individual through Freud, evading reductive psychological and ontological arguments of act and relation forming psycho-synthesis. This dissertation of two hundred pages was withdrawn by Adorno for being to close to his promoter's transcendental system and too far away from mediating Kant and Freud in clear terms. They relate by a self-imposed limitation, by a critical schema of dualism separating identity and existence entangling in metaphysics ideologically silenced. Adorno seeks to show how metaphysics becomes ideology through Freudian metapsychology, which is speculative. The epistemological gap lies in the 'divided Self' of thought and existence, the fact that thought is alienated from Being and vise verse is the driving force behind Adorno model of human subjectivity. Adorno traces idealism's effort to transcend metaphysical dualism to Freudian wishfulfillment. He collides Kant's dialectic of reason and its semblance of totality against desire's unattainable unconscious satisfaction. Both Kant and Freud reveal the hidden source for sensibility in the mind, as Kant says, isolated and divided as its truth content. Psychoanalysis captures the Kantian subject of percept and concept through the medium of desire, completing a limited ridged logic into a deformed Being. A Frankenstein scenario takes hold of the secular subject. The Kantian temporal subject is known only as a reconstructed 'past Self' descending into the abyss of time and the Freudian subject is divided and hidden from itself by a timeless unrelenting id. The universality of a priori categories and instincts erect the individual between identity, will and desire. Adorno's subject floats in a dialectic of reason fragmented by unconscious thoughts and defenses opening to his notion of individuality by negation.

Adorno says Kant's block on reason's totality is a Freudian slip having been beyond the block to issue it, while persevering metaphysics in a negative wishfulfillment limiting knowledge to make room for faith. Kant's critical reason, its self-censorship, represses metaphysics by an epistemology denying rational consciousness existence and existence awareness. Its radical hypothesis of subjective constitution leads to extreme isolation. Kant's transcendental subject is alienated from empirical Being and his architectonic of reason becomes delusive semblance, fantasy and deception. Kant's refusal to relate his subject with the individual captures the problem by refusing to resolve it. His criticism of metaphysics is directed at forced unities, false reconciled unions and deluded singularities that have no existence. Like subjective idealism, psychoanalysis works logic and immediate sense into a dialectic to grasp consciousness divided from itself. Adorno's critical theory uses Hegel's dialectic of identity and master-slave with the material weight of the Freudian unconscious to falsify the social subject and its ideal of individuality. The dialectic between the individual and the social captures the Self as Other of unconscious mentation. The focus on contradiction in the individual comes out in social practice revealing the inverted world of power relations and self-deceiving systems enslaving while liberating (repressive de-sublimation (Marcuse)), regressing while advancing ideas of freedom and individuality through determine laws of collective agreement. Kant's possible and actuality reality setting up his a priori deduction of pre-reflective faculties, and Freud's id and ego capture the dialectic of freedom and determinism. Kant limits his subject before contradiction and antinomies of thought and Freud picks up here to bring Being to thought through the unconscious as an undetermined form. The unconscious is negative by self-censoring lacking awareness. Consciousness mediates between fiction and facts through unconscious censorships, repression and denial. Freud's notion of necessary fiction demands a critique of current thought and modes of Being denying conscious evolution through imagination by a fixed anal retentive literalism concerned with the bottom dollar. Criticism is therapy. Freud's theory shows how society is dependent on individual psychology and how the fundamental nature of the unconscious figures into civilization, institutions, norms and practices. Adorno bends Kant's transcendental pre-reflective a priori to the soma, the dialectic of individual and social adhering to a "radical psychoanalysis, by focusing on the libido as pre-social, phylogenetic as well as ontogenetic, reaches the point where the social principle of domination coincides with the psychological repression of the drive."[RP] Critical of revisionist psychoanalysis, Adorno stresses that "Freud has destroyed the myth of the organic structure of the psyche counts as his greatest merit. He has thereby recognized the nature of the social mutilation more than any direct parallelism between character and social influence could have done."[RP] Adorno affirms irreducible consciousness (transcendental subjectivity) in the negative, nonidentity actualized in the unconscious, against what Horkheimer calls 'common-sense psychology'.

Adorno uses psychoanalysis to attack everyday materialism and self-saming systems and practices embedded in private interests, repressed instincts and violent regressions. He tries to leave metaphysical poles of knowing and Being open in ambiguity to be comprehended as tension and activity in the real world. Idealism's quest for immortality lies at the heart of unconscious rage. Its secular deification comes true in social turmoil exposing anti-nature in the very forms of self-preservation unconsciously censoring truth and Being from the subject of desire. Kant advances self-conscious reason as the 'totality of the limited' measured by the other, the thing-in-itself as its critical self-limiting function. Knowledge of Being is a tautology of thought and thought has no existence without their relation through transcendental subjectivity. Kant denies this subject Being and Being awareness and his epistemology tries to square a circle. What is possible becomes impossible in Kant and his epistemology gives way to an ideology of science and metaphysics of faith. The poles of origin and validity, time and logic break apart in Kant's theory of apperception, sabotaged by an empty mind and deluded reason lacking origin in nature and substance in concepts. The system falls short of knowing the whole by only knowing knowledge itself. Kant's 'subjectivization of objectivity' advances the notion of pre-experiential forms of possible reality setting up the continuum of appearances and then limits these forms to immediate sense and actuality as the reality of universals. Nietzsche says that Kant's elaborate proof of transcendental forms only goes to prove sense reality correct betraying his project to circular reasoning. His 'reality principle' is based on dominate empirical matters hand.

Bleeding surplus ideation out by force of the immediate and the mundane undermines transcendental schema. Kant's a priori determines an unchanging bleak reality in order to avoid delusion and war. He pulls his punches to maintain his theory of sufficient necessary reason by way of empirical reality, the very reality he seeks to judge through universals. He warps the whole into confirming the present, the status quo and common sense by force of immaterial forms and categories. Kant's own reduction of Aristotle's ontological difference of possible and actual reality struggles to find a reality principle, a unity of judgment and relation between forms of thought and sense data to achieve agreement. He treats reason like unconscious wishfulfillment and Freud carries this to the individual as the subject of desire, unconscious inhibition and frustration. Kant refuses to link thinking and Being through the individual as Freud finds the antagonism the departure to truth. For Kant this would be a particular empirical fact and not universal concord capable of expressive existence. With Kant it's always a twofold relation of thought and precept that conjure reality through compromise. Kant's transcendental subject is divided to control the difference between thought and Being, possible and actual reality, dreams and immediate sense experience forming critical correspondence (Schematic of relation). Freud connects them to the individual without reducing one to the other. The unconscious has no origin. Because the unconscious fabricates relations, Kantian semblance of reason's totality finds its object correlate, its nonidentical other in desire and frustration. It's the empirical immoral subject Kant sees in reason. Kantian a priori becomes Freudian projection, cathexis and wishfulfillment. Kantian freedom, immortality and God are brought to sex, drugs and pathology in everyday life. Freud performs the elusive unity of The Kantian subjective manifold of faculties by refusing to answer it consciously with identity, logic and sense experience. Idea and instinct are mutated by desire. Mind and body are brought to an impasse mediated by an act of faith, a synthetic a priori judgment and conversion hysteria. Immaterial though forms, patterns, networks, computations. The logic of self-conscious reason becomes physical through the other of unconscious desire, balancing between life and death the Kantian-Freudian subject of contradiction no god can endure (Hegel).

Adorno follows the modern subject through epistemologies and therapies seeking first principles and coherent foundations covering up the antinomies and contradictions of reason and desire. He follows the invention of the Self, from Greek philosophy into the Christian concept of the individual to the secularized scientific subject of representation and unconscious repressed. He uses the divided Self to contradict both idealism and positivism without abandoning reason to an uncritical reality principle in the wrong against the individual. Freud puts theory to practice by substantiating thinking with desire, ideation with instinct. Desire brings identity-thinking to existence by contradicting it, crossing meaning and sense. Freud registered a dialectical construction of human subject by refusing psychophysical parallelism, reducing mind to act, to indifferent nature or convoluted 'spirit.' Adorno notes how transcendental idealism and psychoanalysis reject psychologism's attempt to reduce mind to an empirical platform of cause, subtracting representation, ideation for impulse and feedback. The Freudian subject is a critique of naturalistic reduction being both an instinct and an idea driven to madness by their irreconcilability. Contradiction of mind and negation in Being sets the movement and process of self-awareness. Consciousness cannot be reduced without the unconscious. The transcendental subject and Freudian psychic reality defy by origin. Freud and Breuer unlocked conversion hysteria and then later Freud's 1916 claim of psychic reality as a 'revolution' in psychology through ideogenic causality (seduction fantasy) is a great discovery. Although Freud upholds natural scientific claims and hopes, in what Habermas calls a 'self-misunderstanding', his theory secures the opposite. Neurotic behavior cannot be pinned to neuron without dismantling the socio-cultural order of freedom under law. The Freudian subject is not cognitive behavioral it's both and at odds with itself. Freud mediates cognitive and behavioral acts through their difference to capture the movement of the Self. Denial of reality and world finds the Self of desire. He finds the Self through Other, not by sequential succession and reduction, but by abrupt negation, confrontation and alienation. Natural reduction of consciousness as missed its own proposition of the "I think" driving scientific cognition seeking to make conjecture an unconscious somatic activity.

Adorno pushes the extremes of knowledge and desire against the middle to find the individual. He upholds Kant's theory of mind to attack the 'empirical' social subject as wishfulfillment. The transcendental subject thinks us. For transcendental idealism what "is supposedly most obvious, the empirical subject, would actually have to be considered as something not yet existing; from this aspect the transcendental subject is "constitutive."" [CM] The transcendental and the unconscious think the man on the street. Adorno attacks Freudian revisionism for turning the ego to a socially condition thing of health, wealth and happiness. They suppress the dialectic forming the subject. "The more psychoanalysis is sociologized [soziologisiert], the blunter its operation for the knowledge of socially determined conflicts becomes."[RP] Adorno attacks psychological therapy forcing integration and assimilation to a system and society locked in self-destruction.. Adorno brings idealism's hostility towards psychology to psychoanalytic psychology hostile to self-determined conscious thought and reconciled conflict free personality. According to Adorno, Kant, German idealism and phenomenology all maintain a philosophy of mind controlling psychology by subtle dialectic, namely time. The critical tradition links with psychoanalysis in attacking psychologism in reducing thought to nature through individual acts. Both insist on subjective presupposition and surplus ideation tracing combinatory patterns into an organizing spirit of sense and meaning. Their theory of consciousness evades a "physiology of the mind" as Kant puts. Adorno will also add here, that a critical sociology would not reduce society too quickly to nature either. "The human race is not, as has sometimes been asserted, a chance phenomenon of natural history, a freak due to hypertrophy of the brain."[DE] Psychologism took consciousness into a physical parallel by asserting the individual's observable traits as the locus of thought and lost both consciousness and the Self looping the feedback. Adorno says the transcendental subject and its variations are truer to the individual than prevailing psychology because representational consciousness and its unconscious correlate have causation. The Freudian psychic reality proves itself by defying a 'reality principle'. One is reminded by Epictitus (50-120AD), who stated: "The thing that upsets people is not what happens but what they think it means." Kant's universals and Freud's desire make the person "incarnate closer to the transcendental subject than the living individual he must immediately take himself to be." [CM] Adorno defends the transcendental subject in its abstraction as a condition for truth and Being. Theory corrects praxis because "objectivity of truth really demands the subject. Once cut off from the subject, it becomes the victim of sheer subjectivity."[AE]

The late modern subject is cohesively drained of ideational dynamics. It's a robot, an AI, a tautology and second nature. Kant's proven true, there is no original thought or concept in man only a copy of nature. Meaning is reduced to appearances and the subject takes on a literal sober bourgeois bootstrap philosophy. Adorno's theoretical subject, used to critique the real social subject, is antagonistic to the analytic continuum of processing data, acquiring habits and paying bills bejeweled in consumption and domination. The myth of this subject comes out in real consequences. The unconscious reminds identity of its limits and its longings, it mediates between the individual and the social, where metaphysics becomes art or ideology, enlightenment or terrorism. The unconscious breaks relations and mutates categories into their opposite. Desire deforms instincts into a history of broken promises. The ego to id, idea to instinct is identity and existence turned flesh. The analytic subject of Kant turns dialectical and metaphysical by imposing reason on reality as Freudian desire imposes a subject unaware of reality. Both capture consciousness in its semblance and delusion by force conjuring faith and necessary fiction as escape routes around the reality principle as gain from illness. Kant's twofold process incorporates nonidentical elements into a force field understanding and heterogeneous Self mitigating an antagonistic whole. Unreconciled Self as Other, of idea and instinct [Triebtheorie] is the propulsion driving consciousness.

Adorno psychoanalyzes the enlightenment's progress and finds self-destruction in its reality principle, its own middle course of practical common sense regressing consciousness. Unconsciousness rules the day in both senses of the term as full of everything and nothing. The world is, according to Adorno and Horkheimer, a 'gigantic analytic judgment' going nowhere fast. Modernity's equivocation of reason and power reduces ideas to instinct and progress to self-preservation without knowing it. The reduction of the Self to the apparatus of contradictory free identity and immediate sense reality conceals the subject and then enslaves it to hysteric money making.

Adorno's dialectical materialism balances between Kant's transcendental subject and the Freudian subject driven by Hegelian dialectic bringing it social criticism. Subjective presupposition is kept alive in self-negation. Adorno brings the transcendental system to sex and death to change the discourse, make the 'ontological turn.' The transcendental subject to Being unaware of itself departs to body as an objective correlate. Adorno maintains metaphysics of subject-object to undermine the ideology of forced reconciled unity. Psychoanalysis is used to show the correlative Being of the "I think", 'I think something' into the "id thinks me' manifesting an inversion of pure thought into Being by tension. For Adorno, philosophical reflection and psychoanalysis maintain control over psychology because, as Adorno notes, psychology cannot deal with horror. Moreover, practical reason and common sense are implicated in self-destructive behavior because they form the compromised status quo, appearances, but they are not what they seem. They silence the discussion where it ought to start in their lack of sufficient reason and speciously absent self-interest. Adorno's negative dialectics is a transcendental unconscious working against identity-thinking prevailing in naturalism and scientific positivism. His anti-system enacts a noumenology (science of otherness) within practice, showing the leap of faith, societal faith in science, and other contradictions shaping the here and now. Freudian psychology provides a way out of the paralogism of rationalism and empiricism and the mind-body arguments in psychology and psychologism. It brings the transcendental to the empirical without spiritual or material dominance by capturing the process of consciousness mediated by extremes.

The collision between abstract logic and personal burden and pain, the unattainable and the immediate, the determined and the chaotic entwine to form Adorno's individual. Contradiction mediates the Self through Other in the social collective. The Other is Hell (Sartre). It exposes the myth of the subject through its object choice. For Adorno, the vital relation between the individual and social collective has fallen into narcissism, fetishism and power because the collective is unaware of itself as a individual. Its worse, the collective unconscious no longer bothers with the ideology of a Self. Nowadays "there are no more ideologies in the authentic sense of false consciousness, only advertisements for the world through its duplication and the provocative lie which does not seek belief but commands silence."[P] Adorno employs essentialism against prevailing appearances by materialism with Freudian instinct. Appear is everything. "Today, ideology means society as appearance." [P] Adorno's critique of modernity stresses the need to change, increase and advance consciousness on its own terms and narratives with better illusion, better 'necessary fiction' then the concurrent theme of war and fear. The myth has to become a better myth than sex, drugs and rock and roll. The rules of the game have to change. The Freudian theory understands that money is shit. And this captures the moment now. Adorno relates to the Nietzschean sense of realizing human potential by embracing its pathology, neurosis and madness to overcome man, the dilemma of infinite worlds in a finite body with sex on the mind as a dirty trick. Nietzsche uncovered the unconscious forces of the individual in the 'doomed One', the self-knower and self-hangman of Zarathustra. Man is something that must be overcome.

Adorno's takes metaphysics of thought and Being to the duality of conscious unconscious material to reach the everyday individual as a social construct. Finding objective mind in society defining the individual as its praxis brings the inward division of sex and death to violence, murder and war. Our attempt to become natural has suppressed the anti-nature of the process. Adorno says the "a priori and the social interpenetrate" and the individual's unconscious forms society and reality by inverse principle of power and debt. The dialectic of the individual and social, lying in the mind and in the panicked heard, is connected. The intersubjective agreement relies on the intrasubjective unity of idea and existence forming the individual. Kant said he found the secrete source for the sensible lying in the mind and Freud materialized that in everyday problems of subjectivity, the limits of knowledge harassed and mocked by its other

Self. Kant's starry heavens above and the moral law within is mediated by earthly desire and unattainable satisfaction. Self-consciousness is suspended between two nothings (Nietzsche). Inject capitalism, tyranny and war as its repressive side lacking consciousness and society becomes a nightmare.

Critical theory builds on the philosophical 'school debate' between rationalism and empiricism, where metaphysics turns to ideology. This debate used psychology to mediate precept and concept, mediating innate idea and given phenomena of Self and Other. Kant argued that Leibniz used psychology and Descartes used ontology to bring a unity to reason and nature under dogmatic forms privileging act and relation above law and cause. Freud moves the epistemological axis of logical universal thought and individual act, contradiction and spatiotemporal succession, into anomalies as an intuition of the intellect. In personal acts, in Freudian slips, instincts are perverted by desire for unknown reasons that define the Self. This 'other Self' makes or breaks the conscious one. As Kant wrestles with philosophy and psychology to contain metaphysical dualism, he attacks rational psychology attempting to bridge thought and thing by individual acts, by materializing code, program and agreement in a concrete thing. Being is simply empirical for Kant and not the source for his subject. His advance and then limitation of the subject holds a ridged its untruth but because it's empty clashing with its possibility, its immortality in variations of the same found through his own analytic matrix. Kant attacks the use of psychology bridging the epistemological gap as a paralogism of pure reason pretending to be a Self and object in one, false admixture. Kant valued psychology as an empirical science but not as the source for self-consciousness. The ego can not be the source for a universal, singularity, otherwise, as Adorno's says, we would have an ontology of pure pain. This is where Husserl and early Heidegger enter as well. Horkheimer or Marcuse, said that the school debate is still active and vital for the critique of instrumental practical reason. The school debate keeps open the understanding's roll in mediating concept and object, individually, categories of identity, as theory and practice. The school debate on 'origin,' finding necessary truths, hides a more uncomfortable truth, more brutal and historic reality in direct force. The school debate forms the antinomies of reason, where war breaks out between contrary propositions of infinite regress. Suppressed in praxis, repressed in theory and confounded in current progress, the impotence of this epistemological debate on origin, on possibility and progress is vital to capture the regression of thought and Being to indifference today. What is happening is possibilities are overwhelmed by actuality, theory deleted for praxis carte blanche. Adorno says modernity has de-subjectified the subject into a closed program. Modernity has abandoned the subject and the individual to the market place and to scientific dissection like "so many things in a bag" (Hegel).

The inverted world of the unconscious puts the philosophical debate on epistemology into a critique of the moment. Adorno follows Freud's intrapsychic division to Hegel's slaughter bench of history and highway of despair mitigated by Kant's logical one. Hegel attacked modernity, prima philosophia, Kant's 'odd science of empirical logic' and the modern subject and links it to the grey on grey administered world taking control of human relations without thinking, sheer automation. Hegel rejected the modern subject contradict free, demonstrating how contradiction forms self-conscious reason from within the tension of the individual thinking the universal. Hegel's dialectic self-others the Self to secure a beyond to identity and existence based on logic and time. But Hegel steps out of dialectics and loses the critical self-othering of its movement to a fixed absolute. Adorno keeps the dialectic going in the individual. Adorno takes the master-slave dialectic in Hegel to critique the present and break the Self from positive reduction to an unreflecting social Self. Hegel's inversion of identity is perfected in Freud's dialectic of identity between the voyeur and exhibitionist. Identity seeks its opposite. Pleasure lies in the imaginations ability to twist precept and concept.

Kant, in the end, critically maintains the difference of thought and Being to uphold agreement by denying the individual the source for truth through psychological acts and facts not reflected through transcendental law. In Freud, consciousness is not the source for the Self until it fathoms the nonself, not as something empty but as something dynamic and full. The unconscious holds content. The tension between the subject's immaterial ideation and its individual's immediate sense keeps identity and sense divided, thinking and Being apart to the dismay of both as irrational character formation and object-choice. Kantian Copernican Revolution is right for the wrong reasons, reducing space and time to the mind is true in the reverse through a timeless unlimited unconsciousness. Kant limitation of consciousness with the metaphysics of the thing-in-itself makes sense through the Freudian dissemination of the cogito. The unconscious is an archeological site for Kant's architectonic of reason, showing the nemesis of Self, the ruin of ancient systems in a dialectic of make believe. The Freudian subject and individual must bridge the ontological difference of possible and actual reality, dreams, terror, and the one and only transcendental foresight of death.

All the bagging of the Self is preserved in Freud within terms everyone understands without the naiveté of evidence based 'clinical' epistemology, without a 'primitive realistic epistemology'. The transcendental is forced on the empirical by irreconcilable ideas and needs incapable of realization in the here and now of existence. The Freudian categories make the 'body' correlate without parallels or equivocations. There is no 'reconciliation' only mediation. While the individual struggles for reality society turns it into fiction, idol worship and power. Critical theory turns on individual how the "awakening of the self is paid for by acknowledgement of power as the principle of all relations... [And] the all-powerful self becomes mere possession - abstract identity."[DE] Psychoanalysis brings epistemology to a critique of society and the everyday because its theory gets the individual right against reductive, statistical, quantifiable methodology as bedfellows consumption and self-destruction. Adorno uses psychoanalytic theory to explore the enigma of consciousness as a possible resource of insights into breaking the analytic spell. Human subjectivity runs on a dialectical-ontological combine of possibilities and actualities, dreams and horror under the certainty of death. When the individual bears it as its essence, it becomes a time-bomb logic, an original terrorism. Thinking about thinking leads to a dilemma and to otherness and to the unconscious as hope and despair. Practical reason is the middle ground of ruin.

Adorno's Authoritarian Personality uses Freud's bourgeoisie psychoanalysis to bring out an inferior consciousness in Nazis ideology. He uses it to draw out the cross road between metaphysics and ideology. Psychoanalysis is a weapon and Adorno uses it on notions of progress, system of integration and methods of creation and profit. Psychoanalysis is dialectical and can be liberating and enslaving, a propaganda playing on the relation between theory and praxis. Psychoanalysis is a logic of mind identifying and manipulating the conscious-unconscious divide by applied transcendental repetition through instinct. It's the objective side of Kant, the dark Kant, the 'all destroyer' (M.Mendelssohn). Kant and Freud represent two irreducible poles for Adorno. Kant's warning about second nature becomes true in Freud. Like Husserl's egology and Heidegger's Daseinanalytic, he describes a turn to immediate reality, the moment and intentional acts mediated through memory and history. Idealism and psychoanalysis work the subject as contradiction to get to the subject of experience in objective terms. There is no outside of consciousness (Husserl). Revealing consciousness is an unconscious affair carried out daily. Adorno works Kant's transcendental logic into Freudian metapsychology, the schema of categories and concepts find the object world deformed by the representational activity of consciousness. 'Identity-thinking' stigmatized with its own impossibility, its lack of existence and space. Unconscious meaning is desperation in the unchanging saga of Being and non-Being. Identity negated by desire and objects misrepresented by instinct, need and eternal longing change the rules of the game, however, and consciousness is maintained in the meanest and shabbiest of things. Freud's unconscious takes metaphysical dualism to the experience of consciousness through a critical process of reflecting on individual acts to prove key universals in human experience. Psychoanalytic uncovering and working through (durcharbeitung) consciousness finding the unconscious gains a true 'Self'. Freud's therapeutic resolve is not about overcoming and reconciliation but a critical process of thinking against oneself defining Adorno's notion of negative dialectics.

Psychoanalytic theory superimposed over the Kantian subject spin Adorno's 'revolution. Kant's transcendental deduction uses time to erect the subject counterbalanced by a dialectic of presence and regression, depth and deception. Freud subverts this into desire, immediate gratification timeless instincts, crude identity through nonidentity to get to 'acts' of repression to bring truth and Being together in the individual. Kant's self-limiting critical reason blocks itself from the individual doing the thinking as desire hides the other within. in Adorno the subject is unfree and society refuses to allow it to think its own unfreedom. The individual bears a freedom punishable by social contract, determined by force, by a collective unconscious enthralled with a Hollywood Self. Adorno admits one freedom in the ability to think our own unfreedom in reliance on a society mediated by the pathology of capitalism. We are unfree by the idea of the unconscious materialized by society. But the unconscious is both free and determined. While society, institutions and groups ideologically advance ideas of freedom the individual is shackled with the reality of it. Psychoanalysis corrected the science of psychology with the notion of the unconscious. Its theory works appearances, the everyday to enlightenment. Adorno's critical theory knows the "force of consciousness extends to the delusion of consciousness. It is rationally knowable where an unleashed, self-escaping rationality goes wrong, where it becomes true mythology. The ratio recoils into irrationality as soon as in its necessary course it fails to grasp that the disappearance of its substrate – however diluted – is its own work, the product of its own abstraction... Regression of consciousness is a product of its lack of self-reflection." [ND] Psychoanalysis sees through reconciled subject and world dictated by the status quo. The present is not what it seems. Seen through the 'Culture industry' with "its self-declared diminished mark of intelligence" and seen through the corporate world sets the "freedom to choose what is always the same."[DE] Confronted with its own truth, Adorno tells us, the ideology of the modern Self says no more than that one becomes what one is [Werden was du bist]. Marcuse also said that. The difference between Kant and Freud is the theoretical freedom to resist the moment for the movement of the individual person mitigating mystery and misery. Freud's psycho-synthesis is a labor of contradiction, where the id lies so the ego becomes. "Wo Es war Wo Ich Werden."

References

[MM] Theodor W. Adorno, 'Minima Moralia: Reflections from Damaged Life,' trans. E. F. N. Jephcott (New York: Verso, 1978), p. 65;

[BUTS] Theodor W. Adorno, 'Der Begriff des Unbewussten in der transzendentalen Seelenlehre' [The Concept of the Unconscious in the Transcendental Theory of the Psyche], in Gesammelte Schriften [Collected Works], vol.1, ed. Rolf Tiedermann (Frankfurt am Main: Suhrkamp, 1986). BUTS

[SP] Theodor W. Adorno, 'Zum Verhältnis von Soziologie und Psychologie' [In the Relation of Sociology and Psychology], in Gesammelte Schriften [Collected Works], vol. 8(1), ed. Rolf Tiedermann (Frankfurt am Main: Suhrkamp, 1986), pp. 42–85. English translation by I. Wohlfarth: 'Sociology and Psychology', New Left Review 46 (1967): 67–80 and 47 (1968): 79–97; hereafter cited as SP

[FP] Theodor W. Adorno, 'Freud in der Gegenwart' [Freud in the Present], in Gesammelte Schriften [Collected Works], vol. 20(5), ed. Tiedermann (Frankfurt am Main: Suhrkamp, 1986), p. 646; all translations are mine; hereafter cited as FG

[RP] Theodor W. Adorno, 'Die Revidierte Psychoanalyse' [The Revisionist Psychoanalysis], in Gesammelte Schriften [Collected Works] 8(1), ed. Rolf Tiedermann (Frankfurt am Main: Suhrkamp, 1986), Translated. by Nan-Nan Lee

[ND] Theodor W. Adorno, 'Negative Dialectics', (1966) trans. E.B. Ashton, The Continuum Publishing Company [1977]

[DE] Theodor W. Adorno and Max Horkheimer, 'Dialectic of Enlightenment', trans. John Cumming, New York: The Continuum Publishing [1988]

[CM] Theodor W. Adorno, 'Critical Models: Interventions & Catchwords', (1963.1969), trans. & with a preface by

Henry Pickford, Columbia University Press [1998]

[AE] Theodor W. Adorno, 'Against Epistemology: A Metacritique', trans. Willis Domingo, Basil Blackwell Publisher Ltd [1982]

[AM] Theodor W. Adorno, 'Metaphysics: Concept & Problems' ed. Rolf Tiedermann, Trans. Edmund Jephcott, Stanford University Press, Stanford California 2000.

[NN] Nan-Nan Lee, 'Sublimated or castrated psychoanalysis? Adorno's critique of the revisionist psychoanalysis: An introduction to 'The Revisionist Psychoanalysis'' Philosophy and Social Criticism 2014, Vol. 40(3) 309–338

The Weight of Philosophy in Otto Rank's Psychoanalysis

Julio R. Costa, MS

Introduction

Among the early psychoanalysts who, together with Freud, formed the Vienna Psychoanalytic Society, Otto Rank, together with Hans Sachs, had a special position, in that he was not a member of the medical profession. Because he departed from Freud's views on psychoanalytical theory and therapy, his work requires comprehensive analysis in order to further probe its acknowledged profundity.

Considering the fact that Otto Rank was the only member of the Vienna Psychoanalytic Society to hold a doctorate in Philosophy, we aim in this article to make clear how that field had a decisive impact on Rank's ideas, and moreover, how Nietzsche, Schopenhauer and Kant influenced his work.

Considering these philosophers, along with Freud, as having provided a broad foundation for his work, it may be said that Rank:

> 1. Accepted the fictional nature of human constructions, from Nietzsche;
>
> 2. From Schopenhauer, adopted the will as the foundation of the world and of human beings' contact with the world; and
>
> 3. With Kant, considered the numinous to be the locus of the *being*, such that ideologies and their social structures are doomed to fail and must, with the passage of time, be discredited; while the human person's being is located in the Kantian numinous, and therefore has a worth that can never be discredited.

An Overview of His Theory

Rank considered that the creative impulse in the individual, which contains in its core the will, propitiates a process in which people become more and more distinguished and differentiated. All this development unfolds through the individual, for as long as he fights, conquers, creates and interacts with others. Therefore, the individual becomes an affirmative agent, who learns and recreates the community's values. In the process, the development of the will and progressive individuation tend to turn the individual, as far as permitted by the human constraints, into the creator of his or her own personality and, symbolically, the creator of himself or herself. This implies the individual's intention to self-perpetuate, mainly symbolically, outlasting the ideologies of the different historical contexts and cultures.

These great systems of belief, which Rank called *ideologies,* eventually become ineffective and are discarded in the trash heap of history. However, the termination of every ideology causes no harm to the individual's being, inasmuch as Rank, influenced by Kantian epistemology and ethics, placed the being within the numinous – as will become clear below.

It should be pointed out that anthropologist Ernest Becker has offered the most widely known recognition of Otto Rank's contribution. Becker's theory deals with the cultural constructions necessary for the individual to confront his or her condition of finitude. To overcome a handicapping fear that arises from the awareness of one's own constraints and eventual death, the human person, in his or her interaction with others, builds mechanisms that will preserve and enhance self-esteem and the ability to effectively interact in the social world. This viewpoint does postulate a consoling role of cultural elements, as a way of self-deception. On the other hand, we can see in Rank's work *the positive affirmation of will and meaning.* In this article, we will focus on this positive aspect, understood as affirmation of life, which could, through philosophy, be seen as deriving from the *primacy of the will,* the *fictional aspect of human constructions,* and the person's being as part of the Kantian *noumenon.*

Therefore, it is very relevant to an understanding of Rank's psychoanalysis that all this replaces self-deception with affirmation of life and meaning.

Culture and the Being

It is important to highlight the fact that when Rank spoke of the different cultures and mentioned the diverse religions and symbolic systems of the peoples, he observed a respect for those social constructions and never debunked them or had recourse to irony. When he talked about cultures, whether Western or of a completely different tradition, he never once discredited them, like somebody who compares them with what he considers to be modern Western rationality.

A reading of Rank reveals to us a melancholic and stoic intellectual in his analysis of the heroic expression of the will deep within the person, in the being. In contrast, we see the fragility of the social expression of the being throughout history, due to the fictional nature of social constructions in the face of the individual's will – which is the very foundation of life.

The question of the fictional nature of things is derived from Nietzsche, while the will, as the foundation of being, is derived from Schopenhauer. Kant's "determine thyself by thyself" provides the ethical criticism in Rank's theory, preserving it from Nietzsche's scepticism and Schopenhauer's pessimism while maintaining the critical nature of these authors' views.

According to Rank, we must recognize that a human being needs to express his or her being, a differentiated being capable of interacting and integrating with a community. Furthermore, it is of fundamental importance that this program of being guarantee the perpetuation of those values that permit the expression of one's subjectivity in the world. It should be stressed that what one is looking for is the perpetuation of the values of subjectivity and its dignity, with a degree of abstraction that will lead us to the Kantian noumenon.

Thus, what will be a problem for the being is the fragility and failure of the social constructions of perpetuation of subjectivity, which Rank designates as *ideologies.* Although also shared by the individuals, they are very close to established social structures, and eventually become ineffective in guaranteeing the symbolic perpetuation of the subject. We observe that the symbols that were pertinent for a culture, that provided an expansion of the being (here considered as the person), have needed to be replaced.

From Dogmatism to Criticism, via Scepticism and Pragmatism,

Apart from some Schopenhauer's influences, there was no metaphysics in Rank. However, what could easily be perceived was his estrangement from Freud, principally in relation to the materialism that the latter represented. Actually, that was Freud's main distinguishing feature vis-à-vis the understanding of psychology at the time.

As pointed out by E. James Lieberman, Freud's success lay in the creation of a system of investigation and comprehension that broke away from religious or supernatural ideas, i.e., from dogmatism:

> Freud – atheist, neurologist, and former hypnotist – championed a psychology without spiritualism and metaphysics, in order to meet the requirements of the new scientific materialism, and called religion an illusion without future. Rank respected religion whether or not it is illusion. (Lieberman, in Rank, 1998, xviii).

At this point, we need to clearly understand how and why Rank respected the elements of culture, "whether or not they were illusions." We see that psychoanalysis expressed an evolution from traditional *dogmatism* to the *scepticism* of Freud's rationalism and scientific attitude.

The fact is that to be consistent with his own position, Freud would have had to discredit the traditional symbolic codes, considering them to be an illusion. What Rank was to do, to be consistent in his respect for culture "whether or not it is an illusion," would be to take one step from scepticism to *pragmatism*, and move on to *criticism*. In this process, the scepticism was to be that of Freud, whom the young Rank had enthusiastically supported; the pragmatism, on the other hand, was to be that of Nietzsche. Finally, we have Kant's criticism – where we may find the roots of what we could consider an *ethics* present in Rank.

Let's start with the question of pragmatism. It says that we assume to be true whatever it is relevant to know. Truth is seen as agreement between thought and being. At certain times, however, this affirmation has been undermined and questioned. That was when the question of philosophical pragmatism (which grew out of scepticism), with its stress on the useful, was raised. In the quote from Lieberman, the idea of pragmatism is clear: whether or not it is an illusion, religion does have utility in human society. This was the attitude shared by Rank, and for him the roots of this idea of the value of utility were basically in Nietzsche. In addition, as representatives of pragmatism, we may cite Schiller and Vaihinger, in philosophy, and, in psychology, William James.

So what was it like, this pragmatism in Nietzsche? It is necessary to stress one point: according to Nietzsche, agreement between thought and being can never be achieved, because of human historicity. Self-awareness is the least developed "organ" in the human being. For living beings, who need to *act* to establish themselves in the world, the primordial force is not intelligence, but the *will to power*.

So the human being is a being who needs to act; only in order to act better does he need to think. Thus a judgement derived from thought becomes true to the degree that it conserves, expands and stimulates life. This then becomes the parameter of validity of a judgement – its *practicality*. According to Nietzsche, what we must evaluate is whether or not a determined truth judgement is at the service of the will to power, i.e., of the expansion of life.

It may be seen that Rank fully internalized the pragmatic point of view; the contents of culture do not need to have their validity confirmed *per se*, because the important thing is their utility in providing the person with a symbology of perpetuation, a basis for "being more", in general.

However, Rank does not stop with pragmatism. If it is necessary to guarantee the expansion of being, it is quite natural for us to ask, what being are we talking about, if we consider metaphysics to be impossible? It is at this point that Kant's criticism comes in.

Kant also experienced the passage from dogmatism to scepticism as a personal journey, mainly in relation to Hume, within British empiricism. While he did agree with Hume with regard to the contingency of knowledge – from which it was inferred that there never has been and never could be a metaphysics – Kant considered the ethical consequences of scepticism to be unacceptable. Actually, all German idealism (in which Kant included himself) found itself engaged in defending reason against the doubt and relativism of British empiricism. Kant, specifically, saw himself as driven to *defend reason against scepticism*, and this is very important for our understanding of Rank. Kant defines this as a critique of the very possibility of knowing, in order that speculative illusions, characteristic of dogmatism, might be avoided, along with the reduction of everything to experience, in the case of scepticism.

It is well worth returning to pragmatism in order to see how much of Kant can be found in Nietzsche, precisely in relation to the possibility of knowing.

Knowledge and Fiction

Nietzsche's pragmatism focused on the life to be lived immediately; it was space without the infinite and time without eternity. It abandoned the metaphysics of Schopenhauer, to whom Nietzsche in his youth had referred as "my master." Thus, in his early works, such as *On Truth and Lie in an Extra-Moral Sense*, the young Nietzsche had asked, "what can we know for sure about the world, and to what extent can we really know about the world?"

Nietzsche's doubt already was very broad: how can we be sure that the world reveals itself to our senses as it really is? We are not as yet asking whether our senses are capable of perceiving the world, but rather if the world itself, understood as the true world, fully reveals itself. Furthermore, the world causes a nervous stimulus to our senses that may not exactly reproduce the external stimulus; this excitement will trigger a thought in the brain, and we do not know how faithful this thought will be to the nervous stimulus. And we do not know how faithful the word that expresses the thought will be to that thought.

Based on these perspectives, we can say that we only have approximations, or, in Nietzsche's critique, collectively shared illusions. As he said:

> What is truth? A mobile army of metaphors, metonyms, and anthropomorphisms, in short, a sum of human relations which were poetically and rhetorically heightened, transferred, adorned, and which after long use seem solid, canonical and binding to a people: truths are illusions which we have forgotten are illusions; metaphors which have been used up and drained of sensory force; coins which have lost their image and are now considered as metal, no longer as coins (Nietzsche, 2014, p. 66.).

For us to understand pragmatism in Rank, it is important to discuss how strongly this doubting of the capacity to know saps the foundations of any system purporting to be absolute, with emphasis on the moral and the social. Nietzsche, however, followed this path to discredit not only social systems but also the very individual, to the extent that consciousness of oneself is extremely weak in relation to the forces of nature, and also because its constructions have no basis. When Nietzsche told us not to have any egoism, he meant that that which our consciousness thinks important for us is nothing compared to what the forces of life and nature are, as it were, planning for us, and that our will – the will to cultivate our fictional "I" – has no bearing on the flow of events. But Nietzsche also told us not to abandon egoism only to fall into altruism, for the will of another similarly has no power, in the grand scheme of things, on whatever life has reserved for him, - not to mention the fabrication that his supposed self-conscious awareness really does exist.

In the course of this paper, we shall see why Rank accepted Nietzsche's critique of the absolute foundation of social systems, while at the same time rejecting his critique of consciousness and of a person's being.

The Human a priori *and the Numinous*

It was Hans Vaihinger who said that "there is more Kant in Nietzsche than one usually thinks". In his opinion, this comes from that radical doubt regarding the capacity to know the world. This doubt, according to Vaihinger, originated from Immanuel Kant's *Critique of Pure Reason* (2011), which discusses the issue of the phenomenon and the thing in itself.
In the *Critique of Pure Reason*, Kant analyzed the possibility of knowing, and, seeing knowledge as contingent upon the human *a priori*, challenged the possibility of a metaphysics, in the sense of *knowledge* of God, the world and the soul. One also must remember that Kant, as a philosopher of the Enlightenment, aimed at attacking all dogmatism.
But we need to understand how he intended to protect reason against skepticism using something that could support skepticism. The answer is in his later work *Critique of Practical Reason*, in which he laid the foundations of morals, introducing criticism as an alternative to both dogmatism and skepticism.

Kant sought an ethics that could be found by a man of the Enlightenment, in which the dogmatic, supernatural drivers of morals should be replaced by categories that could be rationally argued.

Kant's reference to the "Copernican revolution" aimed precisely at showing the subject's reason as the driver of knowledge of the object. The subject's capacity to know dominates the object. We shall see that the fact that reason no longer bowed before the object of knowledge, always remaining faithful to its own laws and consistent with itself, was extremely important. Reason became *law-giving reason*. This was not so when the object dominated the subject and the latter's act of knowing.

This development was necessary for Kant, due to dogmatism's failure to apprehend reality, particularly through the metaphysical attempts intrinsic to dogmatism. One aimed to *know* in such a way that could be as effective and verifiable as the knowledge stemming from logic and mathematics. Kant thus had to study reason itself, its innate characteristics, rules and boundaries.

Kant posited that nature is always questioned by means of requirements already encompassed by human reason, that is, in *a priori* forms of knowledge. The human being knows the real through such forms, which exist *a priori* in reason, and which his capacity to know places above the data of sensory experience. Everything real is thus a human construct stemming from sensorial experience submitted to the *a priori* forms of pure reason. That which is beyond the reach of reason is the thing in itself, the ultimate reality, which the human being cannot know, but can think about through symbols.

Kant differs from metaphysical thought in that the *subject* and *subjectivity* have no "substance," but there is a *consciousness of oneself* that accompanies every cognitive action and every conscious experience. These cognitive actions are established within boundaries that outline the experience of phenomena, for it is impossible for consciousness to have reference to that which is beyond phenomena (the thing in itself). But this consciousness of oneself has to be assumed. Accepting that we have no immediate experience of the objects of our senses, but only reach them through representations supplied by those possibilities already encompassed by reason, we conclude that *consciousness of objects* is no more or less worthy than consciousness of oneself, because they are simultaneous.

We must note that only the phenomenon, the world of phenomena immediately available to human beings, can be *known*. It can be both known and thought of. In contrast, the world of moral determinations is not the object of sensory experience; it can only be thought of. It is the world of the noumenon, separate from the phenomenon. Phenomena thus exist in the visible world, and the noumenon in the *intelligible world*, which is supersensible. However – and this was very important for Kant – the supersensible world was not metaphysical or supernatural; it was a world that could only be conceived of by means of symbols that the reason needs to postulate. It is necessary within the realm of *practical action,* in accordance with reason; it becomes, therefore, *moral action.*

It is noteworthy that in this intelligible world, which is "comprehensible only in the moral aspect" and where all determinations are moral, Kant follows Plato's ancient notion of a world of ideas (Kant, 2012, p. 107). Kant said:

> Because we here treat (or judge) only ideas that reason created for itself, whose purposes (if any) lay far beyond our horizon, and because, even if we must assume them useless for speculative knowledge, they need not because of this be void in every sense, but the very law-giving reason puts them within our reach with a practical purpose, not for us to ponder on its objects, on what they are in themselves and according to their nature, but for us to think to the benefit of moral principles focusing on the ultimate purpose of all things (whereby these ideas, which would otherwise be utterly empty, receive objective practical reality). (Kant, 2012, p.112).

Rank said that the human being is a "theological being," but he never discussed God, but rather culture in relation to the idea of God as a means for the perpetuation of the individual and his or her subjectivity. We could say that Rank used these concepts as if they were Kant's *regulative principles* and Vaihinger's *fictions.* This will likewise be reflected in the fictional character of human constructs in Nietzsche, in whose work we can also find the presence of the Kantian thing in itself:

> We have to establish this principle: we live only by our illusions – our conscience emerges on the surface. Many things are hidden from our eyes. There is no reason to fear that man will come to know himself *fully*, that he will at every instant penetrate all relationships of strength ... that are necessary for life. ... They are only formulae for forces that are utterly unknowable. (Nietzsche, 2013, p. 349).

If we take these so-called illusions as the Kantian regulative principles, Otto Rank's work takes on a new dimension. Kant saw the regulative principles as ideas that are not knowledge but rather establish guidelines and milestones for procedures in the act of knowing. *Constitutive principles*, however, lay the foundation for the objectives and possibilities of knowledge based on sensory data.

These fictions would also entail accepting as the noumenon the sphere where he places the being, in view of the respect with which he treats the subject – which Rank never discredits and whose sincerity he acknowledges.

Will, Affirmation and Autonomy

Although Kant made no room for metaphysics, Schopenhauer, even when criticizing Kant, created a metaphysics, by considering the will as the ultimate reality. It will be because of Schopenhauer that certain considerations approaching the metaphysical will appear in the work of Otto Rank.
Let us remember that in Kant, speculative thought (as expressed in the *Critique of Pure Reason*) recognizes the world of phenomena as its boundary and stops there, acknowledging that it cannot know the thing in itself. However, Schopenhauer saw the thing in itself as being the will, and thus pushed thought beyond that boundary, now seeing the will as the thing in itself.

Being a metaphysical concept for Schopenhauer, the will does not depend on anything biological; indeed, Schopenhauer avers that living beings came to existence to fill the void that the will contained in itself.

In his considerations on the human being, Schopenhauer stated that that which is not phenomenon in the individual is the will, and that the thing in itself also is the will. The will reveals itself through its representation, emerging as the world and being thus perceived by the subject – and this is why Schopenhauer thought the world is assured for the subject.

Schopenhauer's concept of the will, as the foundation of the world of phenomena, is present in Otto Rank. Indeed, Rank wrote that the individual is

> ... the temporal representative of the cosmic primal force no matter whether one calls it sexuality, libido, or id. The ego accordingly is strong just in the degree to which it *is* the representative of this primal force and the strength of this force represented in the individual we call the will (Rank, 1978, p. 4).

One must here note that Rank really did take into consideration the human subject and the being, because therein, implicitly, lies the Kantian ethics. This takes us again to Rank's common ground with Schopenhauer's metaphysics, because this distancing of the being from the social and historical context becomes not only implicit, but necessary.

Thus, Rank reflects Nietzsche's pragmatism in an amalgam with Schopenhauer's metaphysics, in the primacy of the will in relation to consciousness and the intellect:

> ...will, guilt and consciousness maintain themselves differently, for the will, however one comprehends or interprets it, remains a constantly operating force, while consciousness above all is a quality, a state, and as such is passive and temporary, yes momentary (Rank, 1978, p. 90).

If Schopenhauer's ideal was the annihilation of the will because it is the incessant compulsion that should not exist and causes pain, in Nietzsche one finds the enjoyment of the immediate power of life, without the need for any ultimate absolute or purpose.

Within this context, it may be said that Rank sustained

1. The neutral aspect of the primacy of the will;

2. The negative aspect of its compulsiveness; and

3. The positive aspect of the will as a pragmatic affirmation of life.

Furthermore, influenced by Kant's Enlightenment aspects, Rank added his epistemology and ethics, so that we may add the following:

4. The self-determination aspect, whereby the individual transforms compulsion into liberty, guiding the will by means of a project of *affirmation* grounded in the being, which is considered as numinous.

It is very important that at this point, the will is no longer subordinated to the phenomenon, but rather to the noumenon.

To illustrate the presence of Kant, let us focus, for example, on the issue of time as *form*. In Kantian epistemology, the matter of the phenomenon constitutes the sensation, and forms are the structures that make it possible to give order to the materials received from experience (Mora, 1996, p. 305). For Kant, time is an *a priori* form of the internal states of human beings, i.e., the form of the succession of representations in the human being as an arrangement of internal perception. It is conceivable that Otto Rank kept the Kantian concept of time as a form of conscience, while at the same time we can see in him the presence of Schopenhauer's concept of compulsion as the origin of pain:

> Therefore, from the standpoint of the psychology of emotions, consciousness shows itself as a time problem in the sense that time represents the form of consciousness and by means of this time factor makes the different contents pleasurable or painful. Will as the constant driving force strive accordingly to prolong its pleasurable perceived affirmation through consciousness, to make the feeling of happiness lasting, that is, redeeming. Insofar as this prolongation succeeds, it is perceived as painful because compulsory... (Rank, 1978, p. 89)."

As we can see, the inner states unavoidably change; for Kant, this is the very ground of our perception of time.

The Numinous and the Contingency

One must understand that Kant had accepted Hume's skepticism, but could not accept its moral consequences. Thus, what he deemed impossible to attain by speculative reason he attained by practical reason, permitting him to defend reason against skepticism. This made it possible for Kant to legitimately refer to the "'*homo noumenon,*' whose pilgrimage is in eternity (Kant, 2012, p. 114)" – and this without any metaphysics, only referencing the moral world.

Where does this touch Otto Rank? Exactly in the "ineffable

spirit" mentioned by E. James Lieberman in the introduction to Rank's book *Psychology and the Soul*, referring to the form Rank employed to deal with intangible concepts, which Freud, loyal to his scientific view, could only consider illusions.

The experience of the numinous, pertaining to the moral world, is found in the regulative principles. According to Hans Vaihinger, the fictions mentioned by the early Nietzsche are equivalent to regulative principles, outlining the boundaries for understanding an inexact and ever flowing reality. Moreover, Denis Thouard remarked that the numinous may be thought of *symbolically*:

> Imagination appropriated this, compelled by an impulse that may be subjectively understood but cannot be objectively followed. These domains are left for myth, religion, literature, which are entitled to suspend reference (Thouard, 2004, p. 75).

For Kant, *knowing* and *thinking* are not equivalent. Phenomena may be known and thought of, but the numinous can only be thought of. This brings momentous consequences. One might think that something that exists only symbolically should not be taken into consideration. To exist only as a symbol would be tantamount to not existing. But according to Kant, that which can only be thought of symbolically *must* be thought of symbolically, and will have a legitimate place in people's lives. It is exactly in this manner that we can reach the supersensible world, where all determinations are moral and expressed by means of the symbolic life.

In this way, we can correctly grasp Rank's attitude towards culture.

Otto Rank often stated that the human being wishes to escape from purely material and biological determinations in his quest for spiritual determinations. "Spiritual" here means the same as "cultural," the fruit of the being's choices in the universe of moral determinations, where human will can act. According to Kant, all of this alludes to the numinous, not to illusion. The legitimate use of reason leads us to the noumenon, to the unconditioned; reasons allows us to think of it without the presumption – or the need – to obtain from it any sensory data, because the latter belongs to phenomena, while a moral law, which stems from reason, requires not the phenomenon but the noumenon.

Through the noumenon, Rank spoke to us of the being, which brushes up against the various ideologies of immortality, contingent on the different contexts of history, which have helped individuals to seek their own symbolic perpetuation. But the individual, as a being, does not depend on these ideologies to *be*, but rather to present himself to the world. The being remains unscathed, presenting itself as detached from social contexts, which are doomed to fail. And it is here that subjectivity will be protected: it concerns the numinous and is not undermined by the world of phenomena.

It is important to make clear that only the being has a fundamental quality in the moral sense – which is important in Rank's thought, in that *the individual does not have to submit himself or herself to the phenomenon*, given that one's being resides in the noumenon. Only this can detach the individual from contingency; and this permits Rank to question the limitations of the several ideologies of immortality that have followed one another throughout history, without discrediting the human person and his or her being.

The importance of this notion of a "detached" being lies in its shedding of all aspects that could be mistakenly considered "essential" within the world of phenomena. In this sense, Rank followed Kant's moral self-determination. In other words, human beings must be morally conditioned to nothing in the sensory world. The life-heightening and life-propagating property, and the ensuing affirmation of the being, reside not in any aspect of the sensory world, but rather in how the will expresses itself in order to attain this affirmation. We thus see that criticism has penetrated pragmatism.

Affirmation and Dignity

Using the very internal laws of reason, which are simultaneous to perception of the sensory world, a position of respect for human beings and their dignity becomes the correct one to take. Rank, in his narrative of the obsolescence of ideologies of immortality over time, in what he termed the "eternal drama of life," at a certain point mentions a "lowering of the curtains" in the historical saga, when one can exist only in and of oneself:

> The subjects of my former interest – the hero, the artist, the neurotic – all come back once more on stage, not only as participants in the eternal drama of life but also after the curtain has come down: unmasked, undressed, unpretentious. Not debunked by any means, just human, while I myself do not pretend to pull their strings, to tell them what to do and say, nor to interpret them to the audience (Rank, cited by Lieberman, 1993, pp. 387-388).

One may therefore say that Rank considers the being to be outside historical contingency, where human beings would exist even after "the curtains of the drama of life have come down," where people would exist "naked, without masks, without pretensions," and where they could be "just human," and still in no way be discredited.

Only in the universe of the noumenon, where all determination is moral, can the human being reclaim his right to moral dignity, without the need for any self-deception. Likewise, this makes it possible to bring the experience of ethics into the world of phenomena, of contingency. Otherwise, if social life were a monolith of power and domination, each member of society would forever be an accomplice in his or her own domination, with no possibility for the exercise of reason to show another way; because a critique of power would be impossible for the faculty of reason.

Thus we may understand the degree of Rank's wisdom in incorporating Kant's epistemology and ethics, and thus placing the being of the human person outside of contingency. We also better understand the wisdom of Kant's introduction of criticism, which makes it possible to avoid both dogmatism and scepticism.

Taking as our starting point the philosophers that influenced Rank to take his position, we may say that reason demands that the being be outside of contingency, remaining untouched by it; it needs to be where Kant placed the super sensible: in the moral universe. Finally, it becomes possible to acknowledge the importance of the human symbolic repertoire and its many manifestations, "whether or not they are illusions," for human culture, meaning and values remain as affirmations so long as the being dwells in the numinous.

References

Kant, I. (2008). *Crítica da razão prática.* São Paulo: Martins Fontes.

Kant, I. (2011). *Crítica da razão pura.* São Paulo: Ícone.

Kant, I. (2012). *Filosofia da história.* São Paulo: Ícone.

Lieberman, E.J. (1993). *Acts of will: The life and work of Otto Rank.* Amherst: University of Massachusetts Press.

Mora, J. F. (1996). *Dicionário de filosofia.* São Paulo: Martins Fontes.

Nietzsche, F. (2013). *Escritos sobre psicologia.* Rio de Janeiro: PUC-RIO.

Nietzsche, F. (2014). *Obras incompletas.* São Paulo: Editora 34.

Rank, O. (1998). *Psychology and the soul.* Baltimore: The John Hopkins University Press.

Rank, O. (1978). *Truth and reality.* New York: W.W. Norton & Company Inc.

Thouard, D. (2004). *Kant.* São Paulo: Estação Liberdade.

Artificial Intelligence and the Concept of the Self

Gary Kolb, PhD

August 15, 2016

The advancement and development of technology is progressing at an astronomical rate, accompanied by changes in our individual and social structure. Chaos is an appropriate word for what seems to be happening in the world today politically, spiritually, and economically. There has also been a shift in the sense of security on both individual and national levels. Technology has infiltrated many aspects of daily lives. It has changed how a person develops a self-concept to how we communicate with others. It has increased the potential for addiction. The development of technology that could support Artificial Intelligence (AI) has fueled debate between scientists, theologians, philosophers and others focusing on the possibility that computers (machines) will develop consciousness which up to this point has been an exclusively human characteristic.

Introduction

In the earliest stages of the study of Artificial Intelligence (AI), very few people had more than the sketchiest idea of what is involved in the process (Boden, 1977, p.3). In the beginning, most people were skeptical of the value of AI. The lay person may have feared that machine models of the mind would alienate us from our proper humanity (Boden, 1977, p.425). Now, philosophers, theologians, scientists, futurists, and inventors are all involved in the discussion. Much of the information in this article comes from the Gilder-Forbes Telecosm conference held in 2002. The participants included: Ray Kurzweil , inventor and futurist; John Searle, philosopher; Michael Denton, biologist; Tom Ray, zoologist and theorist; and William Dembski, philosopher and mathematician.

Artificial intelligence

Kurzweil was an advocate of Artificial Intelligence (AI) and believed that the intelligence of non-biological entities (machines) will exceed human intelligence, including musical and artistic aptitude, creativity, physical movement through the world, and response to emotion, in the next century (2002, p. 12). He predicted that "by 2019, a $1000 computer will match the processing power of the human brain" (2002, p. 12). Kurzweil envisioned computers with the ability to understand languages and read models of knowledge contained in written documents. He wrote that ultimately, machines will be able to gather knowledge on their own from the physical world, gathering data from many sources and sharing it with each other (Kurzweil,2002, p. 12). They will be able to read on their own, model and understand what they have read.

According to Kurzwiel, mastering the software of intelligence is a matter of "tapping into the blueprint of human intelligence by reverse engineering, or copying, the design of the human brain" (2002, p. 32). Scanning the brain involves mapping the locations, interconnections, and contents of all the somas, axons, dendrites, pre-synaptic receptacles, neurotransmitter concentrations, and other neural components at levels which can be accomplished with high-resolution Magnetic Resonance Imagery, optical imaging, near-infared scanning and other non-invasive techniques (Kurzweil, 2002, p. 32). Researchers have already developed integrated circuits that precisely match the digital and analog information processing of neurons, and have "built a variety of integrated circuits that emulate the digital-analog characteristics of mammalian neural circuits" (Kurzweil, 2002, p. 36). Additional research has discovered "the potential for electronic neurons to precisely emulate biological ones" (Kurzweil, 2002, p. 36). Research started with developing functionally equivalent recreations of single neurons which then evolved into clusters.

Qualities of human thinking can be combined with certain advantages of machine intelligence. "As we combine the brain's pattern recognition methods derived from high-resolution brain scans and reverse engineering efforts with the knowledge-sharing, speed , and memory accuracy advantages of non-biological intelligence, the combination will be formidable" (Kurzweil, 2002, p. 39). Kurzweil explained that "within several decades information-based technologies will encompass all human knowledge and proficiency, ultimately including the pattern-recognition powers, problem-solving skills, and emotional and moral intelligence of the human brain itself" (2005, p. 8).

Kurzweil used the term Singularity to describe "a future period during which the pace of technological changes will be so rapid, its impact so deep, that human life will be irreversibly transformed" (2006, p. 7). In Singularity, people will be able to transcend the limitations of biological bodies and brains. By the end of this century, "the non-biological parts of intelligence will be trillions and trillions of times more powerful than unaided human intelligence" (Kurzweil, 2005, p. 9). Singularity will represent the culmination of the merger of our biological thinking and existence with our technology, resulting in a world that is still human, but that transcends our biological roots. There will be no distinction between human and machine or between physical and virtual reality post-Singularity (Kurzweil, 2005, p. 9).

Clark, who identified himself as a cognitive scientist, wrote that "the more I have learned about the brain and the mind, the more convinced I have become that the everyday notions of 'minds' and 'persons' are open-ended plastic systems fully capable of including non-biological props and aids quite literally as parts of themselves" (2003, p. 8). He claimed that as technology becomes more portable, pervasive, flexible, reliable, and increasingly personalized, our tools will become more and more a part of who and what we are we are (Clark, 2003, p. 10).

Consciousness controversy

If technology develops in the ways that Kurzweil predicted, will machines also become conscious? Consciousness in machines will be a critically important issue in the development of machine intelligence (AI) in the twenty-first century. If consciousness is just a certain type of intelligent skill, for example, the ability to reflect on one's own self and situation, then the issue is not difficult because any skill or capability or form of intelligence that one cares to define will be replicated in non-biological entities within a few decades (Kurzweil, 2002, p. 44). Any computational process sufficiently capable of altering or organizing itself can produce consciousness. However, the essence of consciousness is subjective experience, not objective correlates of the experience (Kurzweil, 2002, p. 44). Will future machines be capable of having spiritual experience? How can consciousness be measured? There is no objective test that can absolutely measure consciousness. Fundamentally, it is not possible to penetrate the subjective experience of another entity with direct objective measurement. Only the correlates of subjective experience, such as behavior, are measurable (Kurzweil, 2002, p. 45).

Dembski, a philosopher and mathematician, pointed out that the debate about whether or not humans are machines has been going on for the last 200 years (2002, p.98). French Materialists of the Enlightenment believed humans were machines (2002, p. 98). LaMettrie, one of the French Materialists of the Enlightenment, authored a book titled *Man the Machine* (Dembski, 2002, p. 98). Modern materialists hold the view that the motions and the modification of matter account for human mentality. Materialism has its faults, but it is a predictable philosophy. "If matter is all there is, then the mind must, in some fashion, reduce to matter" (Dembski, 2002, p. 99). "While Enlightenment philosophers may have thought of humans in terms of gear mechanisms and fluid flow, contemporary materialists think of humans in terms of neurological symptoms and computational devices" (Dembski, 2002, p. 99). Humans aspire for freedom, immortality, and the beatific vision. If in order to find ourselves, we need to transcend ourselves, then spiritual materialism is possible, since human aspirations are spiritual (Dembski, 2002, p.100). Dembski stated that "human beings need to be transcended, not by going beyond matter, but by reinstating themselves in more efficient forms of matter, to wit, the computer" (2002, p. 100).

Dembski contended that we have come to view ourselves as machines, so it is no accident that our society looks for salvation in technologies such as behavior modification, psychotropic drugs, cognitive programming, and genetic engineering (2002, p. 103). However, the problem with machines is that they are incapable of sustaining what philosophers call substantial forms. "A substantial form is a principle of unity that holds things together and maintains its identity over time" (2002, p. 103). A machine configured in one way could be just as easily be reconfigured in other ways. A machine is subjected to constant tinkering and need not bear any semblance to past incarnations. What a machine is now and what it might be in the future are entirely open and discontinuous, whereas substantial forms maintain identity over time (Dembski, 2002, p. 104). "A machine is entirely characterized in terms of the constitution, dynamics, and interrelationships of its physical parts; 'spiritual' cannot refer to some non-physical aspects of the machine" (Dembski, 2002, p. 130). In addition, attributing spirituality to machines on the basis of future actions is equally problematic, since the only access to a machine's future is through its present. Machines break and malfunction, and it is impossible to predict the full range of stresses that a machine may encounter and that may cause it to break or malfunction (Dembski, 2002, p. 105). Dembski proposed that "contemporary spirituality places a premium on religious experience and neglects the more traditional aspects of spirituality as revelation, virtue, tradition, morality, and above all communion with a non-physical God who transcends or physical being" (Dembski, 2002, p. 106). Within traditional spirituality we are aware of God's presence because God has freely chosen to make his presence known to us. God cannot make his presence known to a machine by acting on it and thereby changing its state. If a machine comes to awareness of God's presence, it must be self-induced. "Machine spirituality is the spirituality of Self-Realization, not the spirituality of an active God who freely gives himself in self-revelation and thereby transforms the being with which he is in communion" (Dembski, 2002, p.106).

Searle, a philosopher, emphasized that actual human brains cause consciousness by a series of specific neurobiological processes in the brain, while a computer succeeds by manipulating formal symbols. The computer is not designed to be conscious, to duplicate the actual causal powers of the brain (Searle, 2002, p.67)." Searle pointed out that all of the advances made in technology are due to the ingenuity of programmers and engineers (2002, p. 64). Increased computational power in a machine gives no reason whatever to suppose that the machine is duplicating the specific neurobiological powers of the brain to create consciousness" (Searle, 2002, p. 76). Technology enables us to build tools to do things we cannot do, or cannot do as well or as fast without the tools (Searle, 2002, p. 96).

Denton, a biologist, proposed that if living organisms are analogous in all important respects to artificial mechanical systems, there are no serious grounds for doubting the possibility of "spiritual" machines. However, if living things are not machine-like in their basic design, if they differ in certain critical ways from machines, none of the characteristics of living organisms, including intelligence, are likely to be incorporated in non-living mechanical systems (Denton, 2002, p. 80). He firmly believed that living things are more than just a sum of their parts, even though most modern biologists view living things as analogous to machines with the parts determining the properties of the whole, the mechanistic/reductionist approach. Denton wrote that there is more to reality than the material world and that biological organisms transcend physics and chemistry, agreeing with the vitalist perspective. While biological organisms may depend on lower levels, they can't be reduced to them (Denton, 2002, p. 5).

Many biological phenomena can be reduced to mechanical explanations and, despite the fact that machines have become more life-like as technology has advanced, it is undeniable that living things possess abilities that are still without any significant analogue in any machine that has yet been constructed (Denton, 2002 p. 84).Living things have the remarkable abilities to replicate themselves and to change their forms and structure without any external guidance or control (Denton, 2002, p. 87).Organic systems have a unique order that is missing from mechanical systems. There is a reciprocal influence of all parts of the organic whole on each other and on the whole in which they function (Denton, 2002, p. 88). "The parts of machines do not undergo complex reciprocal self-formative interactions, but have essentially the same properties and form in isolation as they do in the mechanical whole that makes their design possible" (Denton, 2002, p. 94). The capacity for conscious self-reflection which also includes morphing, self-regulation, self-assembly and organization, are all higher plateaus of functioning that make humans different from machines (Denton, 2002, p. 97).

Ray, a zoologist and evolutionary algorithm theorist, disagreed with Kurzweil's theory that the entire organization of the human brain could be re-created on a neural computer of sufficient capacity (2002, p. 121). It is unfeasible to 'copy' a complex organic organ into silicon without losing its function (Ray, 2002, p. 121). Additionally, Ray argued that "the structure and function of the brain or its components cannot be separated" (2002, p. 122). The brain is a chemical organ with a broad spectrum of chemical communication that has evolved in exquisitely subtle and complex functionality based on the properties of these chemical systems. The brain is composed of a variety of relatively distinct, but densely inter-communicating subsystems.

"A metallic computation system operates on fundamentally different dynamic properties and could never precisely and exactly 'copy' the function of a brain, since the materials of which computers are constructed have fundamentally different physical, chemical, and electrical properties that materials from which the brain is constructed" (Ray, 2002, p.123). Ray accepted that the level of computing power needed to map a brain is likely to be reached in the future, but "no amount of computer power will be intelligent in a relevant sense unless it is properly organized and organization is a software problem, not a hardware problem" (2002, p. 124). He expected that "intelligences which emerge from the digital and organic media will be as different as their respective media, even if they have comparable computing performance" (Ray, 2002, p. 125).

Effects of technological advancement on the concept of self

Some of the predictions for the future of computers may be hard to imagine, but when cyberspace came into existence during the 1960's, our world changed forever. The internet has made new social experiences possible. Before the internet, self-concept was developed in reality. Through face-to face interactions with others, people learned about themselves. The interpersonal self results from the direct perception of the relation between the self and another person (Stern in Neisser, 1993). It forms from the social interactions with other people which provide objective information that is directly available to each. Technological innovations of the cyber age have altered fundamental processes of social interactions. Technology has altered perception and experience, and sense of self (Goren, 2003, p. 487). People can gain a sense of who and what they are, not just through experiences in reality, but also through online experiences. Developing a self- concept is no longer solely based in reality. Self-concept also develops in the fantasy of online encounters and relationships. Technology has provided the means for a person to present a fantasy version of himself or herself to others. Clark believed that technology can allow us to learn more about what really matters in the on-going construction of our sense of place and of person-hood (2003, p. 115).

Kourosh stated that new technology provides greater opportunities for both growth and regression (2008, p. 105). The question arises, how might this adaptation change or modify an individual's way of believing who he or she desires to be? Is Artificial Intelligence the next step in modifying the self perception?

Is this concern true or could be we become trapped into a transition of fantasy? Is this a new form of creativity or a process of mesmerizing one into acceptance of a mysterious and unpredictable venture? Is this transition a natural process of evolutional for advancement or a restrictive process for conformity? What is gained or what is lost in major adjustments to the perception of ourselves? Most importantly, are we addressing these questions today? Are the questions appropriate to future projections of research in technology?

Fantasy can become an addiction. The fascination with a mechanical device is intriguing and may institute thoughts of power or control in one's life. Egan believed that the infiltration of fantasy as the capability to preoccupy the mind and which could lead to an unhealthy venture into our reality (2008, p. 381). According to Weiss and Schneider, many technology-based activities have addictive potential, since they evoke feelings of extreme pleasure and satisfaction while serving as a source of profound, although temporary, distraction (2014, p.135). They noted that the problem of addiction has always been driven by human technological advances. "Technology in all of its forms delivers an increasingly wider array of powerful experiences that are, for some emotionally, psychologically, and/or physically unmanageable" (Weiss & Schneider, 2014, p. 135). Technology offers highly distracting, emotionally involved behaviors. The contribution of fantasy may, very well change our perception of ourselves through repetitive and reinforced patterns of behavior over time. We might speculate that artificial intelligence, with its simulation capacity for human processing, its influence on thought and emotional patterns and ultimately its ability to direct behavioral decisions, could become a method for population control?

Conclusion

What is the future of Artificial Intelligence? Will there be configured, fully non-biological brains that are copies of human brains? Will nanobot technology provide fully immersive, totally convincing virtual reality where virtual people interact with humans? Will brain implants expand memories and vastly improve all of our sensory, pattern recognition and cognitive behaviors as Kurweil suggested (2002, p. 49)?

Are we becoming more intelligent with new information available sooner or are we becoming more stressed? Are we becoming more efficient and smarter with newly accumulated knowledge, or are we falling trapped into a funnel of compliance for survival?

According to Plato, ignorance or error about reality is among the worst disasters than can befall us. From ignorance or error, many other pains and disasters follow, and fantasy contributes to that worst disaster (Egan, 2008, p. 321). Maybe what Plato was advising is a cautionary movement into the unknown and on its net effect on us.

References

Boden, M. (1977). Artificial intelligence and natural man. New York: Basic Books, Inc.

Clark, A. (2003). Natural-born cyborgs: Minds, technology and the future of human intelligence, New York: Oxford University Press.

Dembski, W. (2002). Kurzweil's Impoverished spirituality. In *Are we spiritual machines?*, Ed. J.

W. Richards. Seattle, WA: Discovery Institute.

Denton, M. (2002). Organism and machine: The flawed analogy. In *Are we spiritual machines?*,

Ed. J.W. Richards. Seattle, WA: Discovery Institute.

Egan, K. (July, 2008). Conference: Achieving educational goals with imagination. Tract: d:27 Paper: d:776.

Goren, W. (2003). America's love affair with technology: The transformation of sexuality and the self over the twentieth century. *Psychoanalytic Psychology* 20: 487-508.

Kourosh, D. (2008). Video games: Play and addiction, a guide for parents. NY: Universal, Inc.

Kurzweil, R. (2002). The evolution of mind in the twenty-first century. In *Are we spiritual machines?*, Ed. J. W. Richards. Seattle, WA: Discovery Institute.

Kurzweil, R. (2005). The singularity is near when humans transcend biology. NY: Penguin Books.

Nusselder, A. (2009). Interface fantasy: A Laconian-cyborg ontology. Cambridge, MA: The MIT Press.

Ray, T. (2002). Kurzweil's turing fallacy. In *Are we spiritual machines?*. Ed. J.W. Richards. Seattle, WA: Discovery Institute.

Searle, J. (2002). I married a computer. In *Are we spiritual machines?*, Ed. J.W. Richards. Seattle, WA: Discovery Institute.

Weiss, R, and Schneider, J. (2014). Closer together, further apart: The effect of technology and the internet on parenting, work, and relationships. Carefree, AZ: Gentle Path Press.

On My Antecedents

Ellie Ragland, PhD

*On My Antecedents**[1]

Jacques Lacan decided that the best way to position himself as to how he began to practice and teach psychoanalysis was to explain his entry into the field. His training for this included the study of medicine, in particular, of psychiatry (51, 1-2) which he completed at the medical school of Paris from 1926-1930. Stijn Vanheule writes that Lacan studied at psychiatric clinics other than Sainte Anne and first worked under the supervision of Henri Claude as well as that of Gaetan Gatian de Clérambault at the Special Infirmary of the Paris Police Headquarters.[2] Henri Claude (1869-1945), a psychiatarist and neurologist, was Chair of mental illness and brain disorders at the Sainte Anne Hospital in Paris from 1922-1939. He also created psychiatry and psychoanalysis as disciplines at the University of Paris.[3] Gaetan de Clérambault (1872-1934) was a psychiatrist who worked at the Prefecture of Police from 1905 until 1920 when he became Head of the Institution.[4] Lacan served as the Chief of Psychiatry at the Sainte Anne Hospital in Paris from 1932-1936, the youngest person to have ever held that distinguished post. Having begun his clinical training at Sainte-Anne Hospital in 1927, Lacan subsequently worked both with Clérambault at the Préfecture de Police and at the Hospital Henri-Rousselle, after which he returned to Sainte-Anne to work under Dr. Claude.[5]

In referring to his doctoral thesis in medicine, written in 1932, Lacan referenced many examples of "paranoiac knowledge." Working within the context of the many psychiatrists and thinkers when he wrote on paranoia, Lacan had an abundance of influences, including Jean-Paul Sartre. One of the earliest articles on paranoïa was written by Karl Jaspers.[6] Jaspers started out as a psychiatrist, but quickly became discontent with the clinical diagnoses and methods used by his field's approach to mental illness. In his lifetime Jaspers influenced not only psychiatry and philosophy, but also theology. His notions of the limitless freedom of existence led some to label him an existentialist, a label he denied. One of Jasper's major contributions to psychiatry was his detailed study of patients, an approach which came to be called the biographical method. He argued that one diagnoses by form, not by content. His masters were Nietzsche and Kierkegaard, as well as Kant. His principle followers in phenomenological hermeneutics were Paul Ricoeur and Hans-Georg Gadamer.

But Lacan did not rely only on the theories of the above-mentioned persons, he was also indebted to Freud for his essay on narcissism.[7] By referring to Freud he gave an original meaning to the *cause* of paranoïa. In a note (57, #1) he gave the title of his thesis as *De la psychose paranoïaque dans ses rapports avec la personnalité* .[8] The director of the thesis, Professor Heuyer, wrote him a letter with one sentence of judgment on the text: "One swallow does not make a summer" ("spring" in French). He also said "in connection with my [Lacan's] bibliography, 'If you've read all that, I pity you.' In fact, I [Lacan] had read it all."[9] We also know that Lacan sent a copy of this thesis to Freud in England and received a post card from Freud saying that the thesis had reached him. This was the only contact ever made between the two psychoanalysts.

Lacan's thesis was published by Seuil in Paris in 1975 under the title given above. It still does not exist in English. Explaining that even though he referenced 30 cases in the thesis, Lacan said his main focus was on the paranoid incident concerning Aimée, a common woman who had pretentions to being a writer. Aimée became convinced that a famous actress was intent on kidnapping her baby son. One evening, when the actress exited from the theater, Aimée, who believed that the actress had taken her place as the celebrity Aimée thought she ought to be, stabbed her. She did not kill her, but was consequently incarcerated in an institution for the mentally ill.

Lacan was heavily criticized by Elisabeth Roudinesco in her second volume on the history of psychoanalysis, *The Battle of 100 Years*, [10] for a myriad of things. [11] Perhaps her skepticism regarding Lacan's teaching stemmed, at least in part, from his using the case of the young paranoid woman, Aimée A., as

Lacan called her. Not only did Aimée think the celebrity had plagiarized her literary journals and also believed her to be a threat to her young son. Roudinesco is known to have been a good friend of the adult analyst, Didier Anzieu (1923-1999), Aimée's son. Roudinesco may well have borne a grudge against Lacan for choosing Aimée's case to demonstrate the psychosis of paranoïa. This antipathy is reflected throughout her volume II.[12] Indeed, the Surrealist poets were as enthusiastic about Aimée's poetry as was Anzieu, the son. Later, Anzieu himself, unknowingly entered analysis with Lacan and withdrew quickly after the two discovered their proper identities. By 1986 Anzieu the analyst made his opposition to Lacanianism clear. Roudinesco says in her book that "few of Lacan's contemporaries discussed the thesis at all, or examined the theoretical and clinical consequence of the claims he made.... The only person to review it in depth upon its publication was Henri Ey (1932)" (Vanheule, p. 20). But Dr. Ey was not the only psychiatrist to praise Lacan's thesis. Pierre Janet too admired it. As mentioned above, Lacan's thesis owed a great debt to the psychiatrists of his generation and before. He referred frequently to Karl Jaspers who was also a philosophy professor and whose *General Psychopathology* was translated into French in 1928.[13] Jaspers influenced Lacan immensely. Indeed, Lacan was involved in editing the French version of Jaspers book from the German (Leguil, p. 34). Many theories and reflections in Lacan's thesis come directly from Jaspers treatment of psychosis, according to Leguil.[14] Even though many of Lacan's early ideas on psychopathology can be said to owe almost everything to Jaspers, Lacan's later ideas inscribe themselves against "the binary founder of *Psychopathologie générale*" (Leguil, C., 35). By the binary, Lacan means sciences of nature and those of the mind which owe a debt to both Max Weber and Wilhelm Dilthey. Max Weber (1864-1920) was a sociologist, philosopher, and a political economist who is credited, along with Ùmile Durkheim and Karl Marx, for giving birth to modern sociology. His method was antipositivistic and gave place to the study of social action through interpretive means, not empirical ones. He was interested in the purpose and meaning people attach to their own actions. Not surprisingly, Weber and Jaspers were great friends (*Wikipedia*). Weber wrote on many things, one of the most important being his idea that the Protestant aesthetic gave rise to capitalism.[15] Wilhelm Dilthey (1833-1911) argued that nature gives birth to law while the human sciences give rise to an understanding of human and historical life. His goal was to expand Immanuel Kant into a *Critique of Historical Reason* and do justice to the full scope of lived experience. [16] Lacan used ideas such as these to account for mental illness as attesting to a rupture with comprehensive communication. When he finally rejected this binary—between nature and mind—it was based on the idea that psychic *causality* came from the phenomena of the mind (Leguil, C., 35). In 1946 in "Presentation on Psychical Causality" (1946) Lacan defends his concept of what causes madness. This 1946 *Écrit* appeared as a "blasphemy opposed to Jasperian' orthodoxy which does not permit causality to mix with matters of the *sense of meaning* in order to become psychic" (Leguil, F., pp. 6-7). Lacan clearly separated himself from Jaspers' idea that madness could be conceived of as putting understanding itself into peril. If, for Jaspers, in 1913, "we do not know the causes" of mental illness (*General Psychopathology*, p. 438), Lacan, in 1946, finds a cause proper to psychosis. Indeed, Lacan's answer resembles one of Sartre's existential ideas; that of the original choice (Leguil, C., pp. 35-36). This precedes one of Lacan's future ideas—an orientation based on what he calls "the subject" (Leguil, C., p. 36). Lacan will argue that causality is an unconscious belief in some delirious idea. His theory is that there is a discourse on *being* defined as a contingent relation to meaning (Leguil, C., p. 77). While on the one hand madness comes from unconscious identifications, on the other, Lacan will say, it comes from a first choice made regarding one's mode of being (Leguil, C., p. 76). In *Seminar III* on *The Psychoses* Lacan says that "the big secret of psychoanalysis is that there is no psychogenesis." [17] Leguil stresses that Lacan has already hinted at this idea in 1946 when he says that the unfathomable decision of being is itself without cause. One can neither explain it nor understand it. Indeed, this very contingency of choice gives its human value to madness (Leguil, C., p. 77).

Later Lacan will attribute the decision to become psychotic to a child's primary identification with an overbearing mother who makes her infant everything to her, foreclosing the difference-in-being between herself, the infant, and the outside world; that is, she refuses to accept the law given by the third term of the father's name signifier. Yet, recently, Jacques-Alain Miller has argued that the father himself can sometimes be the cause of psychosis, as in the case of Daniel-Paul Schreber.[18] Interestingly, Leguil points out, Lacan finds in Sartre the formulation that permits him to recognize madness as a "psychic causality" against any organic cause (Leguil, C., pp. 36-37). This idea unites Lacan with Sartre, beyond their divergence regarding Freud (Leguil, C., p. 37). As Clotilde Leguil argues, Lacan's idea of an initial choice that is "contingent and unjustifiable" is, indeed, Sartre's description of the phenomenological *Être pour-soi* (p. 37).[19] Sartre had developed the idea of an original choice in 1943 and used it again in 1947 arguing that the free choices a person makes identify her totally with her destiny.[20] Although Lacan does not refer to Sartre as one of his antecedents, Clotilde Leguil makes clear in her book on Sartre with Lacan that the influence is clearly there in Lacan's early writings on madness.

The influence of Sartre—both pro and con—aside, Dr. Henri Ey thought Lacan's treatment of the Aimée case was brilliant. Although Lacan praised Dr. Ey in his "Presentation on Psychical Causality" for his intellectual support and for stressing the importance of studying madness (p. 125), he critiques him severely for his idea of "psychogenesis." Lacan argue that he and Dr. Ey were initially on the same side, but stresses that they have since parted company. Having praised Dr. Ey for his work applying Jackson,[21] Lacan points out that his view of mental problems is false, is "organicism." ("Presentation...," p. 124). Such a view is supported by theories of a mechanistic, Gestaltist,—all material theories wherein biology is the cause. This is why, Lacan claims, he has chosen as his master in psychiatry de Clérambault. He also cites Spinoza who claimed that "a true idea must agree with its object" ("Presentation...," p. 125).

Roudinesco gives no importance to Lacan's thesis, but does point out that Lacan, like Freud who forty years before him gave wide scope to hysteria as a psychic phenomenon, gave paranoia, and more generally psychosis, an important place within psychoanalysis. While Freud had long been perplexed by the cause of psychosis, Lacan gradually established a theory which was to be elaborated many times as to its cause and possible treatment. Lacan's earliest theories were based on the early idea that psychosis was rooted in psychic synthesis or "personality," a term Lacan would get rid of as he elaborated his notions of the ego and the subject (Roudinesco, p. 114). While Lacan thinks, like Sartre, that the subject is irreducible to any mechanistic idea of causality, he thinks, like Freud, that the subject is determined by his unconscious identifications (Leguil, C., p. 39). So far reaching were Lacan's early thoughts on paranoia in connection with the ego that he believed at the time of his thesis that the human ego itself was paranoiac. Once he began to work with the gaze in the 1960s, one can see why Lacan would link the divided nature of the ego—between the ideal ego and the ego ideal, as theorized in the Schema L—[give the schema from S. I-I will send you the scanned image of this schema from page 243 in S. II in English. I cannot do graphics myself.] to the power of the human gaze to make individuals paranoid in relation one to the other. But the human propensity to being sensitive to the Other's gaze is not the same as *clinical* paranoia in which the individual believes delusional things about others and the Other, not merely the imaginary fantasmatic ups and downs of jouissance regarding what the other/Other may think or say about us.

As I have said above, certain critics of Lacan's thesis have suggested that it is a rewriting of Karl Jaspers' *General Psychopathology*.[22] In *Seminar III* (1955-1956) Lacan takes issue with Jaspers in saying that Jaspers had a false notion of what "understanding" means. While he praises him for wanting to restore meaning to the chain of phenomena in a life, he finds no "common sense" or "*relation of understanding*" to general psychopathology in his work. Lacan had already begun such a critique of Jaspers in 1946.[23] Jaspers believed that certain things are self-evident, that sadness comes from lacking what one desires. Lacan's point is that one can have everything he or she desires and still be sad. Jaspers, interestingly enough, played an important role in Jean-Paul Sartre's early thoughts, as well as in Lacan's, although Jaspers' influence on Sartre fell prey to the same result as with Lacan; Sartre separated himself from Jaspers[24] by declaring that an individual's choices are free and existential.[25]

Although Lacan worked with a small group in the 1930s who called themselves members of the *Evolution Psychiatrique* (51, 3), Lacan makes it clear that his offspring—his articles and thesis—had nothing to do with the Surrealist environment of the moment which viewed his thesis as an inspiration for Salvador Dali's "critical paranoia" and René Crevel's *Le Clavacin de Diderot.* Crevel (1900-1935), a Surrealist homosexual writer, was influenced by Denis Diderot's (1713-1784) atheism, materialism, and idea of a "natural" freedom and wrote *Diderot's Harpsicord* in 1932 in praise of Diderot's ideas. Crevel, who was excluded from the Surrealist movement by André Breton for his homosexuality, was also an editor of the Enlightenment work called the *Encycopédie* in which religion was critiqued in footnotes.[26] Indeed, the cofounder and main editor of the *Encyclopedia* (28 vols.) was Diderot, also a philosopher and writer.[27] Although Lacan's own new ideas were published in the first issues of a Surrealist journal called *Minotaure*, they had no relation to Surrealism as David Macey erroneously claimed in his book, *Lacan in Contexts.*[28] Those works include "*Le probléme du style et la conception psychiatrique des forms paranoïaques de l'existence*" ("The Problem of Style...") which presents the thesis of "Schizographie" which argued in 1931 that the paranoïac experience and its world-view constitute an "original syntax." Macey claims that this view is similar to ideas of Salvador Dali (Macey, p. 213), rather than that Lacan's ideas influenced Dali.[29] Lacan also published "*Motifs du crime paranoïque: le crime des soeurs Papin*" ("Motives of Paranoiac Crime...") (57, #2). In this article Lacan talked about the press reports of the brutal murder of a lawyer's wife and her daughter by their servants, Léa and Christine Papin. But, more generally, Lacan's article relates to his theory of the cause of paranoïa. Macey claims that Lacan's article elevates the Papin sisters to the level of heroines, as did the Surrealists. But this is not true. Lacan argues, as is reprinted in his thesis, that the Papin sisters were narcissistic psychotics who were paranoid and that their crime comes from *this cause*. In no way does he praise the sisters (Macey, p. 213).[30] In Lacan's treatment of the Aimée case and the Papin sister case, one sees the difference between psychoanalytic thinking and creative intellectual theories.

Lacan considered the Papin sister crime at the end of his thesis, relating it to his use of Freud's work on narcissism which gave the stamp of originality to his thesis.[31] Freud made a distinction between ego instincts and object instincts which, for Lacan, changes the outlook on what can cause psychosis at all, that being, in one of his early thoughts, narcissistic identification. This distinction gave Lacan the foundation for his addition of the many psychological ideas to the biological theories in vogue that were seen as the cause of psychosis. It is of revolutionary importance that Lacan, finally, does not find the cause of psychosis in the physical organism itself. The idea that psychosis is organically caused is a view still held today by the International Psychoanalytic Association and its offshoots.

The Papin sister crime, committed in Le Mans, rocked France. Two sisters, Christine and Lea, maids and lovers, killed the wife of their employer, M. Lancelin, and the daughter, Geneviéve. The sisters had often donned the gowns and jewels of the ladies when they were out of their home. But the occasion of the crime was not a confrontation with the sisters over the clothes. Rather a blown fuse caused Mme. Lancelin to blame the event on the maids. An argument ensued and resulted in the sisters' beating the mother and daughter to death.[32] Lacan interpreted the crime as a narcissistic murder based on the sisters' inability to attain their own ego ideals represented to them by the wealthy mother and daughter, ideal egos. When the sisters were jailed and separated, each one became dramatically psychotic, showing that left alone neither could resist going into the alien graveyard of the Other—the sphere of language and society—itself a paranoid principle behind any ego structure.[33] (Cf. also Lacan's *De la psychose paranoïaque*..., pp. 389-398). While most interpretations of the Papin sister crime refer to a split between reality and fantasy, Lacan teaches that "reality" refers to any person's imaginary interpretation of the world (Ragland-Sullivan, "Jacques Lacan, Literary Theory, and *The Maids*...," p. 117). Lacan gradually comes up with different interpretations of the cause of psychosis. For example, the mother's *foreclosure* (*Verwerfung*) of the signifier of the father's name normally imposes the law of "no" and the sense of a *difference* existing between two individuals first linked by a symbiotic *sameness*. When this "no" is foreclosed, the child (can choose to) remain in a *mental* symbiosis with the primordial mother, a symbiosis which is retained as an mental Oneness throughout life for the child, obviating the dialectic of lack (ᴲ). That is, Lacan claimed that the learning of "no" and of limits teaches the human subject that it is not a totality, but a being who *lacks* wholeness. Psychosis can also be caused by a rejection of a cruel father as in the case of Daniel Paul Schreber.[34] But at the time of writing his thesis, Lacan was influenced by Freud's idea that narcissism was a cause, not by his own later theories that lack was itself an effect of ego division.

Lacan's "Logical Time and the Assertion of Anticipated certainty: A New Sophism" appeared in *Les Cahiers d'Art*. Lacan tells us that this article, which later appeared in the first version of his *Écrits* published by Seuil in Paris in 1966, was requested by Christian Zervos to fill up space in his journal during the period of 1940-1944.[35] Zervos (1889-1970) was an art critic, writer, and publisher who was known for his journal and for his Catalogue of Picasso's art. Lacan's sophism which appeared in this journal is a reply to the sophism posed by Jean-Paul Sartre. Lacan's point here is that the stake in deciding whether one of three prisoners—who cannot see their own backs—has a black or white disc on his or her back, and thus can leave the room on the basis of certainty, is not *time* per se, but an intersubjective judgment based upon observing the others' hesitating or waiting time. Calculations made within the gaze of the Other/other always concern an intersubjective calculation of the other's movements, words, experiences, in an effort to fit in with the Other's expectations. The first prisoner to figure out that none of the others can decipher the riddle any more than he or she can, exits the room. And so goes desire's calculations in intersubjective life situations for everyone.

The origin of Lacan's interest in paranoïa comes from the work of Gatean de Clérambault, whom he called his only master in psychiatry (51, 4). Lacan met de Clérambault who treated the criminally insane while he, Lacan, was Chief of Psychiatry at the Sainte Anne Hospital where he treated the mentally insane. Gatean de Clérambault (1872-1934) was the psychiatrist in charge at the Special Infirmary for the Insane of the Paris Prefecture of Police from 1910 to 1934. He believed that the fundamental cause of psychosis was *mental automatism*. He also believed that delusion underlies all forms of psychosis. In his view, delusions were derived from *elementary phenomena*. These were organic in origin according to him and included thought-echoes, verbal enunciations of actions, and forms of hallucination. De Clérambault's notion of "mental automatism" details a metaphorical, mechanistic ideology, then.[36] But, Lacan says in *Seminar III* that when de Clérambault analyzes elementary phenomena, he looks for their signature in serpiginous—that is in phenomena such as eruptions on the skin—structure and in neologisms (Lacan, p. 34). Lacan argued, later, against de Clérambault, that *elementary phenomena* are reducible to nothing other than themselves, the unconscious being the fundamental language, not as de Clérambault thought, simply a biologically imposed flaw. (S. III, p. 19). Lacan, thus, dispensed with de Clérambault's notion of "mental automatism" in *Seminar III.*[37] Yet, in *The Psychoses* Lacan tells us that de Clérambault's studies on the idea that toxic substances éaused psychosis was, at the time, original and indispensable. In his work on mental automatism, de Clérambault was innovative enough to claim that such automatism is "*that which doesn't correspond to a train of thought*" (S. III, p. 6). Lacan advanced the idea, rather, that linguistic metonymy lies at the basis of psychotic language and controls it, rather than metaphor.[38]

In an article entitled "Metaphor and Metonymy," Russell Grigg explains the difference between metaphor and metonymy as rethought by Lacan. Having explained that there are three types of metaphor: substitution, extension, and appositive, Grigg points out that Lacan's emphasis, unlike Roman Jakobson's[39] on other linguists, was on the new meaning created in metaphor (p. 68). In the article on Jakobson (1896-1982) just referenced, it is noted that he was both a linguist and literary theorist. Indeed, he was the pioneer of the structuralist vogue of language that influenced other fields as well until the end of the 1970s. Departing from Jakobson's structuralism, Lacan focused, rather, on Freud's use of condensation and displacement as dream techniques, using condensation for metaphor and displacement for metonymy.[40] Grigg takes up, not only Lacan's differences from Jakobson on the tropes of metaphor and metonymy, but, in addition, the importance Lacan gave similarity in metaphor and contiguity in metonymy. Metaphor can create something innovative, while metonymy depends upon a semantic implication in a sentence, such as "crown" for "king" (p. 69). In speaking of metonymy, Lacan even refers to "an effect of sense." In metaphor words replace one another — like one thing—rather than referring to a semantic relation of two (pp. 68-69). In psychotic language, the effect of something already there is necessary as opposed to the fascination of creating something strikingly different.

Not only did Lacan reshape Jakobson's ideas, he modified de Clérambault's as much as he did Freud's or any other thinker he cites. He also praised de Clérambault for having made psychological distinctions in the paranoïas, thus clearing up some of the fog and ambiguity that had surrounded the diagnosis of paranoïa (S. III, p. 18). Lacan also praised de Clérambault for having understood that the erotomaniacal delusion of a paranoïd individual is addressed to another so neutralized that he or she is inflated to occupy the dimensions of the world of the one deluded (S. III, pp. 18 and 43).[41] That is, a psychotic person is so influenced by his or her intimate other that no difference can be made between the psychotic's interpretation of what the other's thoughts are and those he or she has. The other, for a psychotic, does not manifest just one point of view, but the *only* point of view; that of the psychotic.

In his thesis, Lacan claimed that two bases are typical of psychosis: an intellectual deficit and an egocentric tendency (p. 381). His idea of intellectual deficit will change once he begins to study Daniel Paul Schreber's *Memoirs* and Freud's comments on them. These are represented in Lacan's *Seminar III*.[42] In trying to assess Aimée's subjective text, Lacan says the concept of "mental automatism" comes closer to what he would call a *structural* analysis than to any other clinical approach in French psychiatry (51, 5). What he meant by structure at this phase of his thinking is, however, based on the structuralism common to linguistics and anthropology that existed at that historical moment and bears no resemblance to his own later theories in which structure is topological.[43] Lacan's early notion of structure was put forward in a period when he called the basis of any *repeated* phenomenon "structural." For Lacan, de

Clérambault brought a breath of fresh air into the problems of semiology, however, as manifested by writers such as Roland Barthes who, interestingly, insisted that one word matched one thing. Lacan spoke of a determinism in semiology that he rejected as it became ever more enmeshed in problems of rationality as shown in Barthes' efforts to undermine realism for its prolific descriptions of things.[44] One might even suggest that Barthes's efforts to reduce one thing to one meaning is a symptom of psychosis evident in his language.[45] Such rigid, metonymic use of language is common to psychotics.[46] Their use of language is literal and concrete, lacking the substitutive flow that characterizes metaphor.

At this point Lacan compares de Clérambault's thought to Michel Foucault's *Naissance de la Clinique : une archéologie du regard médical* (57, #3). [47] Foucault's point of view, developed further in *The Order of Things*,[48] uses archeology to describe the moment when a field of knowledge becomes an *épistemé* that reorganizes knowledge. For example, the nineteenth century differed from the eighteenth century and before when theological leanings supported theories of knowledge. The new field of knowledge which Foucault places under the medical gaze, separates body from identity, thus becoming able to exercise an almost magical power of healing over the biological organism. Today, one can critique this field of knowledge which has taken on a totalizing power that has ultimately led to a biological reductionism in the practice of modern medicine, especially in the USA.[49] But as early as 1931, Lacan, arguing against organicism as cause, was awarded his diploma of "médicine légist" which qualified him as a forensic psychiatrist (Macey, p. 211).

Having praised de Clérambault, Lacan says that his influence on his own thinking came from an even higher caliber of genius than de Clérambault's, that of de Clérambault's teacher, Emil Kraeplin (1856-1926), a German psychiatrist (52, 3)[50] (S. III, p. 17). Kraeplin was considered the founder of modern scientific psychiatry as well as of psychopharmacology and psychiatric genetics. Biological and genetic malfunctions cause mental illness, according to him. His influence over early 20th century psychiatry was replaced by Freud's influence later on.[51] Although Kraeplin argued against Freud's theories of psychological causes of organic illnesses, maintaining, rather, that the cause was biological, he, nonetheless, led Lacan to Freud (52, 4). As we know, Sigmund Freud (1856-1939) is the father of psychoanalysis. But before founding psychoanalysis, he was a neurologist, a medical doctor, who started his work on aphasia, cerebral palsy, neuroanatomy, and so on. So advanced was his early medical work that he was named "Professeur Extraordinaire" in 1902. Some of the ideas he created later as he developed psychoanalysis are detailed in the twenty-eight volumes of his *Standard Edition of Psychology*:[52] free association, transference, the Oedipus complex, the importance of dreams and wishes, the unconscious, repression, the libido, the death drive, narcissism, and so on.[53]

In his own early career Lacan wrote a paper entitled "Structure des psychoses paranoïaques" which was published in the *Semaine des Hopitûax de Paris* on July 7, 1931 on pages 437-445 (Macey, p. 211). The paper identifies three types of paranoid psychosis: constitutional paranoïa, delusion of interpretation, and emotional delusions. While the typology owes much to Clérambault, Lacan's notion of structure begins to displace de Clérambault's idea of a mental-automatism syndrome as the central category that causes paranoïa. Nonetheless, Clérambault accused Lacan of plagiarism even though Lacan had called him his master (Macey, p. 211). Lacan's next paper was co-authored with J. Lévi-Valensi and P. Rigault and entitled "Écrits 'inspirés': Schizographie". It was based on a paper he had read to the Société Médico-Psychologique on November 12th of 1931. Lévi-Valensi had become known for his work on pulmonary disease and sleep apnia.[54] Rigault is not remembered. Lacan's co-authored paper was subsequently published in *Annales Médico-Psychologiques* in December of 1931. It was also republished in his thesis, *De la Psychose paranoïaque dans ses rapports avec la personnalité...*[55] . It examined one of the thirty cases included in his thesis, that of "Marcelle C.," a primary-school teacher who was diagnosed at the Psychiatric Clinic as suffering from erotomania, paranoid delusions, and mental automatism. Lacan argued in this paper that certain forms of language can be symptomatic of the evolution and internal mechanisms of psycho-pathological conditions. He even compared certain Surrealist experiments in automatic writing with the writings of "Marcelle" (Macey, p. 211).

Roudinesco claims that Lacan's thesis drew no attention other than that of Dr. Henri Ey. Lacan was, nonetheless, awarded a bronze medal and a "*mention très honorable*" for his thesis which was published in Paris by Le Franćois in 1932.[56] Not only Dr. Ey, but Surrealist poets and Pierre Janet commented favorably on it as well.[57] Janet's approval is important. He (1859-1947) was a pioneer in psychology, psychiatry, and philosophy. His specialties were dissociation and traumatic memory. He is ranked with William James as one of the founding fathers of psychology. He had studied under Jean-Martin Charcot at the Psychiatric Laboratory in Pitié Salpêtrière Hospital in Paris and earned a degree in medicine in 1893. He was appointed a lecturer at the Sorbonne in 1898 and lectured at the Collége de France until 1936. He was one of the first to connect past events of a subject's life with present-day traumas and he coined the terms "dissociation" and "subconscious," as well as anticipating the idea of transference.[58]

Lacan, gratified by such interest, is known for risking a bold proposal: that Aimées's psychosis was one of self-punishment. But despite his marks of originality, Lacan himself was ambivalent toward his thesis. In 1933 he said that the originality of his work stemmed from the fact that it represented the first effort in France to present an exhaustive study of the mental phenomenon of paranoid delusions based on the concrete history of the subject.[59] Although he referred frequently to his thesis, in 1969 he said that he would blush to see it reprinted and in 1980, he said that it was with great reluctance that he had allowed it to be reprinted in 1975.[60] In 1975 he explained his reluctance by stating that there is no relationship between paranoid psychosis and personality; they are the same thing.[61] This idea makes more sense if one studies the more recent diagnostic category advanced by Jacques-Alain Miller on ordinary psychosis.[62]

The clinic which drew Lacan was that of the symptom's *formal envelope*.[63] Miller speaks of the connections of his antecedents—de Clérambault, Kraeplin, and Freud—as impressing Lacan with their "faithfulness to the formal envelope of the symptom." Lacan said in the *Écrit* that Miller mentions that the psychotic symptom swings back to creative effects. In his thesis, Lacan cites the Aimée case where artistic writings abound. He compliments Aimée by saying there was a high enough quality in her writings to allow one to mention the famous Surrealist poet, Paul Éluard, who collected her works under the (reverent) heading of involuntary poetry (52, 5).[64] Paul Éluard (1895-1952), first a Dadaist and then a Surrealist, and finally a Communist, became known for his poetry on women as revealed in *L'Amour la Poésie* (1929) and *La vie immédiate* (1932), among many other works, where he invokes woman's mysterious charm. And Éluard's interest in woman and creativity is built upon in Lacan's work on the psychoses where he explains that much creative poetry comes from the use of the literary trope, metonymy, which Lacan links to psychotic language.[65] (Cf. S. III: chs. XVII and XVIII, pp. 214-230).

Lacan complimented Aimée on demonstrating the function of ideals in a series of reduplications—herself/the actress, etc.—and says that the notion of structure works in this case, perhaps, as the imaginary reduplication that lies behind Aimée's psychotic act. This idea of a *structure* seems to him to be more fruitful for understanding Aimée's paranoïa than what the clinicians of the 1920s, who followed the psychiatric ideas of Édouard Toulouse (1865-1947), would have advanced. Indeed, such psychiatrists lowered the value of Aimées's work by inscribing it simply in passion (52, 6). Toulouse had become a doctor by writing a thesis on melancholy which resulted in his creating the "*Ligue d'hygiène mentale*" in 1920. In 1996 the group inspired by Toulouse became known as the "*Ligue francaise pour la santé mentale*". Stressing the importance of both social and emotional impact on the mental, Toulouse was influential, even on the Sainte Anne Hospital where Lacan was to become the Chief of Psychiatry.[66]

Although Lacan in no way owes a debt to Toulouse, one might do well to remember that Jacques-Alain Miller has called Lacan's early notions of structure Lacan's *own* myth.[67] We recall that the act that led Aimée to a mental hospital was her violent effort to stab to death the famous movie star with whom she identified. We also recall that Aimée, whose real name was Marguerite Pantaine Anzieu had developed the delusion that the actress named Huguette Duflo wanted to harm her son and was plagiarizing her literary work (Vanheule, p. 14; Lacan, 1932, p. 157). Interestingly, Aimée ceased to have her erotomanic delusion about Duflo—erotomanic in Lacan's thought including jealousy and revenge as motives—following her act of aggression against the actress.[68] Lacan says this initial identificatory redoubling was a kind of conjugation of her poetic space which later appeared in her copious writings (52, 7). That is, her paranoid delusion later took up residence in writing, rather than in relation to another person.

The Aimée incident took place in the 1930s. And Lacan says that studying it brought him closer to understanding"acting out" *(passage à l'acte)*. That is, one may *fantasize* murder as in "acting out," but to commit it, or try to, plays on another register of structure than imaginary fantasy; it concerns the dimension of the real wherein there is actually "passage to the act." The structure in question in passing to the act would be that of psychosis which Lacan elaborates as paranoïa in his thesis. Although such a structure, at this early stage in his theorization of the cause of psychosis, would be rooted in imaginary fantasy—which belongs later to the category of neurosis—Lacan took up the idea of punishment, the wish to commit an aggression against oneself, as related to the fact that psychotics often commit suicide .[69] And Lacan explains this "passage to the act" by the word "self punishment," a word he first heard from Franz Alexander and Hugo Staub. These Berlin-style criminologists, as well as psychiatrists, also led Lacan to Freud, as did Kraeplin. Alexander (1891-1964) was the more famous of the two men. He was a physician and a psychoanalyst and was considered to be the founder of psychosomtatic medicine and psychoanalytic criminology. He is also credited with being the forerunner to Erik Erikson's work. Hugo Staub is known mostly for his co-authorship with Alexander of *The Criminal, the Judge, and the Public: A Psychological Analysis*.[70] The reason Lacan could be so affected by German criminology and psychiatry, and eventually by Freud's oeuvre, was that he was fluent in German. Indeed, he had won the French national prize at his Lycée, École Stanislaus, for his excellent performance in the German language.

The "self" punishment in question regarding Aimée would be a reaction to *not being* what she imagined herself to be as a symbolic ego ideal, something based not only in the imaginary, but in the Other as well. Indeed, in "On Narcissism: An Introduction" (1914), Freud made a cursory reference to a distinction between the ego ideal and the ideal ego as belonging to group psychology.[71] On pages 102-103 of the *SE* Freud writes that narcissistic object-relations can veer towards group psychology in the case when one's ego does not fulfill its own ideal. He thinks the "self punishment" in question appears as a kind of guilt or fear of punishment by the parents, or as a fear of losing their love, especially in cases of homosexuality. Lacan says, rather, that no one "is" who one imagines oneself to be narcissistically in the Other; that is, organic functions cannot explain the "specific cause of psychosis" (52, 8) (1932, p. 347). Lacan's point is that if one kind of knowledge [*connaissance*] can provide evidence of another function, this leads to a richness of understanding that no academic or avant-garde thinker could resist (52, 9): He says "the original experience that determines psychosis is the one which reveals to a subject his own insufficiency, humiliating him at the ethical level" (1932, p. 92). He will, of course, modify this idea of the cause of psychosis rather quickly. Indeed, Aimée's act concerned an inability to distinguish herself from an imaginary other as Vanheule argues in the first chapter of his book (*The Subject...*: 17). But Aimée had another paranoid motive other than just her jealousy of the actress. Her fear regarding the safety of her son was traceable to the still-birth of her first baby, a girl.

In thinking about how psychoanalysis should be rethought and practiced, Lacan argued against the knowledge-based biases. He argued that they must be eliminated and replaced by the analyst's *listening* to language itself. That, says Lacan, is fundamental to psychoanalysis. The later Lacan will argue that the psychotic is *invaded* by jouissance. But in the 1930s, Lacan's notion of knowledge was phenomenological. "In the beginning of his career Lacan was particularly influenced by phenomenology. His dissertation [or thesis] explored the 'human significance' of psychosis and attributed the paranoid psychoses to phenomena of personality and to a dialectical movement of the psyche, as against deterministic genetic and environmental factors. If it were not for his special attention to psychotic language and to narcissism..., one could read this 1932 text as a prefiguration of R. D. Laing's existential-phenomenological psychoanalysis. By 1936, however, Lacan had enunciated his basic concept of the mirror stage, which he...describe[d] in 1949 as formative of the function of the '*I*'" (Ragland-Sullivan, "The Maids...," p.100). Lacan says in "*On My [Our] Antecedents*" that he had not really thought about the fantasies that existed regarding the idea of what the ego is until 1936 when he presented his paper on "The Mirror Stage as Formative of the I Function as Revealed in Psychoanalytic Experience" (52, 11). In a note at the end of this *Écrit* he tells us that he presented this paper at the Congress in Marienbad (August 3, 1936), making his first pivotal intervention into psychoanalysis even before having received the title of analyst (52, 11). Even though he contributed some of the theses contained in this mirror-stage piece to a volume of the *Encyclopédie* franéaise, as requested by Henri Wallon (1938), he did not give a written rendition to the Report on the Congress (57, #4). [72]

In his article given to the French encyclopedia, Lacan argued that "concrete psychology" must be supplemented by a reference to ethnography, history, law, etc., and that psychoanalysis itself has to adapt to the resultant complex theoretical framework. He also refers to an account of the mirror-stage paper in which he acknowledges a debt to Wallon (1879-1962).[73] Wallon was a social and developmental psychologist, a Marxist communist politician, a physician who worked with mentally retarded children from 1908-1931. He was also a Professor at the Sorbonne, The École Pratique des Hautes études, and the Collége de France.[74] Lacan's chapter on the "complex" given to Wallon draws on his own earlier work and anticipates the *Écrit* "Aggressivity in Psychoanalysis" (1948).[75] In the text given to Wallon, Lacan talks about the weaning complex, an intrusion complex, and the Oedipus complex. He defines "complex" as an ensemble of reactions ranging from emotion to behavior that is adapted to its object. The complex reproduces ambient reality within which the subject develops in two ways: Lacan represents the subject's development insofar as it is distinct from earlier stages in the subject's own psychical existence, and also insofar as it reproduces elements the complexes supposedly "fixes." What is fixed, requires a greater objectification of reality, according to Macey (p. 216). The "complex" is an early formation of what Lacan will later call structure. But in what he gave Wallon he refers to anthropology and sociology, to Malinowski, Frazer, and Durkheim (Macey, p. 216). Bronislaw Malinowski (1884-1942) was a Polish anthropologist, as well as one of the most important ethnographers in the 20th century. He worked in many exotic places, including the Trobriand Islands. After World War I when he was able to leave Australia and return to England, he became Chair of Anthropology at the London School of Economics. From 1933 to his death he taught at Yale University.[76] Sir James Frazer (1854-1941) was a Scottish social anthropologist who influenced the modern study of mythology and comparative religion. His most important book, *The Golden Bough* (1890) argues that society goes through three phases: from primitive magic, to religion, to science. Not only did Frazer study the classics, he also studied the law at Trinity University and later lectured at Cambridge and Oxford. He was influenced by the work of Claude Lévi-Strauss who was one of the developers of the concept of structure in vogue at this time. But, historically speaking, Darwinian evolutionary thought was chosen over Frazer's own picture of social evolution.[77] Émile Durkheim (1858-1917) was a sociologist, social psychologist, and a philosopher. Along with Max Weber and Karl Marx, he is said to be the father of sociology. He set up the first European department of sociology. His interest in epistemological realism took him from Auguste Comte's positivism to a hypothetico-deductive model. He argued that sociology was a science of institutions and that society at large was a "collective consciousness." His theory of social realism used empiricism over Descartes' method of mind. He taught at the University of Bordeaux in 1887 and became Chair of Education at the Sorbonne in 1902 and Chair of Education and Sociology in 1913. His goal remained to discover the inherent nature of society's laws.[78]

In chapter two of his article on "The Family," discussed above, Lacan takes up hysteria as represented in Freud, but more importantly, he develops his own findings regarding psychosis. In this vein he discusses the ego and its imaginary structures.

His major reference to "concrete psychology" owes a debt to Georges Politzer (1903-1942) and his *Critique des fondements de la psychologie* [79] (Macey, p. 216). Politzer was a philosopher and a Marxist theoretician of Hungarian origin. After meeting Sigmund Freud and Sandor Ferenczi (1873-1933) in Vienna, he decided to move to Paris in 1921. We know that Ferenczi was at first a close friend of Freud's and that he later separated himself from Freud based on theoretical disagreements. He has been said to have influenced some Lacanians with his ideas on interpersonal relations.[80] He is not, however, one of Lacan's antecedents, while Politzer was. Politzer taught a class on communism—that is, on dialectical materialism—while at the university in Paris. Although his masters were Karl Marx and Vladimir Lenin, he also studied psychology in a Freudian vein. Thus, his influence on Lacan brought to bear not only Freud, but Marx and Lenin, indirectly. Politzer was arrested for his communism in 1942 and was tortured and executed by a Nazi firing squad, while his wife was sent to Auschwitz and died there.[81] We know that Karl Marx (1818-1883) was a philosopher, economist, revolutionary socialist, journalist, and the author of two history-changing books. His work on economics laid the basis for our current understanding of labour and its relation to capital. As a founder of socialism, Marx put forth a materialist concept of history. He moved from Germany to Paris in 1843 where he met Friedrich Engels who was to become his treasured colleague. Marx was exiled from France in 1849 and moved to London where he put forth his ideas on class struggle. He came to define communism as a classless revolt of the working class against the bourgeoisie and the aristocracy.[82] Vladimir Lenin (1870-1924) was a Russian communist revolutionary and a political theorist. He became Head of the Russian Socialist Republic from 1917 to 1922 when he became the Leader of the Soviet Union until his death. He has been seen paradoxically as the champion of workers, as well as a dictator.[83]

In "Presentation of Psychical Causality" (1946), speaking of his presentation of the mirror-stage paper at Marienbad, Lacan says that "with the fourth stroke of the ten-minute mark, at which I was interrupted by Ernest Jones who was presiding over the Congress....[even though] the members of the Viennese group...gave my exposé a rather warm reception," he felt Jones' rebuff.[84] One can only imagine that Jones' behavior, given that he was the President of the London Psychoanalytic Society, contributed to Lacan's decision not to publish the mirror-stage piece in the Congress proceedings. Jones' rudeness brought Lacan face to face with a kind of resistance to his theory and technique which presented an even greater problem than he had imagined (52, 11; 53).[85] Macey says that there was no public discussion of Lacan's paper at the Congress attended by 198 participants (p. 214). The paper he read at Marienbad at the 14th Congress of the International Psychoanalytical Association on August 3rd, 1936, was entitled "Le Stade du miroir , Théorie d'un moment structurant et génétique de la constitution de la réalité, conêu en relation avec l'expérience et doctrine psychoanalytique." It was indexed in the *International Journal of Psycho-Analysis* as "The Looking Glass Phase" (Macey, p. 214)[86] Lacan tells us in "On My [Our] Antecedents" that the version included in the *Écrits* dates from 1949 (p. 67, n. 1/ Fink, p. 52, n. 4, p. 57; cf. also pp. 147-148).

In "Beyond the Reality Principle" (August-October, 1936), Lacan thought it propitious to offer a paper, later published as an *Écrit*, about which he says that his students sometimes think they have found in his writing what was already there, but which he himself had not yet developed. In this paper Lacan criticizes Freud's metapsychology, pointing out that Freud saw the libido both as an energetic concept and as a substantialist hypothesis which relates phenomena to matter (*Écrits*, Fink, p. 73). In Lacan's own view of language as sketched out in "Beyond the Reality Principle," he says it is the only imprudence that has never failed him; that of trusting in nothing but the experience of the subject in analytic work. Lacan's "Beyond..." paraphrases Freud's "Beyond the Pleasure Principle" (1920) where the Viennese analyst gave a new meaning to repetition in his concept of primary process.[87] Moreover, Freud related it to what Lacan would call the jouissance of masochism, opening it up onto the question of the death drive. All this is linked to Freud's idea of a secondary process which allows reality to be established in response to the pleasure principle's need for satisfaction by the means of homeostasis (53, 5). Such a view of reality could not be more removed from Lacan's concepts of lack and loss that place an incompletion at the heart of being.

Freud, meanwhile, believed that some final wholeness could be attained in psychoanalysis. Indeed, *Beyond the Pleasure Principle* reoriented Freud's project by assuming that the psychoanalytic act transcends the secondary process to attain a reality not produced in it, even though it gets rid of the illusion that the identity of thoughts can be attached to themselves (53, 8). What the primary process encounters is not what Freud thought, Lacan says, but the *impossible* itself (53, 9). We know that the "impossible" is one definition Lacan gives of the real. But in Freud's work on the primary process, Lacan interprets him as offering a beginning of the *imaginary* dimension whose images are associated with the symbolic and the real and will decorate them. He wrote this just before his "Rome Discourse" (1953)[88] where he said that pots, for example, are empty because they are symbolic, *symbolic* meaning only the word that designates a thing, not the thing itself (54, 2).

Nothing in the subject corresponds to a reality system, Lacan says, or to some typical function of reality (54, 3). The confusion regarding what "reality" is corresponds to a theory of the ego based on Freud's *Group Psychology and the Analysis of the Ego* (1921). There is nothing more in this text than a theory of identification, Lacan maintains (54, 3). Moreover, "Group Psychology"[89] derives from Freud's "On Narcissism" (1914) (54, 4).[90] Orthodox Freudians combine *Wirklichkeit* and *Realitét* which Freud meant as psychical, not some external objective system, Lacan says. The error that arises from those analysts' interpretations of Freud's ideas on reality is not only a confusion between "true seeming" and one's own perception of reality, but a reduction of the ego to itself. Freud does not show *how* the ego is formed, but simply states that it exists (54, 5). Freud then linked the ego to the perception-consciousness system, pointing out that its political forms have tested truth standards of this system (54, 7). Yet, Lacan points out that Freud calls such standards of truth into reference by linking the ego to one's own body—via narcissism—and to the complexity of Freud's three orders of identification (54, 6).

Lacan's mirror stage establishes a decisive moment between the imaginary and the symbolic in a temporal moment when an individual's being and thought are captured by an historic inertia. The responsibility for this lies with what calls itself psychology (55, 1). In critiquing the term "psychology," Lacan did not develop his "Beyond the 'Reality Principle'" as an attack on Gestalt theory and phenomenology. Instead he attacked the notion of psychology that was practiced by the second generation of analysts after Freud (59, 1). Instead of becoming bogged down in such historical notions as theirs, Lacan stressed the moments or phases of "configuring insight*" (55, 3). In Lacan's teaching, the dynamic of the first phase that configures the ego develops out of a biological crisis, based on the diachronic effects that happen to human animals. There is a delayed coordination of the nervous system that derives from man's neurological and physical *prematurity* at birth, in comparison with other animals who can forage for food almost from the beginning of life.[91] And there is an anticipation of the resolution of this particular delay as one watches a human baby go through its various stages of the oral, anal, scopic, and invocatory partial drives to finally become a speaking being (55, 4). But there is no "developmental" harmony in a human being, Lacan maintains, as has been proposed by ethology, "ethology" being the alleged scientific and objective study of animal behavior which usually focuses on behavior under natural conditions. This field of study has evolved into a branch of inquiry dealing with human character and with theories concerning its formation and evolution (55,5).[92] Psychological harmony, as proposed by some ethologists, masks the fact, Lacan says, that in being, *lack* plays a central role. Since lack is created by the first signifier, the phallic one which marks sexual difference as a third thing, an effect of difference itself ,[93] it must have a place in a causal chain from which a subject functions (55, 6). So powerful is this lack-in-being that Lacan places it at the heart of causal noesis—mental capacity or action—which mistakes itself for crossing into reality; that is for passing into the real. [94] For example, a little boy of four years old says "only boys can kiss girls." He has heard this at school. For him this statement becomes a signifier which forms not only his symbolic and imaginary dimensions of understanding, but also marks his sexual politics in the real. When he sees a girl kiss a girl, the function of *lack* (which belies one's knowing it all) raises its head and confronts him with a problem which has been repressed in his real, absent to his consciousness, leaving him with the words that make up his *parlêtre*.

The imaginary discordance between a lack in the order of one's signifiers and "reality" means that more is in play in thought and language than the mirror-stage critical lack which is covered over by, and functions as, the secret to an infant subject's jubilation. On the inverse side of the little boy mentioned above, one can say that when he kisses a girl, he does so with a certain jubilation from the real which makes this sexual act licit for him (55, 8). If he kisses a boy, he would be told by his unconscious that this was an illicit act. Of course, the context is cultural. I merely cite this example in the developing thought of a very young child. Indeed, ego judgments made from the imaginary must stem from another order as well (55, 9). Lacan says "order" at this stage of his thought. He will later say dimension or level or chain or link; not order.[95] In "On My [Our] Antecedents," Lacan says that If analysis stopped at the imaginary level, then the function of ego judgment would remain mythical. To find this in the mirror stage, Lacan says one must take up the imaginary definition of metonymy: the part is mistaken for the whole (55, 11). Thus, metonymy could refer to archaic partial images of the fragmented body as confirmed by the paranoid phase in the phenomenology of Kleinian experience (55, 11) where the breast as a partial object determines, according to Klein, whether or not an infant is given the basis for a healthy adult life by having been given a good breast, or a pathological life by having been given a bad breast. Melanie Klein (1882-1960) was the co-founder of object relations theory, the founder of child development psychoanalysis. Analyzed by Karl Abraham and a close colleague of Ernst Jones in London, she clashed with Anna Freud in the 1940s, splitting the British psychoanalytic school.[96] At the phase of his thought in the *Écrit* on his antecedents, we remember that Lacan was still a member of the International Psychoanalytic Association and would quite probably not want to offend the importance given by his fellow analysts to Melanie Klein's theories.

Nonetheless, Lacan placed the most powerful images of the mirror-stage experience here, in metonymy. He says that for an infant to assume an image of what its body looks like in the mirror concerns evanescent objects, those which appear in the exchange of gazes, for example, which occur when the child turns back to look towards the one holding it and is sees himself as *there* only in reference to the presence of this other (56, 1). This is the moment when the unconscious count from one to two begins in infant perception. Here Lacan refers to a movie which knew nothing of his theories. In this movie a naked little girl looked at herself in the mirror and surreptitiously touched herself in the place where there was no phallus (56, 2). Such an action would result from an imaginary perception of the sexual difference of organs common to young childhood, not to any superiority of the male penis.

No matter what covers the image infant's image of itself in the mirror, the cover commands a deceptive power in diverting alienation—that is, alienation behind words and images already situated in the Other's field—towards the imaginary totalitarian rivalry which prevails for the infant. Lacan says this is because the one like him or her (the *semblable*) fascinates him in a kind of *depressive*, in Klein's thinking, return. The idea of a depressive return resonates with the second phase of Melanie Klein's teaching wherein an infant's development includes hate and love for the mother which gradually, emerges into guilt and mourning—depression—as the infant comes to see itself as "whole." But Lacan disagrees with Klein here, saying that this view offers the figure of a Hegelian murder.[97] That is, two become one—thesis and antithesis merge into a synthesis—and each is cancelled out in a merging and synthesis of bodies. Who is who? Who controls the other? Of course, Lacan did not agree with either view, neither Klein's nor Hegel's [Macey on "Beyond...," pp. 214-215]. As mentioned above in the article on Hegel (1770-1831), he was the German philosopher his historicist and idealist thought shaped continental philosophy and Marxism in the period of his writing Phenomenology of Mind (1807) and other works. It is with his dialectic that Lacan disagrees, with the idea that thesis and antithesis end up in an endless series of syntheses making pseudo-totalities.

When Lacan speaks of alienation into the Other which turns toward an imaginary other, alienation means that one is represented to him or herself by the images and signifiers that first mark him as "this" or "that" and which gradually make up the memory bank—or Other—of his first perceptions and conceptions of who he or she is. The infant's first *misrecognition* of itself in the mirror stage is the confusion of who is who, or how to count unconsciously from two to one. The infant confuses its first sense of not being separate from its mother, or primordial caretaker, in early perception. Two are experienced as one. Lacan argues that it takes three—the image of a third other who is perceived as breaking up the original symbiosis of mother and infant—to make the infant realize that he or she is one, not a combination of two.[98] There is also a right-left inversion which takes place. The idea of this inversion, Lacan says, could only take on meaning in a more in-depth discussion of spatial orientation and he refers this to philosophy, saying nothing has been done there since Kant's basing an aesthetics on the reversal of a glove. And this aesthetics is as simple as turning the glove back around, Lacan says (56, 4). Lacan seems to be referring to Kant's idea that the whole conditions the parts, ultimately providing a unity of philosophy by way of *a prioris* and a transcendental sphere. In his later topological work, Lacan will develop a complex teaching concerning the interconnection of within and without, inside and outside, as well as many other concepts which reconceptualize the meaning of space in human thought and perception.

However, the problematic of inversion leads us away from the sphere of vision itself, Lacan points out, to the one in which the blind man knows he is the object of others' gazes. It takes us also to William Molyneux's problem in which a difference is noted between the philosophically inclined blind man and the fiction of the blind philosopher (1656-1698).[99] As an aside, Molyneux's wife became blind when she was very young and died young.[100] Molyneux (1656-1698) was an Irish natural philosopher and a writer on politics. He was considered a major leader in the 17th century Scientific Revolution. One of his publications takes up the question of England's power over Ireland. The work was condemned as seditious, although Molyneux himself was considered the founder of the Dublin Philosophical Society. [101] His published problem on the blind man who regains sight was taken up by John Locke (1632-1704) in his *Essay*.[102] Locke was an English philosopher and physician. He was one of the most influential Enlightenment thinkers, the alleged father of classical liberalism. His work on social contract theory made him one of the first British empiricists. Not only did his work affect political philosophy and epistemology, it also influenced the American Declaration of Independence. His theory of mind is said to have developed the idea of a self or identity in which there was a continuation of consciousness which filled in the blanks of knowledge given that babies are born, according to Locke, tabula rasa, with no internal knowledge. He argued that knowledge comes from sense perception. It would be this idea that led Lacan to take up Locke's mention of Molyneux in his *An Essay on Conscious Human Understanding* (1690).[103] The problem addressed by Lacan was the idea of blindness as something which would cause one to imagine an ego in a world where nothing is known about planar symmetry. (56, 5). Given his early references to inversion and planar symmetry, it is not surprising that Lacan's later work took a topological turn.

This idea brings Lacan to the phenomenon of specular knowledge (*connaissance*) based on a semiology, the study of signs, that runs from depersonalization to the hallucination of one's double. These have no diagnostic value, even with psychotics, Lacan claims. However, Rosine and Robert Lefort gave evidence of the splitting or doubling of body image that happens in psychosis in their book, *The Birth of the Other*.[104] I think of an example of a patient of my own who had a psychotic break and saw himself walking toward himself, a person identical to himself, except for his being an African American, while my patient was Caucasian. Lacan says these experiences, nonetheless, give a consistent reference point for fantasy in psychoanalytic treatment (56, 6). He is speaking of fantasy here in his text, but doubling in psychosis would concern, rather, hallucination. Lacan is situating his texts, his own texts in a future perfect so that one will know that he had inserted the unconscious into language. In seeing these texts spread out over the years, he says there are not many of them and he can be reproached for having been slow (56, 7). But during this early period in the 1930s and 1940s, Lacan said he had to gain a following and prepare for an audience.

At the time that Lacan was doing his psychiatric residency, there were only three persons interested in psychoanalysis, he tells us (57, 1). Even though he credits this little group, *Évolution Psychiatrique*, which he began attending regularly in 1933, with psychoanalysis's ever having seen the light of day in France, these few people did not call psychoanalysis, as it was conceptualized or practiced at the time, into question. He refers to their lack of interest in worldly matters—which might refer to World War I—and says that such major events did not even confirm a solidarity among them or give a basis for their information (57, 1). Furthermore, there was no teaching on psychoanalysis at this time other than a "fast-track" which existed prior to 1951 when Lacan began his own teaching in a private capacity, even before he began giving his public Seminars to his colleagues in 1953-1954 (57, 2). After the War, he says, the quantity of recruits changed and the crowd who came to hear him give his paper on "Training Analysis" was by standing-room only ((57, 3). Lacan tells us that this crowd attests to the important role he played in launching psychoanalysis in France. But prior to the event where the first crowds came to hear Lacan, the only person interested in his work, he said, was Jean Wahl who invited him to speak at the *Collége Philosophique*. Later Lacan was to publish the "Individual Myth of the Neurotic," referring to Claude Lévi-Strauss's work on myth. This text appeared in French in 1953 and was translated into English in 1979[105] (57, #6). Nonetheless, prior to 1953, Lacan put forth a resumé of his published work dated 1933. He first published this "Exposé..." as an appendix to his article "De la Psychose," and reprinted it in his thesis.[106]

Lacan finishes this introductory view of himself by saying that what is biographical is owed only to his wish to enlighten the reader about his antecedents (57, 5).

Endnotes

1 *Lacan, J.*"On My Antecedents"* (1966/2006). This is the title given in (Trans.) Fink, B. Fink, H. and Grigg, R. *Écrits*. New York: Norton & Co. In the French version Lacan calls this Écrit *"De **nos** antécédents"* ("On **Our** Antecedents"), pp. 65-72 in French; pp. 51-57 in English.

2 Vanheule, S. (2011) *The Subject of Psychosis: A Lacanian Perspective.* New York: Palgrave Macmillan, p. 9.

3 "Henri Claude," *Wikipedia, the free encyclopedia*, March 11, 2014.

4 "Gaetean de Clérambault," *Wikipedia, the free encyclopedia,* Nov. 3, 2014.

5 David Macey, *Lacan in Contexts (*1988), Verso: London and New York, pp. 210-211.

6 "Karl T. Jaspers," *Wikipedia, the free encyclopedia*, Dec. 31, 2014.

7 Freud, S. "On Narcissism: An Introduction," *SE*, vol. XIV, pp. 73-107.

8 Lacan, J. (1932/1975) *De la psychose paranoïaque dans ses rapports avec la personnalité.* Paris: Seuil. It first appeared in Paris: Le Franćois.

9 Lacan, J. (1957-1958/2006) "On a Question Prior to Any Possible Treatment of Psychosis." (Trans.). Fink, B. et al. *Écrits.* New York: Norton & Co.: Cf. note # 5, p. 486.

10 Roudinesco, E. (1986). *La bataille de cent ans: Histoire de la psychanalyse en France. 2 – 1925-1985.* Paris: Seuil.

11 Roudinesco, E. (Trans.) (1996). Mehlman, J. *Jacques Lacan.* New York: Columbia Univ. Press.

12 Personal conversations with the Lacanian milieu in Paris, France.

13 Jaspers, K. T. (1997) *General Psychopathology*, vols. 1 & 2. (Trans.). Hoenig, J. and Hamilton, M. Baltimore & London: Johns Hopkins Univ. Press.

14 Leguil, F.,(1989) "Lacan avec et contre Jaspers," *Ornicar?*, no. 48, Paris, Navarin, pp. 6-7.

15 "Max Weber," Creative Communication Attributions-ShareAlike, License, Jan. 28, 2015. *Wikipedia, the free encyclopedia.*

16 Makkreel, R.(2012) "Wilhelm Dilthey," *Wikipedia, the free encyclopedia.*

17 Lacan, J. (1988) *The Seminar III* (1955-1956): *The Psychoses* (Trans. with notes), Grigg, R. (Ed.) Miller, J.-A., New York: Norton, p. 15.

18 Schreber, D. P., *Memoirs of my Nervous Illness* (1988), (ed. and trans.) by Macalpine, I. & Hunter, R. A., with a new introduction by Weber, S., Cambridge, MA and London: Harvard Univ. Press; Lacan,J. (1988) *The Seminar III (1955-1956): The Psychoses,* (Trans. with notes), Grigg, R., (Ed.) Miller, J.-A., New York: Norton; Cf. also Freud, S. (1911) *Psycho-Analytic Notes on an Autobiographical Account of a Case of Paranoia* (*Dementia Paranoides*), *SE* , vol. XII, pp. 2-82; Lacan, J. (2006), In *Écrits* (Trans.) Fink, B. et al, "On a Question Prior to Any Possible Treatment of Psychosis" (1957-1958); Lacan, J. (2005) *Le Séminaire XXIII (1975-1976): Le sinthome,* text established by Miller, J.-A., Paris: Seuil.

19 Sartre, J.-P., *Being and Nothingness: An Essay on Phenomenological Ontology*, (Trans.) Barnes, H.E. London: Routledge, p. 532 in the French edition.

20 Sartre, J.-P. *Baudelaire,* Paris, Gallimard, Idées, 1947, p. 245.

21 Ey, H. (1936) "An Attempt to Apply Jackson's Principles to a Dynamic Conception of Neuropsychiatry," written in

collaboration with Julien Rouart, *Encéphale.*

22 Cox-Cameron, O. www.psychoanalytischepspectiven, be: 1-45. Cf. also Lacan, J. *The Psychoses: The Seminar of Jacques Lacan, Book III*, 1955-1956. (1981/1993). (Ed.) Miller, J-A. (Trans.). Grigg, R. New York: Norton & Co., p. 6.

23 Leguil, C. (2012) *Sartre Avec Lacan: Corrélation Antinomique, Liaison Dangereuse*. Paris: Navarin <> Le Champ Freudien, p. 37.

24 Jaspers, *General Psychopathology*, Cf. note #vi.

25 Sartre, J.-P., *Being and Nothingness*, Cf. note #xviii.

26 *Encyclopédie, ou dictionnaire raisonné des sciences, des arts et des métiers (Encyclopedia, or a Systematic Dictionary of the Sciences, Arts, and Crafts)* (1751-1772), ed. by Denis Diderot and co-ed. until 1759 by Jean le Rond d'"Alembert. Paris: Briasson, David, Le Breton, Durand.

27 "Denis Diderot," *Wikipedia, the free encyclopedia*, Feb. 4, 2015; "René Crevel," *Wikipedia, the free encyclopedia*, Dec. 30, 2014.

28 Macey, D. (1988). *Lacan in Contexts.* London: Verso.

29 Lacan, J. (1945). *"Le probléme du style et la conception psychiatrique des forms paranoïques de l'existence," Création:* pp. 32-42; *Minotaure*, June 1, 1931, pp. 68-69 (a shortened form); this was also reprinted in *PP*, pp. 383-388.

30 Lacan, J. (Dec. 1933) "Motifs du crime paranoïaque: le crime des soeurs Papin," *Minotaure*, nos. 3/4, pp. 25-28, reprinted in *PP*..., his thesis, pp. 389-398.

31 Freud, S. (1914) "On Narcissism: An Introduction." *SE*, 14: 73-102. Cf.: 79-90 and 101-102. Cf. also "Group Psychology and the Analysis of the Ego" (1921), *SE*, 18, pp. 65-143, especially, pp. 105-110 on identification.

32 Jean-Paul Sartre's interpretation of the crime was a Marxist one, class inferiority, while Jean Genet's play "*Les Bonnes*" ("The Maids") focused on the psychological interaction between the sisters, and Claude Chabrols's film "*Les biches*" ("The Does") is a tribute to the sisters.

33 Ragland-Sullivan, E. (1984) "Jacques Lacan, Literary Theory, and *The Maids* of Jean Genet." (Ed.). Natoli, J. *Psychological Perspectives on Literature: Freudian Dissidents and Non-Freudians: A Casebook.* Hamden, CT: The Shoe String Press.: 100-119. Cf. 114.

34 Schreber, D. P. (1955/2000) *Memoirs of My Nervous Illness* (Trans. and Eds.). Macalpine, I. and Hunter, R. A. Cambridge, MA: Harvard University Press.

35 Lacan, J. (1988) "Logical Time and the Assertion of Anticipated Certainty: A New Sophism." (Trans.) Fink, B. and Silver, M. (Ed.) Ragland-Sullivan, E. (1988). *Newsletter of the Freudian Field*, vol. 2, no. 2, pp. 4-22.

36 Lacan, J. (1981/1992) *The Psychoses: The Seminar of Jacques Lacan, Book III, 1955-1956.* (Ed.). Miller, J.-A. (Trans.). Russell Grigg. New York: Norton & Co: 5, Cf. note # 5 above.

38 Grigg, R. (Fall/Spring 1989) "Metaphor and Metonymy," *Newletter of the Freudian Field,* vol. 3, nos. 1&2, pp. 58-79.

39 "Roman Jakobson," *Wikipedia, the free encyclopedia,* Jan. 4, 2015.

40 Ragland, M.E. (1976) "The Language of Laughter," *Sub-Stance*, No. 13, pp. 91-106.

41 Lacan points out in note #8 in *S. III* (1993) that de Clérambault distinguishes between interpretation delusions... and passional delusions...and erotomaniacal delusions in "*Les délires passionnels; érotomanie, revendication, jalousie,*" p. 18.

42 Schreber, D. P. (1903/2000). *Memoirs of my Nervous Illness.* Cf. note # 14 above. Cf. also Freud, S. (1911) "Psycho-Analytic Notes on an Autobiographical Account of a Case of Paranoia (Demential Paranoides)" in *SE* 12, pp. 9-82.

43 Ragland, E. (2015) *Jacques Lacan and the Logic of Structure: Topology and Language in Psychoanalysis,* (London: Routledge/Taylor & Francis Ltd.).

44 Ragland, E. (2013) "From Barthes' 'Realism Effect' to Lacan's Real." Presented at a conference on "Real Deceptions" from April 24-27, 2013, Pomona College, Claremont, CA, April 26, 2013. To appear in *Mosaic,* forthcoming.

45 Ragland, E. (2013) "The Reality Effect…." Idea implied in the paper given at the conference on Real Deceptions.

47 Foucault, M. (1964) *Naissance de la Clinique.* Paris: PUF. *The Birth of the Clinic* (1973). New York: Pantheon.

48 Foucault, M. (1970) *The Order of Things: An Archaeology of the Human Sciences.* New York: Pantheon Books.

49 Liart, M. (2012) *Psychanalyse et Psychosomatique: Écrit et symbole.* Paris: Hamerton.

50 Kraeplin, E. (1896) *Psychiatrie: Ein Lehrbuch für Studirende und Aerzte.* In *Clinical Psychiatry* (1907).

51 "Emil Kraeplin," *Wikipedia, the free encyclopedia,* Feb. 9, 2015.

52 Freud, S. (1974) *The Standard Edition of the Complete Psychological Works,* (Trans. and Eds.) Strachey, J. in collaboration with Freud, A., et al. London: The Hogarth Press and The Institute of Psycho-Analysis, vols. I-XXIII.

53 "Sigmund Freud," *Wikipedia, the free encyclopedia,* Feb. 5, 2015.

54 "J. Lévi-Valensi," *Wikipedia, the free encyclopedia.*

55 Lacan, J. *De la Psychoses paranoïaque dans ses rapports avec la personnalié, suivi de Premiers Écrits sur la paranoïa (1975),* Paris: Seuil, pp. 365-382.

56 Lacan, J. (1932) His thesis referred to in note # xliii, Paris: le Francois.

57 Hollier, D., *Le Collége de sociologie,* p. 200, n.; cf. also David Macey, p. 212.

58 "Pierre Janet,"*Wikipedia, the free encyclopedia,* Jan. 26, 2015.

59 Lacan, J. "Exposée génêral de nos travaux scientifiques," *Psychose Paranoïque...,* p. 401.

60 Lacan, J. (1969) Preface to the Collection "Points" selected from the *Écrits.* Paris: Seuil,, p. 9 and cover note to the "Points" edition of *PP.*

61 Lacan, J. "Le Sinthome," *Ornicar?,* 7, June-July 1976, p. 7.

62 Miller, J.-A. (1999) *La psychose ordinaire: La Convention d'Antibes.* Paris: La Paon; Cf. also *La psychose ordinaire, collection publieé* par Miller, J.-A., (Ed.) Agalma, diffusion Paris: Seuil.

63 Miller, J.-A. (1991), "Reflections on the Formal Envelope of the Symptom." (Trans.) Jauregui, J. *lacanian ink,* no. 4, pp. 13-21; Cf. Jacques Lacan (2006)"The Function and Field of Speech and Language in Psychoanalysis" (1953) (Trans.) Fink, B. et al. *Ecrits.*

64 Eluard, P. (1995) *Shadows and Sun: Poems and Prose.* (Trans.) Buckley, C. Durham, NH: Oyster River Press.

65 Cf. S. III: chs. XVII and XVIII, pp. 214-230

66 "Édouard Toulouse," (Internet) *en.Wikipedia.org/wiki/.*

67 Miller, J.-A. (2013). "Structure is Lacan's myth as the Oedipus complex was Freud's." personal conversation.

68 Cox-Cameron, O. (Cf. note #8 above) speaks of the many female identifications that may have led to Aimée's obsession with the actress—her older sister, her dead sister, her dead baby daughter, still-born—, but other erotomanic parts of Aimée's delusions were reserved for the Prince of Wales to whom she sent copies of her novels which were, of course, returned, unopened.

69 Vanheule, S. *The Subject of Psychosis: A Lacanian Perspective* (2011). London: Palgrave, p. 17.

70 "Franz Alexander," *Wikipedia, the free encyclopedia,* Dec. 8, 2014.

71 Freud, S. (1914). "On Narcissism: An Introduction." *SE* XIV, pp. 73-102. Cf. also pp. 102-103.

72 Lacan, J. "Au-delé du 'Principe de réalité'" ("Beyond the Reality Principle"), dated from Marienbad-Noirmoutier, August-October, 1936, *Evolution psychiatrique*, 3, 1936, pp. 67-86; reprinted in *Écrits*, pp. 73-92; (Trans.) Fink, B., et al.,*Ecrits*, pp. 58-74; This paper contains an outline of the mirror-stage theory although it begins with a critique of associationism which is described as based on an empirical theory of knowledge inherited from John Locke, and as an idealism that fails to recognize the specific reality of mental phenomena (Macey, pp. 214-215). Such a theory of knowledge is further attacked for its reliance on a "scholastic psychology whose categories are derived from a traditional philosophical discourse." Possibly, says Macey, these criticism owe something to Politzer's *Critique des fondements de la psychologie* (1929) (p. 215). The Freudian revolution is characterized, Macey continues, by its analytic technique (the rules of free association as reformulated by Pichon as the rules of non-omission and non-systematization), which assumes that every facet of mental life is significant. Language is seen as the datum of the analytic experience and is described

in phenomenological terms. Before signifying something, language has to signify for someone and the analyst's role is to recognize a signifying intentionality of which the analysand remains ignorant (p. 215). In addition, Lacan gave a version of his mirror-stage paper to Henri Wallon. It was entitled "La Famille," *Encyclopédie francaise*, vol. 8, Henri Wallon, ed. This long essay, says Macey, comprises an introduction, "L'Institution familial," 8, pp. 40-43 and 40-44 and two chapters "Le Complexe, facteur concret de la pathologie mentale," 8, pp. 40-45 and 40-48 and 40-16. It also contains "Les Complexes familiaux en pathologie," vol. 8, pp. 42-48 and 42-16. This latter chapter was republished as *Les Complexes familiaux dans la formation de l'individu: Essai d'analyse d'une function en psychanalyse* (Paris: Navarin, 1984). Besides his thesis, this is Lacan's most substantial pre-war text (Macey, pp. 215-216).

73 Cf. Henri Wallon, *Les Origines du caractère* (Macey, note # 14, p. 290).

74 "Henri Wallon," *Wikipedia, the free encyclopedia*, Dec. 4, 2014.

75 Lacan, J. "Aggressivity in Psychoanalysis," *Ecrits*, etc.

76 "Bronislaw Malinowski," *Wikipedia, the free encyclopedia*, Jan. 26, 2015.

77 "Sir James Frazer," *Wikipedia, the free encyclopedia*, Feb. 3, 2015.

78 "Émile Durkheim," *Wikipedia, the free encyclopedia*, Jan. 30, 2015.

79 Politzer, G. (1928/1968). *Critique des fondements de la psychologie. La psychologie et la psychanalyse*, Paris: PUF, Quardrige.

80 "Sandor Ferenczi," *Wikipedia, the free encyclopedia*, Nov. 25, 2014.

81 "Georges Politzer," *Wikipedia, the free encyclopedia*, Nov. 16, 2014.

82 "Karl Marx," *Wikipedia, the free encyclopedia,* Jan. 29, 2015.

83 "Vladimir Lenin," *Wikipedia, the free encyclopedia,* Feb. 9, 2015.

84 Lacan, J. (1946). "Presentation of Psychical Causality." (Trans.). (2006). Fink, B. et al. *Écrits*, New York: Norton, & Co.: Cf. pp. 150-151; Cf. also "A la mémoire de Ernest Jones, *Écrits* , p. 697 , "In Memory of Ernest Jones: On His Theory of Symbolism," pp. 585-601.

85 Macey points out that Ernst Jones mentioned nothing of this incident in his own *Life and Work*, vol. 3, p. 223.

86 Lacan, J. "The Looking Glass Phase," *International Journal of Psycho-Analysis,* vol. 18, 1937, p. 78; title only given.

87 Freud, S. (1920), "Beyond the Pleasure Principle", *SE,* vol. XVIII, pp.3-68.

88 Lacan, J. (1953)."The Function and Field of Speech and Language in Psychoanalysis." (Trans.) (2006). Fink, B. et al. *Écrits*, Cf. pp. 237-268.

89 Freud, S. (1921) "Group Psychology and the Analysis of the Ego," *SE*, vol. XVIII, pp. 67-143.

90 Freud, S. (1914) "On Narcissism: An Introduction," *SE*, vol. XIV, pp. 69-102.

91 Ragland-Sullivan (1984), *Jacques Lacan and the Philosophy of Psychoanalysis*, Urbana and Chicago: The University of Illinois Press, cf. ch. 1.

92 "Ethology," *Wikipedia, the free encyclopedia*, Feb. 19, 2015.

93 Ragland-Sullivan, E. "Seeking the Third Term: Desire, the

Phallus, and the Materiality of Language." (Eds.). (1989). Feldstein, R. and Roof, J. *Feminism and Psychoanalysis.* Ithica, NY: Cornell Univ. Press, pp. 40-64.

94 Leguil, C. *Sartre Avec Lacan*, Leguil shows what Lacan's manque-à-être owes to Sartre's manqué-d'être, p. 77.

95 Price, A. (2014), "In the Neighborhood of Joyce and Lacan," *LC Express*, vol. 2, issue 14.

96 "Melanie Klein," *Wikipedia, the free encyclopedia,* Jan. 6, 2015.

97 "Georg Hegel," *Wikipedia, the free encyclopedia,* Feb. 5, 2015.

98 Ragland-Sullivan E. (1984), *Jacques Lacan and the Philosophy of Psychoanalysis*, Champaign-Urbana and Chicago, The University of Illinois Press, cf. p. 2.

99 Grosrichard, A. (1966). "*Une expérience psychologique au XVIIIe siécle,*" *Cahiers pour l'analyse* II.

100 Molyneux William". (Internet) in *Wikipedia.org/wiki* "

101 "William Molyneux," *Wikipedia, the free encyclopedia,* Jan. 24, 2015.

102 Locke, J. (1690/2011) *An Essay Concerning Human Understanding,*(Ed.). Nidditch, P. H. Oxford: Clarendon Press.

103 "John Locke," *Wikipedia, the free encyclopedia,* Feb. 8, 2015.

104 Lefort, R. in collaboration wih Lefort ,R. (1980). (Trans.) (1994). du Ry, M., Watson, L, and Rodriguez, L. (Forword). (1994). Grigg, R. *Birth of the Other.* Champaign-Urbana and Chicago: The University of Illinois Press: 278-288.

105 Lacan, J. (1979) "The Neurotic's Individual Myth." (Trans.).

Evans, M. N. *Psychoanalytic Quarterly* XLVIII, 3: 405-25. Cf. also (Ed. of a series) Miller, J.-A. *Paradoxes de Lacan.* "Le Mythe individuel du névrosé ou Poésie et vérié *dans la névrose."*

106 "Exposé général de nos travaux scientifiques, " in De La Psychose paranoïque..."(1932), pp. 399-406.

Presencing EPIS

EPIS Journal
Guidelines for Submission

Publication Details

Published by The Existential Psychoanalytic Institute & Society. One issue per year. Aims and Scope: Presencing EPIS is a scholarly, peer-reviewed journal dedicated to contemporary psychoanalysis. The journal covers theoretical and clinical issues emerging from existential psychoanalysis, phenomenology, traditional psychoanalysis, cultural studies, Critical Theory, post-structuralism, deconstruction, and fictional literature. The journal covers substantive and methodological issues in psychoanalysis and psychoanalytic psychotherapy, including ethical, political, professional, sociological, and historical ideas, especially as they relate to similar professional practice. Articles address theory, method, clinical case studies, previous articles, and research. The journal also has a book review and forum section for critical commentary on the journal itself.

Instructions for Authors

Papers may be theoretical, clinical, empirical, or methodological, between 2,500-7,500 words. Book reviews are up to 2,000 words and letters to the editor no more than 1,000 words. Presencing EPIS welcomes manuscripts from any country although the official language of the journal is English. All contributions will be anonymously reviewed, either by members of the Editorial Board or by panels of Independent Reviewers drawn from practitioners, researchers, academics or others who have made significant contributions to the field.

Decisions regarding publication will be made by the Editors with advice from the Editorial Board or Independent Reviewers with feedback provided to authors on decisions made. Editors can be contacted by potential contributors wishing to discuss a proposal or seeking advice or guidance on preparation of a submission.

Guidelines for Manuscripts

Manuscripts must be double-spaced on 8.5 x 11 inch pages, allowing for 1 inch minimum margins. The word count should be stated. The title should be brief and indicate the main topic of the article. A list of up to eight keywords should be supplied, as well as a summary abstract of up to 150 words. Names of authors should be given in full on a separate sheet. Authors should provide brief details (up to 50 words) of professional autobiography. Please include address, telephone, fax, and email as well. Where there are two or more authors, please indicate a single contact for correspondence.

Guidelines for Book Reviews

The main theme should be clearly presented but it is not the purpose of a review to summarize the book. Reviews should evaluate the book in relation to other significant work on the subject. Reviewers should assess the book the author has written rather than use the review as a vehicle for their own opinions, and should include criticisms with reference to specific instances in the text wherever possible. Apart from minor editions the Reviews Editor will not alter or cut without prior consultation with the reviewer. The invitation to review a book, however, does not constitute a guarantee that the manuscript will be published. To submit a book review or a book to be reviewed, please contact the Reviews Editor. Referencing Books and Articles: Use Either the Chicago Manual of Style or the APA depending upon your professional affiliation. Only works actually cited in the text should be included in the references. Indicate in the text by putting inside brackets the author's name and year of publication. References should be listed in alphabetical order at the end of the article. Publications from the same author in a single year should use a, b, c, and so forth.

Footnotes and Tables

Footnotes are not normally permitted but endnotes may be used if necessary. Tables should be Word objects, delineated clearly and supplied on separate pages, with an indication within the text of their approximate location. Vertical lines should be omitted and horizontal lines limited to those indicating the top and bottom of the table, below column headings and above summed totals. Totals and percentages should be labeled clearly. Guidelines for Graphic Images: Graphic images must be of professional quality and included as separate high-resolution files. Each image must be attached and named chronologically "figure 1," "figure 2," etc. Images must not be embedded in the manuscript itself. The approximate location of each image should be indicated in the manuscript with a stand-alone sentence: "Figure 1 approximately here," etc. Acceptable file formats: Word Documents preferred. For images in other formats, please consult with the editors prior to submission. Maximum image size: 1/2 page (approx. 6" wide by 4" tall). Images that do not conform to these guidelines will be rejected.

Copyright

Manuscripts are considered on the understanding that they are not being considered concurrently by another journal. On acceptance you will be asked to assign copyright in your article to the journal. Consent for reproduction of your article in collections of your work appearing subsequent to the publication will be given without charge, contingent on full citation of your article herein.

Electronic Offprints

Authors will receive stand-alone PDFs of their articles, reviews, or letters, which they may freely disseminate in accordance with the provisions of the copyright agreement. Authors will also receive a complete PDF of the Journal issue in which their contributions appear, which in accordance withe copyright agreement is not for dissemination without the explicit permission of Presencing EPIS. Responsibility for Views: Presencing EPIS is published under the auspices of the Existential Psychoanalytic Institute & Society (EPIS). Neither EPIS nor its editorial boards hold themselves responsible for the views expressed by contributors.

Address for Correspondence via email

nazarita66@gmail.com
kbradref@gmail.com

Editorial Office

Presencing EPIS
The Existential Psychoanalytic Institute & Society
2026 S. 9th W., #4
Missoula, Montana 59801 USA
www.episworldwide.com

About EPIS Press

We established EPIS Press in the objective of publishing new work in the following areas of inquiry:

1) existential psychoanalysis & phenomenology;

2) traditional & contemporary psychoanalysis theoretical and clinical;

3) critical philosophy as it pertains to psychoanalysis, culture, phenomenology, and philosophy of mind;

4) new literature in phenomenology and psychoanalysis;

5) any related work as it bears on these issues, including neuropsychology and psychoanalysis.

For more information go to

EPIS Press
2026 S. 9th W., #4
Missoula, MT 59801
epispublishing1@gmail.com
www.episworldwide.com

EPIS RADIO

Radio for the thinking person.

EPIS Radio—Radio for the Thinking Person—has become wildly successful, entertaining discussions in psychoanalysis, phenomenology, Critical Theory, and cultural studies. If you know of a person you think we should interview, please have them contact us. Interviews are informative, valuable, and fun.

episworldwide.com
kbradref@gmail.com

EPIS Radio Programs
The Existential Psychoanalytic Institute & Society

Made in the USA
Monee, IL
04 November 2026

67391560R00154